9/11
Holding the Truth

A Compilation of notes, commentary and articles by Andrew Johnson

Focused around the 9/11 research and evidence compiled by Dr Judy Wood

A bus parked on Barclay Street, near WTC 7 – before (top) and after (bottom) the building's destruction

Knowledge is essential to freedom."
— William Ellery Channing (1887)

"When people who are honestly mistaken learn the truth,
they will either cease being mistaken, or cease being honest!"

Other Books by Andrew Johnson

These are available as free PDF downloads, as well as other formats:

9/11 Finding the Truth

This is the pre-cursor to *9/11 Holding the Truth*, documenting the cover up - by the 9/11 "truth" movement - of the truth about what happened to the WTC.

Climate Change and Global Warming... Exposed: Hidden Evidence, Disguised Plans

This book collects together, for the first time anywhere, a range of diverse data which proves that the whole issue of "climate change" is more complicated and challenging than *almost all* researchers are willing to consider, examine, or entertain. For example, this book contains astronomical data which most climatologists will not discuss in full. Similarly, the book contains climate and weather data that astronomers will not discuss. The book contains some data that neither astronomers nor climatologists will discuss. It contains some data that no scientists will appropriately discuss.

Table of Contents

Dedication

Like the first volume of this work *9/11 Finding the Truth*, this collection of articles is dedicated to all those people who have made these same articles possible – this includes my wife and children, my parents and my family, my friends – old and new, researchers and curious people around the world, as well as those who have invented and developed the technology that makes your reading of this possible.

It is also dedicated to all those who want to know the truth about 9/11 and other large-scale deceptions – and to those who have suffered enormously because of them.

A special dedication must be made to Dr Judy Wood, for much of the key 9/11 research, understanding and most of the pictures collected here – please see her website http://www.drjudywood.com/

In considering this dedication, I hope there is a realisation of how we are all connected – in a "pool" of human consciousness. What we each do affects what the rest of us are able to do.

Author Biography

Andrew Johnson grew up in Yorkshire and graduated from Lancaster University in 1986 with a degree in Computer Science and Physics. He worked in Software Engineering and Software Development, for most about 20 years. He has also worked full and part time in lecturing and tutoring and he now works for the Open University (part time) tutoring students, whilst occasionally working on various small software development projects.

He became interested in "alternative knowledge" in 2003, soon after discovering Dr Steven Greer's Disclosure Project. Andrew has given presentations and written and posted many articles on various websites about 9/11, Mars, Chemtrails and Anti-gravity research, whilst also challenging some of the authorities to address some of the data he and others have collected.

Andrew is married and has two children. You can email Andrew Johnson on ad.johnson@ntlworld.com.

His website is www.checktheevidence.com.

You can post questions related to the 9/11 research topics covered in this book in a facebook study group - https://www.facebook.com/groups/911TruthMovement/. Make sure you are familiar with what the group is for, by reading the description (it isn't a debating group).

Acknowledgements

Most or all of the people named below have helped me, either with organizing talks or events to discuss the truth about 9/11 and related topics, or they have distributed 9/11-related materials that I have produced. Or they have helped in some other significant way. There are other people, too numerous to mention who have also helped in some way.

Adam Dwyer

Adam Webb, Sally Kennedy, Alan Matthews

Alan J Mock

Alex Burke

Alex Williams, Rob Jones and the New Horizons (Lytham) Crew

Andy Eardley

Anthony Williams

Atahan Gandu

Ben Emelyn-Jones

"Betsy McGee"

Cindy Laverty

David Clarke

David Woodworth (Woody)

Deanna Spingola

Debbie and Steve in Brighton

Deborah Williams

Dr Abraham Rodriguez

Dr Judy Wood

David Kimball

Dr Morgan Reynolds

Emanuele Montagna (Italy)

Evan Denton

Franco Soldani (Italy)

Geoff Brady

Hilary Kitching

Iain Fugue & Laura

James Wallis

Jeroen Van Straaten and the BEM Crew

Jonathan and Ann Halstead

Keith Mothersson

Mark Conlon

Matthew Hancock

Matt Naus

Maurice Herman

Mel Ve and Biggi Boho

Menna Trinder-Widdess and Matt Campbell

Mike Sacchetta

Neil Geddes-Ward

Ollie Blossom Breezy

Paul Giovanni

Peter Lewis

Ralph Winterrowd

Richard D Hall

Royce Holleman

Russ Gerst

Ryan G Bannister

Steve Collier

Stuart Pound

Stephen Bamber

Tom Farrar Talley

Jonathan Barker

Part 1

Setting the Scene

1. Introduction

This volume is a follow-up to the original compilation of articles I called *9/11 Finding the Truth*. It is recommended that you read that volume before reading this one - electronic versions are available free. In the next section of this chapter, I include the same summary of 9/11 evidence which must be studied and explained.

What 9/11 Truth are we Holding?

To explain the title of this book, I want to point out the established facts about the destruction of the WTC, which were compiled into a Website by April 2008 and later into Dr Judy Wood's textbook *Where Did the Towers Go?* – which I abbreviate to WDTTG. The truth is as follows:

On 11 September 2001, the WTC towers did not burn up, nor did they slam to the ground – about 85-90% of the buildings turned to dust in mid-air.

- A total of 7 WTC buildings were either destroyed outright on the day, or their remains removed in the following months/years.

- Whatever crashed into the WTC towers did not cause their destruction.

- The towers underwent a type of destruction that had never been seen in the "white world" before. The destruction was the result of some type of energy weapon – which operated on principles not recognised in "white world" science.

- A category 3 hurricane – Erin had movements coincident with the events of 9/11 and was closest to NYC at about 8am on 11 September 2001.

If one is to accept these truths, then one must also accept there is a separate "power elite" group that both possesses such advanced directed free energy technology and the means to deploy it. Not only that, as I have been documenting for over 10 years, it can cover up these things to the point that almost no one recognises this massive deception for what it is.

But why do I say "free energy technology"? It is because, from observing the process of destruction of the WTC towers, we can see a catastrophic change taking place. That is, to tear apart steel beams and other materials and turn them to dust, using a process already recognized by mainstream thinking would require an enormous amount of energy. In a conventional process, this energy would perhaps come from some type of explosion, burning, laser or electrical discharge. However, all of these processes would have an enormous amount of associated heat – and such heat was not seen or felt on 9/11. Hence, this energy release or change either came "from thin air" or from within the materials which made up the WTC. This is the "big secret" and some clues to what that secret is can be found in the evidence collected in the WDTTG book and in Dr Judy Wood's presentations. This aspect of the truth is also referred to in chapter 16.

Finding this Truth

I sometimes stop to wonder how I can possibly have ended up writing all this – and how I can have come to know things that I know. Similarly, I am almost baffled as to how I can have come into contact with the people that I have come into contact with. 20 years ago, I was tutoring and lecturing 16-18 year old pupils in Computing and Maths at a College of Further Education in the East Midlands region of the UK. 10 years ago, I was working from home – still tutoring in a Computing subject, doing some Software Development and assessing students with disabilities. I had, by that time, started to uncover a different reality – and had realised that there must be a connection between the UFO/ET phenomenon and what has been called "Free Energy" technology. This was mainly because of Dr Steven Greer's "Disclosure Project" – which brought forward a compelling body of powerful witness testimony, from many highly qualified and highly trained observers. This body of testimony was also, in many cases, accompanied by important pieces of documentary evidence, detailed in Steven Greer's "Disclosure" book and elsewhere. Since then, I have been immersed in a process of following a number of significant "disclosure threads" and have found they are part of a much larger tapestry of reality than most want to acknowledge. I have found that, surprisingly, even people such as Dr Greer (see chapter 6) himself do not want to acknowledge what really happened on 9/11 and that parts of this tapestry are connected to other parts. I have written and spoken, fairly extensively, on the connections between the "free energy" issue and the events of 9/11[1]. This discovery, for me, happened because of the research of Dr Judy Wood into the destruction of the WTC Towers on 9/11[2].

Since about 2004, when I first became aware of problems with the official story of 9/11, I have been investigating the events themselves and their cover up. The first volume, catalogued some of my journey and initial research and how I was invited to join the group called "Scholars for 9/11 Truth." Initially, I was pleased that this "Scholars" group seemed to be questioning the official story of 9/11. I then realized that this group itself was a "set-up" - designed to attract sceptical intellectuals and divert their energy and attention into something which would be, ultimately, deceptive and unproductive.

During my involvement with the "Scholars" group, I came to see that attention was being diverted *away from* the research of Dr Judy Wood. In early 2008, it became clear that Dr Judy Wood had established an important connection to the energy phenomenon or phenomena known as the "Hutchison Effect" and that this was a kind of "flashpoint" for those that were continuing to attempt to cover up the truth about 9/11. It was already clear to us by then that the connection of Steven E. Jones to the inappropriately named "Cold Fusion" research and also to the field of 9/11 research, is a clear indication of the importance of energy research to what happened on 9/11.

It had become clear how well the 9/11 cover up had been planned. It had also become clear how vitally important it was to keep the connection between 9/11 and energy covered up – not only have we seen the promotion of a bogus theory about thermite and/or controlled demolition of the World Trade Centre Complex, we had also begun to see the increasing promotion of the "nuclear demolition theory." I contend that this was because Dr Judy Wood and I had revealed that a process which destroyed the World Trade Centre was related to the process which takes place during Low Energy Nuclear Reaction (i.e. Cold Fusion) experiments.

"More of the Same...?"

In this volume, I further document the attempts to cover up the truth that Dr Judy Wood has revealed. It is nonetheless difficult to comprehend the number of people that seem to be involved in this cover up. There seem to be a disturbing number of people who are willing to lie about and misrepresent the truth of what Dr Wood has said. Essentially, I've just had to write new articles about the evolving cover up. It might seem like I am just repeating things I said in the first volume, but I hope that I am able to show you several more "case studies" which highlight additional psychological tactics, not seen in the earlier articles I wrote. I hope that these will help you identify other methods of deception that are employed to keep important secrets from being revealed and understood. I hope this will then help others to strengthen their psychological and intellectual armoury against the incessant use of tactics of misdirection and deception.

Why This Is Important

A study of the evidence that has been uncovered by Dr Judy Wood not only reveals the truth about how the WTC was destroyed, it then forces us to reconsider at least 3 issues of global importance – the so-called issue of "terrorists and terrorism," the production and use of energy and the truth about global warming and climate change. That is, the events on 9/11 involved the use of an advanced energy weapon technology, which we do know something about. This technology has the ability to produce vast energy changes without generating heat – and appears to be related to Cold Fusion or Low Energy Nuclear Reactions (LENR). Also, it appears that Hurricane Erin was manipulated in certain ways, so that its movements were coincident with certain events.

This essentially proves that all current "accepted wisdom" about global terrorism, energy scarcity and so-called global warming and climate change is false and therefore must be reviewed by anyone who still has

the ability to dispassionately analyse available evidence. I don't think this can be stated often enough or urgently enough.

Brief Summary of Key 9/11 Evidence to Be Explained

Thanks to Dr Judy Wood for highlighting the very basic and important evidence from the WTC disaster, summarised below. Please see her Website for references for these pictures, and much more evidence. Ideally, you should obtain and study a copy of her comprehensive forensic investigation into the destruction of the WTC – *Where Did the Towers Go?*[3]

What caused the towers to turn to dust?

Why was there almost no debris after the destruction?

On the afternoon of 11 September 2001, the "rubble pile" left from WTC1 is essentially non-existent. WTC7 can be seen in the distance, revealing the photo was taken before 5:20 PM that day.

What happened to these cars in the so-called "Toasted Cars Parking Lot"

Before WTC 1 Destruction   **After** WTC 1 Destruction

How did the inflated tire survive the WTC "plane crash" fireball?

This is an official photograph of WTC plane wreckage!

How did this WTC beam get bent into a "Horseshoe" Shape with no obvious stress, heating or buckling marks?

What Turned these Cars Upside Down?

What caused this girder in the Banker's Trust/Deutsche Bank Building to "crinkle up", when FEMA reported there was no fire in that building?

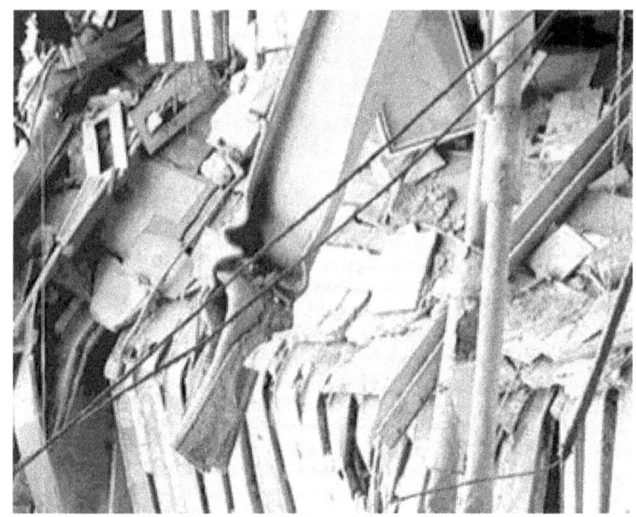

Why was Hurricane Erin closest to NYC at about 8am on 9/11?

Why wasn't this hurricane reported as a potential risk to people living on the East Coast of the US, and in New York?

Why was hosing down of the site – including some equipment, still ongoing in Mid-January 2008?

NYC WTC Site, 17th Jan 2008. Still image from
Samsung MX10 Video Camera. (Andrew Johnson)

The above represents just a "quick summary" of the photographic evidence. However, there is additional video evidence and witness testimony from the WTC Oral Histories to be considered.

Irrefutable – Video Series

Since I published the 3rd edition of *9/11 Finding the Truth*, Adam Dwyer took it upon himself to produce an excellent video series called Irrefutable[4]. He also produced some detailed and powerful graphics[5], in an effort to clearly illustrate the evidence listed above. This video series lasts just over 1 hour and is well worth watching. I have given out many copies of this DVD since 2015[6]. Please contact me if you would like a copy.

A Brief Note about "Calling for A New Investigation"

If you're looking for calls to a government to do a new investigation into the events of 9/11, you've come to the wrong place… Please see *9/11 Finding the Truth*, where I show what "Architects and Engineers for 9/11 Truth" have been up to since 2007. This topic is also revisited in chapter 17. Additionally, a similar UK "outfit" is mentioned in chapter 23.

World Trade Center

What society thinks happened
FIRE

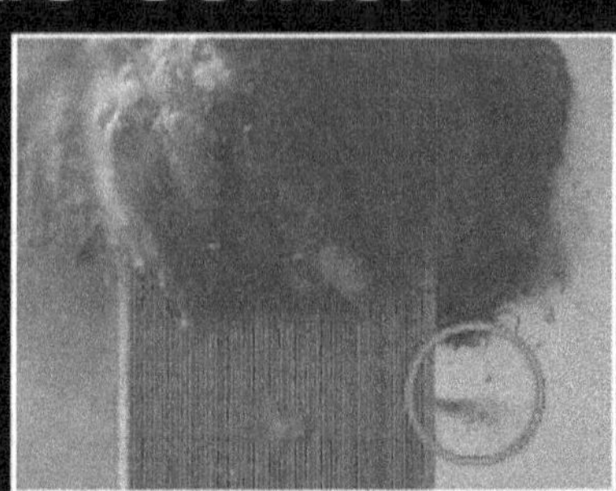
What truthers think happened
BOMBS

What really happened
DUSTIFICATION
WHAT HAPPENED: WHEREDIDTHETOWERSGO.COM   POSTER: DEBAMBOOZLED.COM

WHERE DID THE TOWERS GO?
THE EVIDENCE OF DIRECTED FREE-ENERGY TECHNOLOGY ON 9/11, BY DR. JUDY WOOD
WHEREDIDTHETOWERSGO.COM
THE BOOK
THIS POSTER
DEBAMBOOZLED.COM
THEY LITERALLY TURNED TO DUST IN MID-AIR
"They didn't burn up, nor did they slam to the ground, but turned into dust in mid-air" Dr. Judy Wood - "Although they were demolished
in such a way as to look as if they fell, they did not fall at all" John Lash - "Those towers literally disintegrated, they went into dust."
Jesse Ventura - "A plane hitting the building, should not turn the buildings into dust." George Noory - "Arguably the most important
book of the 21st century." Richard D. Hall - "If you don't have Dr. Judy Wood's book, do yourself a favor; buy it, read it." Mel Fabregas
CLASSIFIED FREE-ENERGY TECHNOLOGY REVEALED

Implications of the Forensic Study & Cover Up – Video

A video posted in September 2017 by YouTube user PeteFD1986[7] gives an excellent overview of the implications of the research of Dr Judy Wood. It also discusses the cover up of the evidence and the related implications of this cover up.

2. Emerging Thoughts

This chapter contains some of my own thoughts and feelings which have come about as a result of writing the articles in this compilation and those in the previous volume *9/11 Finding the Truth*. It also contains some thoughts and feelings expressed to me by various people that have reached, more or less, the same understanding of the 9/11 cover up as I have.

In writing all of these articles, over a period of more than 10 years, a very strange picture emerges. The cover up of 9/11 is like some strange, frightening malevolent beast – with tendrils seemingly stretching across the world and into certain people's hearts and minds. Those who have been "stung" by these tendrils don't seem to have a conscience about what they say or do. Perhaps I am being over-dramatic and they are just victims of their own egos or they have had to make too many compromises in their personal lives and circumstances. From what I have written, you can make your own judgement. Whatever the cause, they have acted in a callous, dishonest and occasionally threatening manner.

Rhetorical Questions

As a way of "setting the scene" for the rest of this book, please consider this section carefully. For those that attend "alternative" conferences and events, or follow various "alternative" radio shows, podcasts, YouTube channels and the like, I have listed the following questions to ask yourselves. These questions have come about as a result of my past dealing with other researchers, hosts and conference organisers.

- Should a platform be given to those who are found to be untruthful?

- Should those found to be lying be challenged, or should we just assume they are mistaken and "clap" anyway? e.g. when a radio show guest is wrong in what they are saying or has an incomplete picture of the facts, should the host attempt to correct or enlighten the guest in a suitable manner? Or should the host just continue and pretend nothing is wrong?

- Does the truth matter?

- Is an opinion more important than truth and evidence?

- If someone presents information later shown to be false, should that person correct the statements about the false information and apologise?

- Are intelligence agencies concerned that access to "alternative" information sources might cause the revelation of closely-guarded secrets to a wider audience?

- Do you value knowing and speaking the truth above having a friendship?

- In a community of "Truth Seekers" is it offensive to state you are a "Truth Knower" – at least in relation to certain topics and events?

"The Truth Needs No Protection"

I have been thinking about the phrase / saying "the truth needs no protection" and wondering if this phrase is itself true! One or two people have said to me things along the lines of, "so, Andrew, are you saying that it is only you and Dr Judy Wood that are telling the truth about what happened on 9/11?" Of course, this is not *really* what I am saying, but it may come across that way, because of the number of people I have challenged to tell the truth. When they have failed this challenge, I have then written about them.

I have begun to wonder what might have happened if Dr Judy Wood had not decided to speak out and make a website and then challenge NIST. Whilst the awareness of what Dr Wood has discovered and shown is still quite limited, it is not insignificant. Whether, at this time (November 2017), it could be described as a "growing awareness" is difficult to say. I also wonder what the awareness level would be if I had not compiled my first book *9/11 Finding the Truth*. Thanks to the efforts of a number of dedicated activists, we now have a firm public record of disclosure. Dr Wood has given talks in several US towns, several UK cities and towns and she has given presentations in two European countries. In "cyberspace," Dr Wood, myself and other figures such as Dr Morgan Reynolds, Jerry Leaphart, Richard D Hall and others have also carried out this disclosure – about what really happened on 9/11 and how it has been covered up.

Of particular note are Richard D Hall's single-handed and highly-skilled efforts to build a "vehicle" which has allowed him to convey important truths to people in the UK and around the world. It is largely due to his work that, in the UK and Europe, knowledge of Dr Judy Wood's book *Where Did the Towers Go?* has grown considerably since the book was published late in 2010.

Similarly, Dr Wood's relentless efforts from the USA - giving many, many radio and "podcast" interviews, has also gradually raised awareness of the evidence which proves that the World Trade Centre was destroyed using an undisclosed technology - which someone knows about. Someone is working very hard to keep knowledge of all this covered up. The cover up works too, but I should not be too surprised really, when things like cures for cancer have been covered up for perhaps 80 years, or maybe even longer.

"Soft" Cover Up and "Hard" Cover Up

Consider regimes in the former USSR and East Germany – they would cover up corruption and a deeper agenda with threats, violence, kidnappings and so forth – perhaps I can call this "hard cover up."

In our current regime cover up is achieved by psychological means – ridicule, marginalisation, ostracism and through using people who've had past misdemeanours and making deals with them, or offering them money - as seems to be the case with Jeff Prager (see chapter 9) and Jeremy Rys (see chapter 0). Perhaps I can call this "soft cover up."

More latterly, one of the blanket phrases has been laid down to cover many potential avenues for disclosure is "national security." As I showed in *9/11 Finding the Truth*, censorship extends to media which should be free and open (such as Huffington Post, Wikipedia, internet forums and even, to some extent YouTube).

Other methods of "Soft Cover Up" are largely psychological in nature and seem to employ a kind of social engineering. I discuss this, in a satirical article in chapter 3.

Threats and Protection

Over the years, I have developed two main lines of thought on whether people like Dr Wood and myself, who are working to break down the cover up, are in danger. One line of thought is that basically we are protected, the other line is that we are no threat to anyone because the number of people who know the truth is miniscule in proportion to the total population of the world Also, people like Dr Judy Wood and myself have no significant power or influence over others – nor would we want it!

I personally have never received any credible threats, nor have I experienced any overtly negative effects on my life by being involved in 9/11 research and related research. Certainly, a fair number of my old friendships have faded quite a bit and I feel more isolated in the way I see things in the world now, making "small talk" much more difficult than it used to be.

Dr Wood has received threats in the past, but has continued to speak about her research. Since I learned from her about her earlier life (parts of which were very traumatic, to say the least), I have concluded that there are powerful POSITIVE forces at work, which have been preventing the evil perpetrators from "having things all their own way." I have sometimes considered there is "a game" going on - which has certain rules. If we play by the rules, we may eventually win the game. The opposing forces think they can win by cheating or being dishonest, but in reality, they cannot win using such tactics. Those of us that are "playing by the rules" automatically gain some kind of protection, by doing things correctly - following their hearts and their intuition and maintaining their integrity, and a balance of their logic and emotions, along with preserving a sense of humour. The opponents can only give the appearance of doing these things - because they have engaged in one or more acts of deception, so they do not have this in-built "spiritual protection."

The Numbers Game

Now, only "a minority of a minority" are aware of what Dr Wood and myself have "packaged up" and presented. There is an even smaller number of people that understand what the implications are. I have had the pleasure of communicating, now, with a fair number of those people - and I might even be able to remember each of their names if I really tried.

However, Dr Wood and myself are no real threat to the "Powers That Be" (PTB) at the moment, because their system is still functioning pretty well - even though some of the "pixels" in their "super-high definition screen of reality" are blinking the wrong colour or have gone dead... Most people can't see these or don't worry that a new picture of reality might be emerging…

Also, the muddle-up/cover up is already in place, so even exposure to a large audience would have a limited effect, unless it was repeated, daily for weeks on end - in the same way that the original false story of 9/11 was and is repeated almost daily.

Education, Credentials, Arrogance, Experience

It seems there is a fine line between education and indoctrination. Some people are proud of not being educated, because they think they have been less indoctrinated. Sometimes, however, they may not realise that they can be indoctrinated by ongoing propaganda in the mainstream media, or other sources of information they may be exposed to on a regular basis.

Is having a formal education useful in finding out about the truth of what happened on 9/11? Or does it hamper an honest investigation of the facts? In my experience, the answer to this question is quite complicated. People that I've spoken to have often mentioned that they intuitively knew, on 9/11, that what they were shown on television was not right/true. However, they have then said that they needed the expertise of someone like Dr Judy Wood to show them *what parts* of the official story of 9/11 *could not be true*. And, of course I also needed to be shown this! So, even though I have had a university education, and I started investigating the official story of 9/11 in 2003, even after 12 months, I still didn't have everything "straightened out" in my mind. Once I did have things straightened out, I was able to use the tools given to me in my education to help me articulate and pass on my understanding to other people – as I'm attempting to do right now!

However, for many who are more deeply embedded in the educational/academic establishment, it seems they are unable to confront or dispassionately analyse the 9/11 evidence for themselves – even close associates of Dr Judy Wood herself have not been able to cope with she has shown them, personally. Although I currently only work part time in education, as far as I know, none of my peers are even aware of any of the research I write about, or articles I have written.

One would hope that the "Peer Review" process in science would help expose the obvious problems with the Official Story not being supported by available scientific evidence. The fact that this has not happened shows that the Peer Review process is not "pure" - but it is driven by vested interests and the traumatised psyche of those unable to accept the deeply troubling truths that are revealed in the evidence discovered and catalogued thus far. Often times, the "peer review" card is played by sceptics – who claim that because "this or that" has not appeared in a peer-reviewed journal, it cannot be true/correct.

The Curse of the Truth?

A number of people that have read Dr Judy Wood's book *"Where Did the Towers Go?"* Have communicated with me to express how much the knowledge they gain from reading this book changes them – changes the way they look at the world and it changes their relationship to it.

Sometimes, it seems like knowing the truth is a curse. I have described this as a feeling of isolation - like you become an "intellectual leper." Most people live with deception on a far deeper level than they seem consciously aware and some just don't seem to care what the truth is. Others seem, on the surface, to care but when they are confronted with certain evidence and truth, they are seemingly unable to process it. It's like the "paper jams in the printer" and no information can be "placed on the paper" - the paper has become crumpled and no new information can be printed on it. Perhaps this is to do with their level of consciousness or the status of their "spiritual awareness" – or something akin to these things.

Since 2008, I have gradually felt more isolated, because of the way I now see the world. This has happened on a personal and interpersonal level and even in the sphere of what is often called the "truth seeking community." For example, my experiences with Web Radio Host Henrik Palmgren have been, to say the least, disenchanting (see chapter 13).

Dealing with the Truth

I know for sure that evil, hidden forces are at work - and they have sophisticated technology and methods at their disposal. Evidence from 9/11 seems to show that they can engineer the underlying fabric of our reality - and hence perhaps achieve any conceivable outcome... I wasn't absolutely sure of this until 2008. Since then, I have slowly come to terms with the implications of that knowledge. It's like you are entering a whole new world and you have to leave almost everything behind in the old one. In knowing and accepting this truth, you cannot go back to the "old world."

One chap who has experienced this same "knowing" told me he feels like…

God reached down and said 'you're going to be lonely.' I wish to call it an immaculate burden...! I think it's some kind of lesson. Maybe you're supposed to learn how to choose wisely the evidence you share and who you share it with…

Maybe something was unlocked in our heads and then you want to bring your loved ones with you but you can't. I honestly don't know if this sucks or not! You feel sorrow as you watch others get their psychology operated on and all you can do is watch and understand. It takes everything you're made of to survive this kind of transition. Some of my friends didn't make it, but they are still friends. Sometimes I wonder what they feel about me now. I don't get too close anymore but I always have open arms.

We hope that friends and family will listen to us because they respect us. Sadly, it does not seem to work that way. People are normally just happier to "go along with the programme."

On the theme of "waking up" and grasping what happened on 9/11, I had been communicating with Claudia Von Werlhof, whom I met in April 2013. I expressed the feeling that it was like I'd gone over a wall or through a barrier that others couldn't cross. She said:

Andrew,

You are the first person I know who speaks about this barrier or wall. It is exactly my experience since I heard about the earthquake in Haiti, was put into contact with (Rosalie) Bertell and read her book "Planet Earth. The Latest Weapon of War." I WAS THROWN over this wall and landed on its other side. Since then I have been living beyond the barrier and cannot make myself heard or understood by the ones on the "normal" side. The change happened like an earthquake within my body, I fell ill, and when I got up everything had changed. It was like a "call" from the spiritual world, the earth herself perhaps, and this is why I founded the Planetary Movement for Mother Earth. I thought it could be the means to move other people over the barrier as well. And it is my experience as well that I failed in trying to do so – until now. I tried to find an expression that would define the new way to look at the world as something like a "planetary consciousness." I know that Rosalie Bertell had it, and this was like a bond between us. When I found out that people who had read her book nevertheless did not climb over the wall, she told me: "There are people who do not understand." But she did not know why.

Yes, it is like an aversion. I know one woman who made the "journey," but was so shocked that she "returned" to the normal side, by denying the reality she became conscious of. I do not know if she succeeded because she would never speak with me again.

An argument against the journey is: What would people do with this knowledge as they cannot do anything against the perpetrators. But: Who knows? Only when being clear about the reality can we start to think and act properly – without that we would always be behind, hopelessly lost in confusion.

The radical poet Ingeborg Bachmann from Austria once has said: "It is a reasonable demand that people should know the truth!"

Yes, because who else? And, most important, whereas we are discussing if or if not – "they" are destroying the planet. There is no choice. We cannot behave as if the world was still the one we knew before.

I think there is a sub-conscious reaction to the truth that is revealed in the study of 9/11 evidence – those that are "ready" to accept it react differently to those are that aren't ready. Perhaps this is to do with what a friend called Pete Taylor Wood suggested:

> *The forces or energies that were employed in the destruction of the world trade centre are the same as those from which life itself arises.*

Why Don't Other Researchers Know the Truth?

In 2015, a 3-hour long YouTube video[8] was released called *JFK to 9/11- Everything Is a Rich Man's Trick*. The narrator and main researcher appears to be Francis Richard Conolly. This was one of the most in-depth analyses of the Kennedy Assassination that I had seen and it quickly seemed to have garnered over one million views. The video presents evidence in a clear, concise manner and discusses some of the parties and interests that were behind JFK's assassination. It introduced many things I hadn't been aware of and the overall presentation of the JFK-related material is most compelling. Judyth Vary Baker – former girlfriend of Lee Harvey Oswald - told me she thought this film was mostly correct.

However, the last half an hour of the film covers 9/11 and in doing so covers the usual disinformation about the WTC undergoing controlled demolition. My reason for mentioning this is to raise the question "If this researcher is so thorough in one area, why are they so hopelessly wrong in another? Why haven't they seen the obvious truth and rejected the disinformation?" It's a common problem.

But it also raises another issue – perhaps they are willing to reveal all the truth about JFK's assassination now - as many or all of the people involved and affected are dead or very old now. It was over 50 years ago. There has never been a real criminal prosecution for the JFK assassination. We can easily fast forward further into the future and see the same situation re the events of 9/11 - with each anniversary seeing a lack of prosecution – because of widespread corruption and dishonesty.

Tom Farrar Talley wrote to me to say

> *"I keep thinking of the 9/11 cover up as having layer upon layer. and now am seeing it as more like a poisonous snake who keeps shedding its skin. Most think of the 9/11 event as being the 'Primary', and the cover-up as the Secondary. Now, I think just the reverse. There could be even more design and planning that went into the cover-up, than the event, itself.*
>
> *It's getting so hard to keep track of all the players; we really need a Scorecard."*

Well perhaps this book and the previous volume represent some kind of "score card…"

Throughout this book, we will look at yet more examples of apparent unwillingness among researchers, speakers and activists to discuss certain 9/11 evidence and conclusions – especially in chapter 12. For the moment, let us mention one person who is willing to tell people some of the grim truth about the destruction of the WTC on 9/11.

Dr Eric Larsen – Thank You!

I would like to mention the work of Dr Eric Larsen, Professor Emeritus (of English) at John Jay College of Criminal Justice (CUNY). Dr Larsen wrote the foreword to the WDTTG book and he described it as "the most important book of the 21st century". I agree - this is the main reason I have composed this volume and the previous one.

Dr Larsen has written a number of books, including *The Skull of Yorick: The Emptiness of American Thinking at a Time of Grave Peril—Studies in the Cover-up of 9/11* (2011). He founded the Oliver Arts and Open Press in 2009. Since then, Dr Larsen has written a number of articles about Dr Judy Wood and her research and these have been posted on a website called Intrepid Report. One of these articles, called "Serpent Songs in America"[9] discusses Dr Paul Craig Roberts. President Reagan appointed Dr Roberts as Assistant Secretary of the Treasury for Economic Policy in 1980 or 1981.[10]

Roberts posted an article in March 2011 called The Perfidy of Government: Evidence v. Denial[11] which is "about three recent books that explain how we lost our economy, the Constitution and our civil liberties, and how peace lost out to war."

Dr Larsen observes and highlights how Roberts suddenly switches from a discussion of the JFK and RFK assassinations to mentioning 9/11. Roberts writes…

> **Niels Harrit, a professor of nano-chemistry at the University of Copenhagen, together with U.S. physicists and engineers published a paper in the Open Chemical Physics Journal in 2009 that proves that nano-themite was used to bring down the World Trade Center towers.**

Dr Larsen suggests (and I agree) that this is a deliberate tactic to insert disinformation once the reader's trust has been established. The reader may think that Roberts is "brave" enough to imply there was a conspiracy to assassinate Kennedy and another conspiracy to destroy the World Trade Centre on 9/11. While he has got the reader to think this way, he deliberately misleads them regarding what happened on 9/11.

Dr Larsen has written another series of articles, published at IntrepidReport.com called "Dr Judy Wood and the Future of the World[12]". This is recommended reading!

Hon Paul T Hellyer – FULL Disclosure

On 18 Mar 2015, David Whitehead posted a video address entitled "Full Disclosure" by retired Canadian Politician Paul Hellyer[13]. I have been following Mr Hellyer since late 2005 when he "went public" with his statements about the UFO/ET cover up[14], **having read** Col Philip J Corso's book, the Day After Roswell[15]. Paul Hellyer spoke at the 2012 Global Breakthrough Energy Movement Conference[16] – and so did Dr Judy Wood [17]– and so did I[18].

Paul Hellyer in 2015 – "Full Disclosure" Video

Although Hellyer incorrectly states that "some of the WTC buildings had been rigged for controlled demolition," he goes on to say, at 16:50 in this video:

> *A new weapon of mass destruction was used to reduce the concrete and steel to dust before it reached the ground, if you have any doubts about this, get a copy of Dr Judy Wood's book entitled Where Did the Towers Go? 500 pages of meticulous evidence.*

Out of the many books seen, in the background, in this video, this is the only one that Hellyer holds up to the viewer. I would suggest this is a measure of the book's importance. Thank you, Mr Hellyer!

Leading the Way

So, Mr Hellyer, who was once Defence Minister for Canada[19], has "shown the way" for others to follow. The first "others," I would argue, should be those in the research community – such as Steve Bassett, Joseph Farrell and Ian R Crane. However, they have consistently "passed" on opportunities to speak about the evidence[20]. I hope that they will do what they have not done yet – *accurately report the evidence we know as <u>the truth</u> and accurately describe the implications of it*. As the years pass, the "force of reason" needed to convey this truth to people will only increase, if the realisation of the truth is not displayed and delivered to the precious few who are listening to those in the research community, rather than listening to the "robotic mouthpieces" following their carefully authored scripts in the mainstream media[21].

And, as I write this piece, there is some possibility that the reluctance to both talk about and listen to this sort of evidence will also increase, as UK PM David Cameron is said to want to "revive moves for tough action against non-violent extremists" (to target "radicalisation")[22]. So, who is going to accurately report what they realise is the truth…? Will anyone younger than Mr Hellyer be "up to the job"…?

Some Notes About Received Correspondence

I do get some "funny" messages from time to time so I may be a little guarded or even "snarky" in my responses, until I learn more about whomever has sent this correspondence. In the main, however, most of the messages I get are positive and express gratitude - which is partly what keeps me going.

One thing that can be frustrating is when basic questions are asked that have already been answered in one or more of the videos or interviews that Dr Wood or myself have given. By now, there are probably a total of about 100 interviews and presentations given by myself and Dr Wood that are freely viewable and downloadable online. Some are more formal than others but by listening to a good number of them, it should be possible to gain a fairly good impression of the sort of people we are.

In most cases, when people write to us, or comment on the videos, we don't know them – there aren't any videos of these people online - and so we can't get to know them (and it would be difficult to find the time to do so if such videos were available). It is sometimes the case, then, that we can give people "short shrift" if they appear not to have studied the available materials well enough. We hope and even expect that if people are interested enough in studying the available evidence, they will devote an appropriate amount of time to complete this study. We have spent literally *years* of our time making this information available either for free or at relatively low cost.

Dr Wood gets many more emails per day. I think it's worth saying that she is not obliged to respond to anyone's email messages (and neither am I). We haven't been "appointed" by any official body to investigate 9/11 or any other topic. We haven't been paid any money and we haven't even been *invited* to do an investigation. Hence, we are volunteers – and have no responsibility to do anything at all. Obviously, we have *chosen* to do what we do because we feel it is of huge importance – so important that we have chosen to sacrifice various things (in my case, mainly a relatively small amount of money and a considerable amount of time).

Also, because of the comprehensive investigation Dr Wood has done into the events of 9/11 and my support of that research, we often get asked to look into other events which may not necessarily have a simple explanation or events that, like 9/11, have in no way been appropriately investigated by those that are paid to do such investigations (be they journalists or officials of one kind or another). I discuss an example of this in Chapter 26.

3. "Compliance and Acquiescence Disorder" – CAD

By an Individual Free Thinker (Andrew Johnson)

3 Nov 2010

This article is a satirical composition, inspired by what is described in the first paragraph. I wasn't quite sure where to place it in this book, but I thought it was worth including, as it relates to critical thinking.

The Diagnostic and Statistical Manual of Mental Disorders (DSM-IV), published by the American Psychiatric Association, has recently included a diagnosis of something termed Oppositional Defiant Disorder[23] which it defines as "a recurrent pattern of negativistic, defiant, disobedient and hostile behaviour towards figures of authority." Though this is included in a section entitled "Disorders Usually First Diagnosed in Infancy, Childhood or Adolescence", there is at least that word "usually."

However, it has become clear over the last few years, that many intelligent individuals have started to exhibit the symptoms of another form of "mental disturbance/disorder."

In simple terms, it manifests itself as a loss of independent thought. Typical symptoms include blindly following authority and believing everything one is told or believing what is shown on TV. Additionally, sufferers tend to accept, without question, the opinions of those who give the appearance of being "experts."

People suffering from this disorder usually watch too much TV or read too many newspapers. Their understanding of many topics commonly discussed in the media is generally shallow. In some cases, for those sufferers who have completed further or higher education they seem to experience an apparent difficulty in applying their usual analytical and research skills outside of their main area of study. They seem to exhibit a kind of "fear" and have a specific reaction when they are presented with certain types of information. This reaction is perhaps best described as Evidence Denial Disorder (EDD). This comes about when they are shown evidence which, under circumstances which would *not* challenge authority or an entrenched view, they would more readily examine and study without an immediate (usually negative) reaction. Some examples are given below.

The Spire – Turning to Dust on 9/11

Scientists who fully understand the laws of gravity, how things burn and even have a good grasp of chemistry and nuclear physics have failed to notice steel girders turning to dust - believing instead, they just 'burned down' – because a few news reports and some official-looking documents said so.

This is probably in part because their mental disorder has also been suffered by many scientists and 'experts' the world over. When the steel turning to dust is shown to these experts, a combination of EDD and CAD kick in – possibly induced by Fear of Loss of Employment (FOLE). EDD can sometimes manifest as a form of Tourette's syndrome – especially in internet media – where strings of insults are "fired" at those challenging the EDD sufferer to explain evidence (of the steel turning to dust).[24]

This is therefore symptomatic of an additional related disorder – Herd Mentality Disorder – HMD. Sufferers of this disorder forget that Science is based on the study of evidence. They believe instead, in specific cases, that the truth is established by *consensus* and that evidence can be liberally ignored to allow conclusions to be made even though they are completely wrong or inappropriate. They think that EDD will create "harmony" and "unity" among a group of researchers, for example.

Also, people suffering from this disorder are averse to intellectual challenges. For example, they are unable to study the evidence and come to the realisation that cures and non-toxic treatments for cancer have been suppressed for about over 80 years[25]. Their compliance and acquiescence prevent them from doing research thoroughly enough to establish this and FOLE will often come into play here.

Similarly, EDD/CAD sufferers are not able to process data relating to the idea of non-human entities interacting with us[26]. All evidence pertaining to such ideas is automatically filtered and/or rejected without it passing through the normal cognitive processing centres of the brain ("cognitive dissonance"). For example, study of DNA evidence[27] – which would normally be quite acceptable in a study establishing a family lineage or to determine whether a person was involved in a crime, is suddenly not acceptable as a way of proving something.

This leads these people to live in a false and limited reality – believing they have unlimited freedom. They fail to see the severe boundaries which are being externally applied to their freedom and so possibilities for the expansion of their consciousness are routinely shut down - usually without the person realising that this is happening.

One has to wonder if the spread of this disorder has come about with the administering of vaccinations, many of which have toxic substances in them[28]. It is possible that this causes brain function to be adversely affected – causing an increased risk of manifestation of any or all of CAD, EDD and HMD.

The internet has been something of a "battleground", where those sufferers of CAD, EDD and HMD often participate in forums, using anonymous handles, and insult those people who focus on presenting evidence and asking HMD sufferers to explain the anomalies[29]. When an EDD, CAD or HMD sufferer is moderator, they too may remain anonymous and then either delete or lock threads where evidence is being presented and CAD sufferers are being challenged[30].

Compliance and Acquiescence Disorder (CAD) can be taken advantage of by those with False Authority Disorder (FAD). FAD results from an inflation of ego and a propensity for exaggeration, or fear-mongering or over-assertion of one's personality. FAD increases the tendency of those suffering from it to ignore evidence (a variation on EDD), "bend the truth" or outright lie - in an effort to improve their standing among CAD sufferers.

The polarisation between those still able to think independently and focus on evidence – wherever it takes them – and CAD, EDD and HMD sufferers seems to be increasing – perhaps as it is realised just what is at stake.

Please note, that this article has been written by someone "affected" by EAA – Evidence Analysis Affinity. If you think you might be suffering from CAD, EDD or HMD, then you probably will have a negative reaction to this article – if this has exacerbated your condition, then please accept this apology and realise that your recovery will only be possible if you study the evidence *before* coming to conclusions.

(Final note: Does this article show that anyone can come up with an abbreviation and a plausible description of something that appears to be a "disorder" when in reality, it is just completely fabricated. The only difference in its presumed validity seems to be where you read it.)

4. Do We Have the Energy to Change the World?

This article was originally written for the Global BEM "Pulse" magazine, to accompany a 2012 conference in Hilversum, Netherlands. The magazine and the conference were about "breakthrough" energy technologies and what was being developed and how they would affect the world. The focus of this article is the same as the focus of this whole book – the connection between classified free energy technologies and the events of 9/11. It was part of my ongoing attempts to illustrate the importance of this to people and get them to think about the cover up.

Most people realise that our ability to access energy sources safely, responsibly and cheaply is fundamental to our (technological) progress as a society. Outside of events like this, a rather limited mindset is present. Even within groups like this, it is assumed that energy supplies are limited by certain factors – primarily the availability of fuel, or where energy is said to be "renewable", then it is limited by environmental factors such as the amount of solar radiation, amount of wind, water flow etc.

In my own lifetime, I have seen the various factors played off against each other – all set in what I call a "paradigm of scarcity." A great many doom-laden forecasts have suggested that our technological progress will be arrested quite abruptly. In the period of about 2003-2005, for example, it again became fashionable to talk about "peak oil." Now, hardly anyone is talking about peak oil.

The issues of energy and the environment are now fully woven together in the public mindset – because it has been "programmed" into people that the only way to get the majority of our energy is – essentially – by destroying the environment in some way. This then "causes" the existence of an environmental movement which at one time was just vocal in criticising the way energy is derived from fuel-based sources. Now, however, it sets government policy in many countries and forces certain controls to be placed on energy usage. However, behind this "green mask" lies a darker agenda – one of control of our freedom. Without a complete view of the "energy picture", the "control agenda" appears sensible and benign, but when more obscure histories from the last 100 years or so are studied in depth, an insidious cover up can be observed.

Many people have discussed aspects of this cover up, but only a very small number of people, including myself, have connected this cover up to what has become known as "The War on Terror." Indeed, others have appropriately re-used this cliché to describe that what we are involved in is a "A War on Terra" – i.e. that some group somewhere has co-opted us into helping us to destroy our own environment. In my presentation at BEM, I hope to illustrate clearly how this energy cover up is more far-reaching than most will discuss or acknowledge. In the 11 years (arguably longer) since Dr Judy Wood first connected the evidence seen in the aftermath of the events of 9/11 to energy phenomena, the number of people openly discussing this evidence is small. The number of people wishing to cover up knowledge of this (now obvious) link is much larger than I would have expected – and it seems that a comprehensive programme has been underway, for some time, which seemingly "rolls out" new personnel and new strategies to help manage the cover up.

In 2003, I discovered Dr Steven Greer's "Disclosure Project" and it confirmed two things for me. Firstly, it confirmed that the UFO cover up was real and secondly that there was a clear link between the UFO phenomenon and "free energy." The evidence indicates some groups appear to have access to advanced propulsion technology – which uses an "unconventional" energy source. Nick Cook's book "The Hunt for Zero Point" discusses the links between free energy and anti-gravity through the work of people like Thomas Townsend Brown. In 2006, I became familiar with Dr Judy Wood's investigation into the destruction of the World Trade Centre on 9/11 and this proved that some type of energy weapon was used to destroy most of the WTC complex on 9/11. In late 2007 and early 2008, more information was discovered showing the connection between the effects seen in the WTC evidence and the work of Canadian Experimental Researcher John Hutchison (see www.thehutchisoneffect.com). This resulted in ongoing character attacks against John Hutchison, Dr Judy Wood and to a lesser extent, myself. Weeks later, Dr Wood began to document the peculiarly synchronous presence and movement of Hurricane Erin near NYC with the events of 9/11, as they unfolded. So now, climate data were linked to the energy effects seen on 9/11 - primarily at the WTC.

At this point, the reason for the implementation of Steven E Jones as a "figurehead" in the 9/11 Research Community had already become clear. However, with certain effects – such as transmutation of elements – being observed both in John Hutchison's research and what Jones called "Cold Fusion" (more correctly called Chemically Assisted Nuclear Reactions – CANR, or Low Energy Nuclear Reactions - LENR), it became even clearer – the cover up needed to be carefully managed.

So here we are, 10 years after all those links were all clearly established – and who is talking about them? I wonder if President Dwight Eisenhower tried to warn people about the likelihood of something like 9/11 being perpetrated. Grant Cameron's archival Research at www.presidentialufo.com shows that it is extremely likely that "Ike" was briefed on the UFO issue - at a high level. The USA's secrecy apparatus was well established by the time Eisenhower left office in 1961 and so perhaps it was his fears about this which caused him to state

> *"The potential for the disastrous rise of misplaced power exists, and will persist. We must never let the weight of this combination endanger our liberties or democratic processes."*

He also said

> *Yet, in holding scientific research and discovery in respect, as we should, we must also be alert to the equal and opposite danger that public policy could itself become the captive of a scientific-technological elite.*

Who were the members of this "scientific-technological elite" he referred to? Perhaps some of them work for ARA and SAIC – two companies that were defendants in Dr Judy Wood's Qui Tam case in 2007.

I have argued and pointed out that one of the main reasons that we do not have Free Energy technology in general use is because such technology has already been weaponised. However, few people will look at the evidence and even fewer will talk about it. For example, I have never heard Dr Steven Greer – who, as described earlier, was instrumental in linking together the energy cover up and UFO cover up speak or write, in any meaningful way about 9/11. Further, his own Free Energy initiatives (SEAS Power, AERO 2012 and Project Orion) when scrutinised carefully do not appear to "do what they say on the tin." I found it very interesting to hear what Bruce De Palma - an inventor of another Free Energy Device – called the N-Machine, had to say about Free Energy and New Age Movements, before his death in 1997 (see: http://www.panacea-bocaf.org/brucedepalma.htm)

> *The CIA operates through various innocent looking fronts – to find out what people are thinking and what they're inventing. Now, what's more innocent than a benign institute – founded on transcendental principles to help New Age inventors bring free energy into the world?*

In this case, he seems to be referring to the Institute of Noetic Sciences (IONS) due to his experiences with the sixth man <u>not</u> to walk on the Moon, Edgar Mitchell.

If we want widespread use of free energy, we must first realise the obstacles in our way. Some of these obstacles can only be discovered by careful analysis and documentation. As well as solving engineering problems, it must be realised there is some type of "system" or "programme" in operation which is influencing people in subtle and not so subtle ways. Can this system be circumvented?

So, do we have the energy to change the world? Yes, we do – and that has been demonstrated thousands of times in the last 100 years. It was most clearly demonstrated, however, in the destruction of the WTC on 9/11. But do we have the energy to make sure that everyone in the world knows this? At this point, it's up to you and me to make sure "the job gets done."

Part 2

How the cover up of what happened on 9/11 is maintained by key people telling…

"Some truth, some half-truth – or anything but the truth…"

Graphics by "Betsy McGee"

5. "Alien Scientist" and His "Alien Science"

Edited/updated version of the 11 Oct 2011 posting.

Alien Scientist is (or was) an anonymous YouTube poster whose channel was created on 7th August 2008[31]. He has posted a number of very interesting videos – largely to do with topics such as UFO's and related secret technologies and so on. His channel does seem to be quite popular, having garnered (at the date of writing of this article) 43,526 subscribers.

In January 2011, he did an interview on the Progressive Technology Hour with William Alek[32]. The blurb for the interview is copied below:

> *The Alien Scientist is a man named Jeremy (approx 30) He prefers to have his last name/identity withheld due to the sensitive nature of his work and how that might affect his career goals as a young aspiring scientist and student of Physics. About 3-4 years ago Jeremy read "Behold a Pale Horse" by William Cooper and became interested in the UFO/Alien phenomenon for scientific purposes. This lead him into researching other conspiracies, such as 9/11. After reviewing much of the available information found online and finding a lack of strong scientific arguments and evidence, he decided to start making and posting his own videos in an attempt to battle the disinformation and counter-intelligence out there using the only proven method for finding the real truth: The Scientific Method.*

A question I then have at this point is "Why is he using this particular pseudonym, AlienScientist?" The title on his channel says:

> *The Science of TRUTH*

In the description it says:

> *Truth does not fear Investigation! DO YOUR OWN RESEARCH!*

So, here is some research and investigation I have done relating to what Jeremy the Alien Scientist has said.

A Video from 23rd December 2008

In late December 2008, I had cause to point out some errors in one of Jeremy the Alien Scientist's videos entitled 'Proof by Stereo-Type The "Conspiracy Theory" method', because it mentioned the research of Dr Judy Wood – a common "target" for misquoting and "muddling up", according to what I have been able to document since 2007[33].

This video was originally posted on AlienScientist's own channel[34], but soon after I posted the comments, listed below, the video above was deleted. (I made a video response to this and posted it on my own channel, but that channel got suspended in June 2011[35].)

Jeremy Alien Scientist's 'Proof by Stereo-Type The "Conspiracy Theory" method' was reposted, on the same day by a YouTube user using the name

"WarCrime911[36]", under the title of "How to Destroy the 9/11 Truth Movement[37]."

Jeremy Alien Scientist says in the above video "John Hutchison is a quack." Funny, in another of his videos he mentions John Hutchison quite a bit[38], but he does not say he is a quack.

I posted some comments on AlienScientist's video (reproduced below).

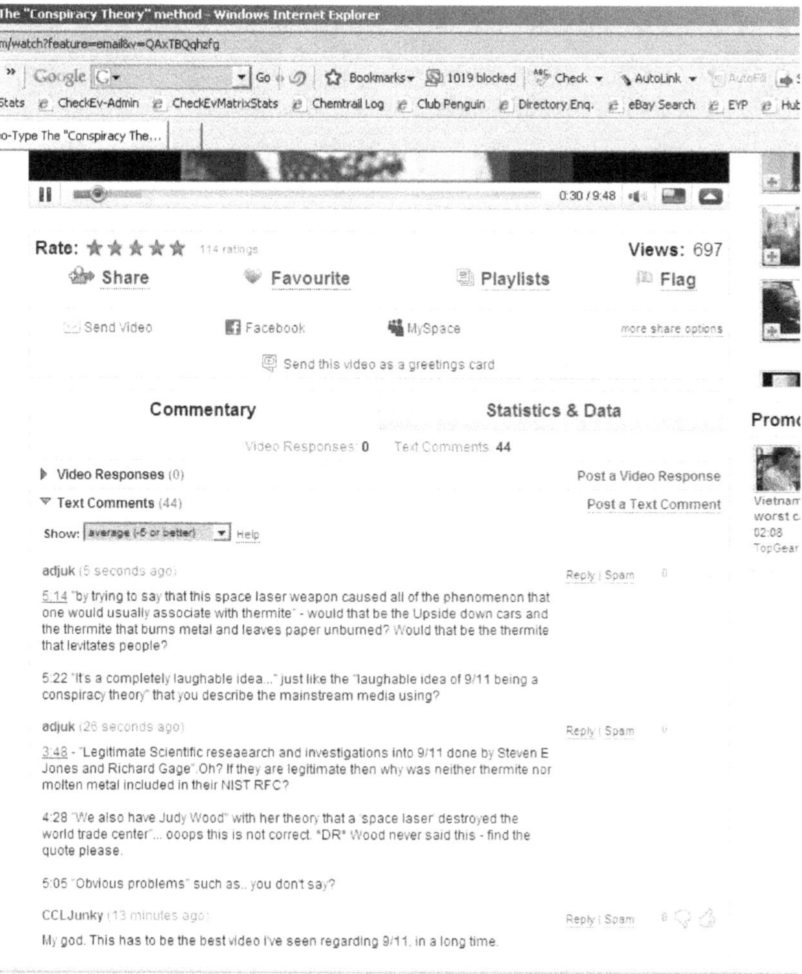

They are not insulting and they are factually correct. Why did he delete them, then block me from commenting on his channel? Did he feel my comments would "expose" him too much? The first 3½ minutes of his video are fine - but then he starts being rude about Dr Wood and Dr Morgan Reynolds - and making false or inaccurate statements. These are two people who have actually tried to prosecute those helping to cover up what happened on 9/11[39].

3:48 - "Legitimate Scientific research and investigations into 9/11 done by Steven E Jones and Richard Gage." Oh? If they are legitimate then why was neither thermite nor molten metal included in their NIST RFC?

*4:28 "We also have Judy Wood" with her theory that a 'space laser' destroyed the world trade center.".. ooops this is not correct. *DR.* Wood never said this - find the quote please.*

5:05 "Obvious problems" such as.. you don't say?

5:14 "by trying to say that this space laser weapon caused all of the phenomenon that one would usually associate with thermite" - would that be the Upside down cars and the thermite that burns metal and leaves paper unburned? Would that be the thermite that levitates people?

5:22 "It's a completely laughable idea..." just like the "laughable idea of 9/11 being a conspiracy theory" that you describe the mainstream media using?

*6:30 Odd - how can aluminium wing struts cut through steel girders? How come only 20% of 117 people within 1/2 mile of the WTC reported seeing or hearing the 2nd "plane." How come only 8% of that 117 reported seeing *and* hearing the plane?*

For those reading this, please see my YouTube videos for an analysis [of] some very important evidence this video misses out. e.g. Google 9/11 and Hurricane Erin

The problem with Jeremy Alien Scientist's "truthful" video is that he is promoting two known liars (Steven E Jones and Richard Gage) claiming they have done "legitimate scientific research," whilst misquoting Dr's Wood and Reynolds conclusions. Judging by the content of his videos, and the way they have been put together (it takes quite a long time to do some of these), Jeremy AlienScientist is not stupid – quite the reverse, it seems.

Though Jeremy AlienScientist talks about "The Science of Truth", the comments and observations on the video above prove that Jeremy AlienScientist has lied, so why is it, then, that he has built up something of an apparent following on YouTube? (More on this later).

AlienScientist's - Sept 2011 Video "9/11 Collapse Hypotheses"

Jeremy AlienScientist made another video called "9/11 Collapse Hypotheses[40]" (now deleted) and he lied again – several times. I pointed out a couple of these lies / omissions (mainly about Hurricane Erin[41]) in a comment

Well-seems AS has stopped saying "Judy Wood's Space Laser" theory!

watch?v=awy8cmcuBlk @ 4:28

And also,if thermite is "proved" why wasn't it in the RFC? 8:55 "violent opponent"? How so? Did you mean "vociferous"? I guess you're struggling with your diction! "Alienscientist?" It's amazing people even take you seriously when noone even knows who u are! Where's your 9/11 legal case?13 minutes & u didn't even mention Hurricane Erin. The questions you ask are answered in the book! Snapshot taken.

checktheevidence 1 day ago

Someone (I did not save their name, but it wasn't AlienScientist in this case) responded:

@checktheevidence, Have you even taken the time to check AlienScientist's 9/11 website? Just look at all the REAL evidence he has compiled!!! and you want to talk about a fucking Hurricane? Who the fuck cares? What the hell does a hurricane have to do with anything related to 9/11?

When it comes time for 9/11 Federal Grand Juries, you and Judy Wood will have no case, no evidence, and no suspects. Meanwhile AlienScientist has done excellent work bringing all that and more out into the light.

That's a fairly extreme reaction to me pointing out that Jeremy AlienScientist – who states that "truth does not fear investigation" – had not mentioned Hurricane Erin in his latest video about 9/11.

Following a discussion with a friend and supporter of our research, Thomas Potter, he decided to file a copyright violation notification with YouTube, because several images of Dr Wood and an image which is on the cover of my book[33]**Error! Bookmark not defined.** were misused, without permission. (Potter has both been accused of being Dr Wood herself or a "paid shill.") In the submission about the copyright violations made in "9/11 Collapse Hypotheses", Potter included these notes:

8:54 The narrator makes an oral utterance that Dr Judy Wood, "who insists that the towers were vaporized to dust..." Dr Judy Wood specifically says that the process was not vaporization as vaporization requires high heat. Vaporization is ruled out because it contradicts the evidence that there was no high heat. It discredits Dr Judy Wood to say she is promoting mutually contradictory descriptions. Therefore, to claim Dr Judy Wood said the buildings were vaporized is slander.

The narrator makes an oral utterance that Dr Judy Wood, "who insists that the towers were vaporized to dust by an unknown, undocumented, unproven effect, which has never been reproduced in a laboratory, and has no scientific credibility to substantiate it." It has been documented (see Where Did the Towers Go? Evidence of Directed Free-Energy Technology on 9/11 http://wheredidthetowersgo.com). The technology has been proven; it has been patented (see Chapter 17 of the book). And it has been reproduced in a lab (see Chapter 17 of the book) as well as the provided references and documentation. And it has credibility. Dr Judy Wood believes that Nikola Tesla has "credibility."

b.) 9:12 The narrator makes an oral utterance that "One of Dr Wood's hypotheses is a space-based weapon powered by..." Dr Judy Wood has never said this was a "space-based weapon" so to claim that she has is slander.

c.) 9:23 The narrator goes on to show a satellite-tracking map and proposes to debunk the false story he claimed Dr Judy Wood had put forth. Again, this is slanderous.

d.) 9:34 The narrator shows a cartoon of a ray beam from space, implying that is what Dr Judy Wood has been hypothesizing. Again, this is another count of slander. Presenting this slander while showing the cover of Dr Judy Wood's book makes this defamatory behavior more damaging.

e.) 9:55 The narrator states, "Even if the Hutchison Effect turns out to be a proven technology, which I don't deny..." which contradicts what he said at 8:54. It appears the narrator has contradicted himself to attempt to confuse those who know of this technology and convince them that it can't do what he is proposing...which is baseless.

This is why the video was removed by YouTube. Over the years, I have certainly grown weary of people like Jeremy AlienScientist either lying outright, or repeatedly getting things wrong – however many times they are corrected or statements clarified for them. This is completely different to "having an opinion" or "feeling a certain way" about something. Some people appear to have trouble distinguishing "an opinion" from "a lie" or "a feeling" and *what real, physical evidence shows and proves*, it seems. As I have stated earlier in this book, "When a man who is honestly mistaken learns the truth, he will either cease being mistaken, or cease being honest."

AlienScientist "Fan" Encourages "Debate"

In March 2010, I was contacted by someone (whose name I have withheld – even though I am doubtful the name he used was genuine) who seemed either to be a "fan" of Jeremy AlienScientist or was associated with him in some way. He seemed very keen for either myself or Dr Wood to "debate" AlienScientist either in an interview or on his forum as regards "theories" about what happened on 9/11. I pointed out to him that AlienScientist had lied and I saw no point in debating with someone who was a proven liar. It again struck me as strange – if Jeremy Alien Scientist wanted to talk to me, why didn't he contact me himself? You can read the peculiar exchange on my website, if you wish.[42] I mention it here because it seemed to me that Jeremy Alien Scientist has "helpers."

Jeremy AlienScientist and Edgar Fouché

Following my discovery of the Disclosure Project[43] in 2003, I started to research into topics related to Antigravity Technology and theories – and I avidly read Nick Cook's book, The Hunt For Zero Point[44] and watched a number of videos online. In 2004, I compiled some of the additional information I had come across into a PowerPoint presentation which I then narrated, using a desktop microphone, to create a video – called "The Case for Antigravity"[45]. (I created some introductory music using a free package called eJay and added some simple graphics.) In the video, I included information on current thinking about gravity and also historical research by figures like Thomas Townsend Brown. I uploaded this to Google Video – which had just come into service. (An updated version of this video was posted in 2010 by Anthony Beckett, following a presentation I gave at one of his Exopolitics

Conference.[46]) Since 2005, several people have re-uploaded this video (a matter I will return to shortly). Fouché was even briefly featured in a 1999 UK documentary about UFOs[47]. In this video, I mentioned the disclosures of a certain Edgar Fouché[48], who gave a few public presentations, starting in 1998, where he gave an account of his knowledge of a secret aircraft – called the TR-3B, developed as part of the "Aurora" Programme. According to Edgar Fouché:

- The operational model of the TR3B is 600 feet across.

- At least 3 of the billion dollar plus TR-3Bs were flying by 1994.

- The craft can travel at up to Mach 9 in any direction (due to reduced G-forces).

- At times a corona of silver blue light glowed around the circumference of the massive TR-3B.

- The TR-3B's outer coating is reactive and changes with radar stimulation and can change reflectiveness, radar absorptiveness, and colour.

- Quasi-Crystals are used in the vehicle's skin.

- Part of the propulsion is by Magnetic Field Disruption (MFD), which has been reverse engineered. Mercury based Plasma, pressurised at 250,000 atmospheres and at a temperature of 150K (-123C) is rotated at 50,000 rpm. (MFD research had started as early as 1955.)

- This reduces the weight of the centre of the craft by 89%. This increases manoeuvrability by 89% as well.

- TR-3B uses Nuclear Thermal Hydrogen / Oxygen Engines for manoeuvring

What struck me about Edgar Fouché's account was the level of technical detail he gave. This level of detail is rare in the accounts of so-called whistleblowers who have appeared on websites such as "Project Camelot" and "Coast to Coast." A couple of years later, Fouché became inactive and had seemingly "disappeared." I included this information in a short booklet that I later made[49].

Edgar Fouché's account is told from his position as someone who was both in the US Air Force and as someone who later worked as a defence contractor. He has posted a number of documents about his background (see http://www.checktheevidence.com/ for details).

Going back to the matter of the "Case for Antigravity" video that I made in 2004/2005, one poster that re-uploaded it was… "Alien Scientist!"[50]. Interestingly, this poster included my original description/summary and then added the following text:

> *This was one of the videos I stumbled upon in my initial research into anti-gravity which lead me into researching Ed Fouché and first revealed to me the existence of Metamaterials and Quasicrystals (which I had no idea about at the time)* **I credit this video for inspiring me to take the research a step further and create the AlienScientist YouTube Channel. I am now paying my respects to the author of this video by re-uploading it here to YouTube** *so that more people can learn about the work that inspired me.*

In 2010, I came across a channel called efearfull [51]– and this turned out to be Edgar Fouché. On efearfull's channel, he stated (in September 2011):

> *Hey, finally I'm going to be a Special Guest on the Alienscientist.com Forum. We're great friends and you can join for free and talk about anything you want including ask us questions. I've been a Special Guest on Open Minds Forum and still am.*

This connection, I think, is important and it led to a later collaboration with Edgar Fouché between the end of 2013 and 2015, details of which are on my website.

Jeremy AlienScientist and Eugene Podkletnov and American Antigravity

Another researcher into antigravity/gravity effects is Eugene Podkletnov[52]. On 12 December 2010, Jeremy AlienScientist posted a full-length interview with Eugene Podkletnov from 2004[53]. How did AlienScientist get this video, and why was it posted approximately 6 years after it was recorded?

Information about Eugene Podkletnov seems scanty - he did a couple of podcasts – for example originally on the American Antigravity Website[54], then he seemed to "disappear." I have archived two Podkletnov Interviews on my website[55],[56]

Curiously, if you look in the audio archives on the American Antigravity Website[54]**Error! Bookmark not defined.** or search for "podlkletnov"[57] (as of the date of writing/posting this article), no results are returned. A trip to the Internet Archive also allows access to a Podkletnov interview from a snapshot of the American Antigravity Website[58]. (Go to the very bottom of the referenced page.)

However, as of 11 Oct 2011, the site prominently features John Searle's research[59], which I do not have a very high regard for[60]. (I think it is worth comparing the way John Searle talks with the way Podkletnov talks). The American Antigravity Website also features an interview with John Hutchison[61] about his research, which I wrote considerably more about in *9/11 Finding the Truth.*

In summary, then, the connection here is between Ed Fouché, the events of 9/11, AlienScientist, Eugene Podkletnov and … gravity (or anti-gravity).

Alienated Scientist

It was somewhat ironic to later discover that this "AlienScientist" who had been "inspired" by my 2005 video, would not "pay me respect" when I pointed out errors and mistakes in one of his other videos (see chapter 0). It became clear that his motivations were significantly different to my own. "Alien Scientist" was not interested in "the truth, the whole truth and nothing but the truth," as I am. He later demonstrated that his main interest in the truth was to *help cover parts of it up.* This YouTube poster, Alien Scientist – later revealed his identity to be Jeremy Rys. It became clear that he was posting lies about what happened on 9/11 and in doing so, he was deliberately leading people away from the truth.) Also of note is Alien Scientist's Facebook Page[62], where it states:

> *A non-profit educational foundation teaching science, logic, and critical thinking skills and how to apply them to complex topics with an overall goal of bettering humanity by promoting the creation of a peaceful, sustainable, space faring society.*

It is unclear what the components of his "educational foundation" actually are, however – beyond a YouTube channel and a website. (i.e. perhaps I have inadvertently created my own "educational foundation" by creating a website and YouTube channel. That is to say, his "educational foundation" description is meaningless in this context.)

Alien Scientist – Connections

In researching Jeremy Rys, two significant connections came to light. Firstly, Rys had a connection to Richard Heene, the father of "balloon boy." The Balloon Boy Story[63] received blanket coverage in the US media for a short period in late 2009. Richard Heene claimed that, without him knowing, his son was carried off inside a helium filled balloon that he had made in his back garden – a home video showed them launching the balloon[64] then panicking after realising their son was "in the balloon" as it floated upwards. The "media drama" revolved around the story of the child being endangered by this situation – as no one knew where it would land. However, Richard Heene was later charged with wasting police time, as he lied about his son being in the balloon. He pleaded guilty to the charge and went to prison in early 2010[65].

The peculiar thing is, a photo on the American Antigravity Website[66] shows Jeremy Rys filming Richard Heene - with what seems to be a good quality video camera.

Jeremy Rys and Richard Heene in 2009

What, exactly, is the connection between these two people (apart from them both being proven liars)?

The other interesting connection is Jeremy Rys' father - Richard A Rys. A page on his website[67] documents:

SUMMARY OF MAJOR PROJECTS

*June 2010 – present - Working with **Invensys** to provide **control systems for 8 PWR style Nuclear reactors** to be located in Fuqing, Fangjiashan, and Hainan China. The projects total about 7300 MW of power. The main role has been to test the control system software and hardware. The control platform is a combination of IA systems, Triconex, and ATOS for the graphical user interface.*

Further inspection of this web page reveals that Richard A Rys works in the energy industry, with a company called Invensys – in a project engineer's role. A quick look at the Invensys Website[68] reveals

*Invensys works with: **23 of the top 25 petroleum companies,** 48 of the top 50 chemical companies, **18 of the top 20 pharmaceutical companies, 35 of the top 50 nuclear power plants**, all of the top 10 mining companies, 7 of the top 10 appliance manufacturers.*

*Invensys enables:, **20% of the world's electricity generation**, 18% of the world's crude oil refining, 37% of the world's nuclear energy generation, **62% of the world's liquefied natural gas production**, 23% of the world's chemical production.*

I am given to wonder if (because I have no evidence that) Richard A Rys knows Tony Craddock[35]Error! Bookmark not defined. . . .

Having established certain facts about Jeremy "Alien Scientist" Rys, let us return to his association with Edgar Fouché.

Alien Scientist supports Edgar Fouché!

On the same day I posted my article (which this chapter is derived from) – 11 Oct 2011, Jeremy Rys posted a new YouTube video[69] to promote his new internet discussion forum, linked to his website. In this video, starting at 0:32, Jeremy Rys states:

> *Former Area 51 Employee Edgar Fouché is a special guest on my forum, so you have the rare opportunity to directly talk with a former employee of the top secret military base at Groom Dry lake and ask him any questions you'd like.*

If Jeremy Rys is using this to promote his new forum, he must think that Ed's information is important and truthful, must he not?

The Alien Scientist Forum and Its Demise - Edgar Fouché Writes to Andrew Johnson

The Alien Scientist Forum[70] ran for almost 2 years - it has been defunct since early November 2013[71]. Around 20th November 2013, Edgar Fouché contacted me via my YouTube channel[72] and we arranged to talk on Skype. He acknowledged our earlier correspondence back in 2010 regarding Jeremy Rys and we agreed to do some interviews. I can only presume that Ed Fouché decided to contact me because I had mentioned him in earlier videos that I had made and I also had some knowledge of Jeremy Rys and how he was "operating." Perhaps his decision to contact me was connected to the demise of the Alien Scientist forum, which Ed had apparently invested a considerable amount of time posting information on (all of these posts are no longer accessible). The interviews with Ed Fouché can be found on my website[73].

Alien Scientist – Further Brief Notes

In my conversations with Ed Fouche, he told me that Rys had been to prison twice. This seems to be indicated in this report[74] from the area where Rys lives[75], which mentions probation,

> *At 10:23 p.m., Jeremy Rys, 1 Cherry St., was put in custody on an arrest warrant. Police went to his home at 9:15 p.m., and his family said he was not home. Police received a call from Rys who said he forgot his phone charger when he went to work, and will call his probation officer in the morning. Dispatch called probation who asked for Rys to be picked up by police.*

Thursday, July 31

At 5:14 a.m., police received a call reporting there were three brown horses approximately six feet tall in the road on Elm Street and almost hit the caller's vehicle. Norton Police Department sent the horses' owner to pick them up, and she took them back to Norton in a trailer.

At 4:04 p.m., police responded to a call on Summit Avenue to assist Mansfield Fire Department with an 18-month-old that ingested fragrance spray. The child was transported to Norwood Hospital.

At 9:52 p.m., police were informed that a male with short brown hair in a blue shirt at Duo's Liquors, 30 Chauncy St., was attempting to pass a fake form of identification. The caller told police the male took the identification from him and ran out of the store before he could call the police. The caller told police the male left in a black Accord, and headed west on Route 106.

At 10:23 p.m., Jeremy Rys, 1 Cherry St., was put in custody on an arrest warrant. Police went to his home at 9:15 p.m., and his family said he was not home. Police received a call from Rys who said he forgot his phone charger when he went to work, and will call his probation officer in the morning. Dispatch called probation who asked for Rys to be picked up by police.

Let us also note this picture:

Jeremy Rys – Left, Richard Gage - Centre

Summary and Conclusion

Jeremy Rys has had a past conviction for which he has been on probation. He has had an association with convicted fraudster Richard Heene.

From the evidence linked and discussed above, I conclude that Jeremy Alien Scientist Rys is involved in managing the disclosure of information relating to antigravity technology – and he is willing to lie whilst doing this. The disclosures of Eugene Podkletnov are "safer" – possibly because what he has said is harder to prove –we cannot personally verify his experiments and there do not seem to be any easily viewable / accessible reproductions of them. Jeremy Rys has now attacked Edgar Fouché and Dr Judy Wood – both of whom have brought forward credible information relating, in some way, to secret energy technology and secret antigravity technology.

Again, it illustrates the fundamental importance of Dr Judy Wood's research – apparently, this is an "unsafe" type of disclosure.

6. SAIC, Dr Steven Greer, Disclosure, 9/11 and the CIA

SAIC-Science Applications International Corporation

SAIC were defendants in Dr Judy Wood's 2007 9/11-related Qui Tam Case[76]. This company was mentioned by several Disclosure Project Witnesses as significant benefactors of Black Budget Programs. In 2013, SAIC split into 2 companies – and so sometimes now go under the name **LEIDOS.** From SAIC's website (page 31 of the referenced PDF), we read[77]:

> *Following the September 11, 2001, terrorist attacks, we responded rapidly to assist a number of customers near ground zero in New York City and in Washington, D.C*

SAIC are involved in research or manufacture of Directed Energy Weapons Systems/Components[78] (Listed as LEIDOS). SAIC oversaw ground zero security from 13.11.01[79]. Another specialty is of SAIC is Psychological Operations (PsyOps)[80].

Dr Steven Greer

As I have written elsewhere, it was my discovery of Dr Steven Greer's research that led me to find out the truth about 9/11. It is therefore ironic that I should later find evidence that Steven Greer himself has become part of the 9/11 cover up and the energy cover up. I have written about his apparent role in the energy cover up in an article on my website called "Something in the Aero.[81]" However, I had also observed Greer's reluctance to talk about 9/11 – such as when he wrote, in 2007, in an article entitled "Transformation of Risk" originally posted on his Aero2012 Website[82]:

> *This overview explains how the current risks of environmental global warming, air pollution and public health challenges, energy resource scarcity and competition, global terrorism and current electric grid obsolescence and vulnerability are transformed by these out-of-the-box technologies.*

Years earlier, Greer posted an article soon after 9/11, on his Disclosure Project Website[83]. He wrote:

> *This is not to excuse in any way the evil, monstrous and inhuman acts of Osama bin Laden or others of his ilk. There can be no rationalizing such horrific deeds. But we can understand it: Why him, why us, why now: why. **Fanatics like bin Laden are hell-bent on running America out of the Middle East** because they view our presence there as a virtual invasion of their land, culture and values. They view us as an imperial power colonizing their region **in order to secure cheap oil, and it is resented**. To a lesser extent, they are concerned about our support for Israel, but bin Laden himself has made it very clear in numerous speeches that their main concern is getting the US out of Saudi Arabia, the land containing the most holy sites in the Islamic world.*

However, on 21st November 2015, at the end of a 3 hour + talk[84], Steven Greer faced a question from a seemingly informed member of the audience. Greer's response seemed to clearly underline his support for the cover up of what happened on 9/11. He did not discuss any real evidence - nor did he wish to. Instead, he said very little of note. One might even perceive what he said as a warning - to NOT look at the available evidence...

Question: There's compelling evidence that not just the towers, but the entire World Trade Centre Complex was destroyed by perhaps a directed energy type of weapon something that was operating on a technology of molecular dissociation - that seems to be very much related to what you've been talking about. Have you looked at that?

*Answer: I have looked at it - you know, I have bigger fish to fry... 9/11 was terrible - um we lost 3000 people... it lead to 2 huge wars and trillions of dollars... [Pause] I will tell you this. I'm not going to get into specifics. I mentioned] a gentleman named Richard Foche 3rd highest guy... Richard Foche at the Naval Research Labs he was in meetings with the then Vice President of the United States - Cheney - and he said "Absolutely it was known about in advance - and there was involvement at that level." And he told me - and I have witnesses, multiple witnesses to this - that if he were to speak of this... (Now he's passed away...) That he, his wife, his children and his grandchildren would all be killed. That's all I am gonna say on the 9/11 issue. But there is a lot to that story - I've never shared publicly what I just said... but the man has passed away. So it's not hard to ... and I think most people... get into these **grand conspiracy theories...** Basically all you have to do is stand down. There's constant threat - there is terrorism out there... you don't even have to hoax an event in that case ... You just have to stand down the systems that would've intercepted it. You understand what I am saying? So it's like when you're doing a 'code blue' ... "Boom! Clear!" You say "clear" before you do the electric shock. So you just clear the system and let it come in and hit... Now, what I think happened on 9/11 is more like what I just described and I have very good reason to believe that because someone of that integrity and rank had a front row seat - and knew about it - and I've never spoken of this before right now. But I think that .. it's disturbing, it's enraging, but it's a minor rounding error compared to what's coming if we don't end this cartel's hegemony on the secrecy related to UFO's, ET's what have you. 9/11 is going to be a very minor blip on the screen. So that's my warning to people - you can take it or not. **But I've known what you've just asked about since it happened. My whole security team lit up** like you wouldn't believe when that happened...*

If Greer had "known what you've just asked about since it happened" (i.e. the use of an energy weapon), why was he pushing the Bin Laden fable in his 2001 article, referenced above? I think Steven Greer knows a lot more than he said here. Even going back to 2005, in an interview for Hustler magazine[85], he says:

Q: Who else is making these phony UFOs?

A: The companies involved are SAIC [Science Applications International Corporation], TRW, Northrop, Raytheon and EG&G. We have enomous intelligence on this. I know the buildings where this stuff is going on. This needs to come out so people know the truth.

Later in the same interview he states:

> *Q: Who's in this covert group?*
>
> *There's a committee of 200 to 300 people who are on the policy board for this issue. Admiral Bobby Ray Inman, who went from head of the National Security Agency to the board of **SAIC** - which is one of the crown jewels of this covert entity - is a member. So is Admiral Harry Trane. George Bush Sr., Cheney and Rumsfeld are involved, as is the Liechtenstein banking family. **The Mormon corporate empire has an enormous interest in this subject**; they have much more power than the White house or the Pentagon over this issue. And there are secret cells within the Vatican.*

I will just briefly mention here that Steven E Jones is a Mormon.[86]

Greer says some interesting things on P157 (or thereabouts) of his book Forbidden Truth, Hidden Knowledge[87]:

> *At a subtle level of electromagnetism, you can transmute elements, and also transfer something from one place to another - and infect or harm someone electronically. This is a very lethal application of a science that could be used to heal people. Unfortunately, right now, the worst elements of humanity currently possess these technologies.*
>
> *When people worry about these technologies being disclosed, I say: "Forget about it. The worst elements already have them!*

From "Testimony of Denise McKenzie, former SAIC employee, March 2001", Page 308 – 309, "DISCLOSURE PROJECT BRIEFING DOCUMENT"[88]

> *Essentially SAIC is one of the crown jewels of the super-secret, black project world and is connected to UFO technologies and covert funding. Former NSA head Adm. Bobby Inman is heavily involved with SAIC, it should be noted. Here again, we see the revolving door between military and corporate projects described by Dr Rosin .*

In 2017, a YouTube video was posted of a radio/podcast interview with Dr Greer, in which he said the following[89]:

> *"In the 90s, I had 3 people on my team assassinated including a... very close friend.*
>
> *[What has shifted now...]*
>
> *There were people in the agency who really wanted us to succeed – and I was gonna shut down this whole project when this happened... and they said "NO! You have to keep going... we need **someone on the outside this has to be known...** our planet that's going off the rails here...*
>
> *I'm an emergency doctor working in an ER, taking care of shootings and all that stuff and I said "You know what? This is just getting to be too ridiculous.." and they said, "**Do you want executive protection?**" and I said "Whatdya mean?" and they said... "**Do you wanna be have a [assisted?] protection - you and your team?**"*
>
> *This was after the **CIA Director Bill Colby - who was going to help us bring out one of these free energy devices and bring it out to the world***

– was found floating down the Potomac river – assassinated. And I said "Well, I really don't like to play that game… it's a very dangerous game – it's called wet works…… But if they're targeting my people, I said 'I believe in self-defence – make it happen.' So, I won't say who this person is… still a very senior person – science director at the CIA – offered this protection and some other folks and I said 'yeah let's do it.' So, since then, we've had no problems.

Is this an admission that Steven Greer is working for the CIA? In the "Sirius" Film he made, released in April 2013, he talked about having a "dead man's trigger" document[90] – to be released if he was ever assassinated. We see, then, some serious contradictions here. It seems Dr Greer is controlled by the CIA and will not tell the truth about 9/11 and SAIC's clear connection to the event.

7. 9/11 Truth "Deafness" in Toronto Hearings

International "Hearings" in Toronto To Discuss *Only* the "Popular" 9/11 Evidence.

11 Aug 2011

This article was written about another fake 9/11 truth event which again served to keep the cover up of the most important 9/11 evidence in place. Nothing else came of this hearing.

As we approach the anniversary of the terrible events of 9/11, some anticipation and chatter seems to be building up in relation to what have been described as "International Hearings" regarding the events of 9/11. Although "news" of these hearings seems to have been posted in February 2011 (http://torontohearings.org/), a couple of people have reposted information about them recently.

Dr Judy Wood and myself have already received a number of messages either telling us about these "hearings" or asking if we have heard about them. I have therefore put together this short article to confirm that I certainly have heard about them – and so has Dr Wood. Here I provide some information which should give you a more balanced view of what these hearings will be about and what outcome they may have.

I couldn't help wondering exactly what will be "heard" at these hearings. They almost sound like a re-run of the "9/11 Omission Hearings" in 2004[91]. A key person apparently involved with these hearings is James Gourley. According to a page[92] on the 9/11 Truth.org website

the final report [from the hearings] will be edited by American attorney James Gourley.

This was quite interesting to us because it was James Gourley who failed to submit a Qui Tam case to challenge NIST's contractors back in 2007, when he was working with Steven E Jones and Richard Gage on their "Request for Correction" (RFC).

Ralph Winterrowd, who has been an important figure in supporting Dr Wood and myself in the 9/11 research Dr Wood has done, telephoned Mr Gourley on 08 August 2011. He asked if Dr Wood had been invited to speak at this conference in Toronto. Mr Gourley confirmed that Dr Judy Wood had not been invited. When asked for the reason, Gourley stated that the "steering committee" had decided not to invite her and Mr Gourley stated that "she is absolutely wrong on every point she makes." Gourley then stated he had written a paper about Dr Wood's research and so had Greg Jenkins and that Dr Wood "had never answered either one of them." Sadly, Gourley is mistaken or he is lying. A response to points Jenkins makes was posted on 02 July 2007[93] (and an earlier response was posted by Andrew Johnson[94]). A response to the "hit pieces" in *Journal of Nine-Eleven Studies* (JONES) was also posted on the same date.[95]

For the hearings themselves, when I looked at the guest list (a more appropriate description than the "witness" list term they used), I wondered if we would hear Richard Gage accuse the only person who has done a forensic investigation into the destruction of the WTC - Dr Judy Wood - of practising "witchcraft"[96]? (I discussed this episode in *9/11 Finding the Truth*.)

Would we hear David Ray Griffin say Global Democracy is the way forward[97]? Or would he suggest we resolve the truth about 9/11 by counting the number of google search results[98]?

 And would Dr Griffin mention that for his book, "A New Pearl Harbour" (first edition) Richard Falk wrote the foreword[99]? Would he mention that his friend Mr. Falk is a Council on Foreign Relations (CFR) member[100]?

Would we hear Steven E Jones say it was safe to dip your fingers in Molten Metal[101]?

Perhaps Dr Jones will suggest that Paint on Thermite was used in the destruction of the WTC…[102]

 I wonder if the "truth troops" - especially Gage, Gourley, Jones and Harrit will mention Thermite a lot - like they usually do. Will they be honest and report how they "passed" on the opportunity to submit their "conclusive" evidence to NIST[103]?

Will Kevin Ryan draw a comparison between the submission he made to NIST regarding the WTC 7 draft report and the submission by Dr Judy Wood[104]?

With that said, I feel I am able to hazard a guess at what would NOT be heard. I doubt the "hearings" will mention how the principle of operation of the weapon which destroyed the WTC is now known[105].

I doubt the hearings will mention Hurricane Erin moving towards NYC for 4 days before 9/11 and making a right hand turn on the 9/12[106].

I doubt the hearings will mention that a legal case started by Dr Wood in 2007 included a proportion of this evidence in submissions made to the court and in the appeal[107].

Mind you, as long as the subjects covered at the "hearings" are "popular" it doesn't matter about the truth does it?

The hearings also seem to have an associated website[108] (Originally 9/11cc.org). I posted a comment on their "contact us" page[109], advising them of Dr Judy Wood's research[2Error! Bookmark not defined.], conclusions and court case[110]. Predictably, someone posted a response thus:

*Although Judy Wood is nuttier than squirrel ***** and has eye pupils the size of Texas, she would get chased out of the ring in one round by the great pamphleteer, Judy Cunningham!!*

The Reason for Documenting This

Here we see a whole conference organised in Toronto to promote disinformation about 9/11. Dr Wood's research was, once again, completely censored. Not only that, but when I remarked on this on the associated website, it wasn't very long before someone posted a personal insult whilst disregarding the information posted. This, again, is just another example of what I demonstrated in *9/11 Finding the Truth* and it is something that is probably still happening today.

8. 9 or 11 "Clues" about Simon Shack and a 3D-Analysis of Flight 175

May/July 2012

September Clues

Around the beginning of June 2007[111], a new video appeared – called "September Clues"[112]. It presented an analysis of the events as they were shown on TV on 9/11/2001. It tried to present the evidence that some of the images we were shown of the events could not have been real. The person who had produced/edited this video used the pseudonym "Social Service" and he seemed to be associated with a band of the same name[113].

Around this time, I had been following the discussion and presentation of the so-called "video fakery" and "no planes" evidence by people such as Nico Haupt, Rosalee Grable and Ace Baker, and so I was very interested in this new video series and I watched all of it.

Over the next few months "Social Service" produced additional "episodes" documenting further anomalies in the video record of 9/11. One of the interesting things he noted that, as the events unfolded on TV, a number of phone calls were made to various TV stations where witnesses claimed to have seen a plane hitting the tower. Oddly, most - if not all - of these calls that were aired were from media people – TV producers, their wives or other staff from TV stations. Some of the callers - like Teresa Renaud - seemed to describe events they could not possibly have seen clearly[114], based on where they said they were when they made the call (this is illustrated in one part of "September Clues").

If you watch the September Clues series[115], you will probably see why I was impressed by the detail that "Social Service" had studied and pointed out in his videos.

Social Service released several updates to September clues and it finally ended up as 8 ten-minute segments and a couple of additional "epilogue" videos. Around this time, it was revealed that Social Service's name was "Simon Shack."

It seemed Shack could be "onto something" - as he was being attacked by quite a number of people – even by "fellow" 9/11 researchers like Ace Baker[116] and Anthony Lawson[117]. One particular area of "confrontation" was the so called "nose out" video[118] – where it was illustrated that in one video, the nose of the plane appeared to have penetrated the whole WTC tower! (Arguments then circulated about the details of this[119].)

Andrew Johnson Offers Support to Simon Shack

In July or August 2008, on a forum, Simon Shack made a request for some web storage space for his videos. At the time, I had set up some web space, and paid a 1-year subscription – but then the people I set the website up for didn't want it and I had no real use for it, so I offered some of the space to Simon Shack to store his video files etc, and I gave him the passwords. Additionally, I purchased a domain name[120] for Simon Shack www.septclues.com - at modest cost.

Sometime after this, because I thought Simon Shack was interested in finding the truth, I asked him if he would be interested in recording a "Podcast" about his "September Clues" research and also about his thoughts on the research of Dr Judy Wood. This research has proved that an energy weapon or weapons, which appear(s) to operate on a principle of "field interference" was/were used to destroy the WTC complex[2]**Error! Bookmark not defined.**. (As I have written elsewhere, it was also used as the basis of a Qui Tam Fraud case)[121]. Simon Shack never responded to my request – and I moved on to other things without repeating it. However, this didn't really matter, because it later became clear what his thoughts on these issues were.

Approximately 1 year later in August 2009, Simon Shack wrote to me[122] pointing out that the web space I had given him was "no longer accessible." This was because the package I had originally bought (for someone else – not me and not Simon Shack) had "expired" and I had chosen not to renew it. I therefore sent Simon Shack the passwords to access the Website control panel so that he would be able to use his own credit card to pay for a renewal – in no way did I block access to the site.

Since 2007, I have given out hundreds of copies of September Clues on DVD. Whilst arguments about details are ongoing, I still find parts of the analysis of the "plane" related video clips compelling. Despite everything, Shack's research helped to illustrate that real planes could not have crashed at any of the 4 sites, it also highlighted other oddities, such as a news reporter going to LAX airport to meet with families and friends that would have been waiting for people to disembark from the hijacked flights (which never made it to LAX airport). However, when he got there, he found only 2 people waiting – and that the airport was going to be evacuated[123].

9/11 Actors!

Over time, I have become more suspicious of what Simon Shack has been doing – especially when he started to claim that *all* the video and images from 9/11 are *fake*. He has made a video called "9/11 Actors" where he has claimed that relatives and friends of victims of the events – such as Bob McIlvane are actors who are simply "going through the motions" when they have been speaking about their anguish at public events[124]. However, Shack presents no other real evidence in this video other than what he interprets as their odd behaviour. This sort of analysis or view seemed to follow on from other (to me, more convincing) videos that showed that people did seem to have been "planted" early on to "cement" the official story – even as it was unfolding[125].

In his "9/11 Actors" Video, at 6:47, Shack declares (with a clever design) "What a Smart Scheme it was. A total simulation upheld by a group of actors doing what they do best: SIMULATION"[126]

9/11 Shills!

Following this, in his "9/11 Actors" video, Shack plays in quick succession a number of photos of various researchers and figures who have spoken out against the official story of 9/11. If you look carefully, at 6:57, you will notice that he includes a picture of Dr Judy Wood[127]. Some of the other pictures that Simon shows really are of actors – such as Charlie Sheen. What subliminal message is Simon Shack trying to embed? (Note: he flashes up pictures and includes no specific evidence to back up any allegations – in fact, he makes no specific allegations in this part of the video.)

Dr Judy Wood Sent Hate Mail, Right?

Earlier on, I mentioned that it became clear to me why Simon Shack was not interested in the truth about 9/11 – as proved by Dr Judy Wood's research. The inclusion of Dr Wood's photo in his "Actors" video, described above, is one reason. On his forum, he made a post that implied Dr Judy Wood had sent him some hate mail through a YouTube account[128]. (This wasn't the first time he had referred to this supposed hate mail.) In this same post he writes:

> *I see that Judy Wood has published a new book. However, her research is based on fake pictures. The sole purpose of her existence is, imho, to provide 'a plausible explanation' for the very stupid-looking WTC 'pulverization' animations.*

So, Shack thinks the research is inconclusive because "the photos are fake." It seems clear, if one reads the language used in the supposed hate mail sent via YouTube that it could not have been Dr Judy Wood. Simon Shack seems to think that because the YouTube channel is there, it must be Dr Wood's. (There are apparent efforts of fellow posters to "bolster" this idea.) However, if you look at this channel, you will see that there are no videos uploaded on it – and it is decidedly "austere."

Simon Shack also stated:

> *"Is this really Judy's YT channel", you may ask... Well, at the time I did ask Andrew Johnson (her research colleague whom I've been in touch with in the past) for clarification.*

That may have been true when he made the post (6th May 2011) – but soon after, he contacted me via Skype text chat and I confirmed to him that this was not Dr Judy Wood's channel (more on this "chat" later).

Also, the message said Dr Judy Wood would "sue" Simon Shack, but Simon doesn't make it clear in the post why Dr Wood would want to sue him. It is not clear now either.

I can confirm that the YouTube channel "DrJudyWood" does not belong to Dr Judy Wood and it does not belong to me. I do not know who it does belong to. Also, as far as I can remember, when I originally looked at this channel, it was only subscribed to one other channel – that of SimonShack (though that has since changed). I can also confirm that Simon Shack is the only person I am aware of that received hate mail from the YouTube channel with the name "DrJudyWood."

Real Names Vs. Aliases and Pseudonyms

People who have seen how I approach things will know that I avoid any kind of anonymity. There are a number of reasons for this, one of the main ones being that the culture of anonymity that was created on forums some years ago is a big factor in making them what they are – for discussing subjects such as 9/11, they are largely a waste of time now. You don't know who you're talking to unless (like me) everyone uses their real name or can be immediately known by the name they use.

As it turns out, Simon Shack is actually a Pseudonym. Simon Shack's real name is Simon Hytten and he disclosed this on his forum in March 2011[129]. (Hytten is Norwegian for "hut" or "cabin" - hence "Shack.") So, Simon Shack has not been using his real name – only a possible translation of it.

It's All Fake!

Mr Shack (Hytten) has now gone to the ridiculous extent of claiming that *all* 9/11 video and photo footage is fake - and he therefore claims it cannot be relied upon to determine how the towers were destroyed. Yes, really! He confirmed this in a Skype chat I had with him[130].

My assumption/thought was that if CGI was used, it would be done well – and not show anomalies such as disappearing wings (we don't see this in Hollywood movies from 2001 using CGI, do we?).

As for the lighting anomalies/colour of the plane, one can make the same arguments for projection and CGI – in both cases, the image shown wasn't particularly accurate.

But there is another reason for me being far less convinced about the plane CGI than I was back in, say, 2009 or so. It's because, as mentioned above, Simon Shack went on to declare all 9/11 footage (not just video of the plane crashes) was fake. This then paved the way for talk of "Vicsims" (which came out around 2011 or 2012 I think) where people started to claim *all* the events were fabricated (using Crisis Actors) etc. Then, we had Sandy Hook where, according to the liar James Tracy "No victims died" etc. (he has changed his claims over time). Now we have a "Flat Earth" PsyOp because it is assumed NASA images are faked / CGI. (The NASA hoax claim is also, of course, related to the proof that the Apollo missions did not go to the moon – or at least, the claims about the named astronauts having been there and being filmed there cannot be true).

I am not sure if or to what extent CGI was used in 9/11 videos and photos - that are claimed to be real. I just know that Simon Shack heavily promoted this idea - and he is not trustworthy (and I can prove this). Similar faulty 9/11 video fakery claims have been made by Markus Allen - and these have been carefully deconstructed by Mark Conlon in a series of articles which I discuss in chapter 23.

Simon's Skype Chat

On several occasions, Simon Hytten has contacted me via Skype text chat[130]**Error! Bookmark not defined.**. On 24th Aug 2010, he asked me:

> *[24/08/2010 22:29:08] simon shack: Andrew, why don't you return to our forum? Tell me frankly now: are you somehow connected to the UK intelligence agencies? Don't get offended now - you know that I'm a quite normal person making my utmost to understand the oddities of this planet.*

Some slightly odd questions. However, I have never posted on Simon Shack's "clues" forum. He did have another forum (z6.invisionfree.com/Reality_Shack) though I am fairly sure I never posted there either. I confirmed to Simon that I do not work for any UK (or other) intelligence services – and that I work for the Open University – as I have stated many times. I encourage everyone and anyone to study what I have posted and I openly challenge them to find errors or misleading statements or any evidence at all that I am anything other than just an ordinary person.

During this Skype chat, Simon Hytten made his position clear:

> *[24/08/2010 22:35:11 | Edited 22:36:36] simon shack: Yes but you must know that people analyzing the fake 9/11 videos- and making scientific conclusions around them - are entrenched in a fallacy? Such as Judy Wood?*

Sadly, Simon misrepresents the truth. Dr Wood's research is based on at least the following:

1) Photographic Evidence
2) Video Evidence
3) Witness Audio Testimony
4) Audio features (e.g. relative silence of towers turning to dust)
5) Weather data
6) Seismic Data
7) Official reports – such as dust analysis (Cahill).
8) Photos from places like FDR drive ½ mile from WTC.

9) personal trips to the WTC site. On each of her visits to the site, for example, she has

    a. taken her own photographs (See Figure 154, page 153 of *Where Did the Towers Go?*)

    b. sampled air quality

    c. made observations about the material characteristics and documented anomalies and changes

    d. documented unusual treatment of the site

    e. spoken with first responders, victims' family members, and survivors who were in the towers shortly before they were turned to dust.

    f. directly observed and documented structural and material changes

10) Magnetometer Data

Conversely, Simon Hytten's research is primarily based on video and photo evidence – some audio and the odd bit of witness testimony. Simon Hytten completely ignores the other 4 or 5 categories of evidence – I have not seen him discuss them *anywhere* in any of his lengthy posts.

Later in the Skype chat, Simon seems to think that Richard Gage is a researcher – and that his "methods" are comparable to Dr Wood's:

[24/08/2010 22:38:28] simon shack: Both Richard Gage and Judy Wood look at the videos and draw conclusions from them. This is a fallacious way of going about the research.

Sadly, Simon does not seem to have read what I had previously posted about Richard Gage and AE911[131]. (I have posted more information since[132] this conversation with Hytten.) It seems that Hytten's mind is already made up about proving what happened to the WTC:

[24/08/2010 22:46:18] simon shack: I - and NO ONE ELSE - will ever be able to prove exactly how the WTC complex was demolished. Do you understand? That's why Richard GAge concentrates on his UNPROVABLE matter.

Again, Simon ignores what I had already written and posted about Richard Gage and recklessly lumps things together in a way which displays ignorance of the facts. He says, "NO ONE ELSE - will ever be able to prove exactly how the WTC complex was demolished." Wow. He sounds sure of himself. Is he afraid of someone doing *just that*? Let's not forget, Dr Judy Wood started a fraud case based on the evidence she collected – Simon Hytten has, to date, not done anything similar.

Simon Says "Believe…"

Also in this Skype chat, Simon addressed the question of the towers' disappearance:

[24/08/2010 22:41:08] Andrew Johnson: How were the towers "demolished"?

> *[24/08/2010 22:41:16] simon shack: Let me believe that they were demolished quite conventionally, ok?*

I found it most interesting that Simon chose to *believe* that the towers were demolished in a conventional manner (despite the evidence which proves they were not – such as the lack of sound and the lack of seismic signature – neither of which are photo or video evidence). His whole study in September Clues is meant to be based on analysis of evidence – of video fakery and so on. So, when it comes to the destruction of the WTC, why does Simon *believe* all the evidence is fake? Why does he *believe* they were "demolished conventionally"? Why does he choose *belief* over knowledge – and evidence?

On the Ball

On 3 Aug 2010, UK Engineer, Researcher and Journalist (in the proper sense of the word), Richard D Hall[133] published his intriguing and detailed "Ball Analysis" (which was updated in 2016[134]). This analysis was inspired by a curious sequence included in September Clues where Simon Hytten notes how it appears that a "Ball shaped object" rather than "a plane shaped object" strikes the tower[135], as shown in live NBC footage, shot from a helicopter. Curiously, this same shot is repeated on the evening news, but with the "ball" being replaced by a "plane." Richard's analysis explores the possible meaning of this.

In a later Skype chat, in 2011, Simon Shack said (presumably referring to the Ball Analysis):

> *[03/06/2011 22:12:26] simon shack: Well - your friend Richard Hall has obviously tried to distort the TV fakery evidence, has he not?*

I pointed out that Richard Hall had merely used a segment from September Clues and re-analysed it – I'd hardly call that "distorting TV fakery evidence." Hall presented it as an idea, not a "definite conclusion."

9/11 Flights - Video *and* Radar

Richard D Hall and I had discussed some of the issues raised above and he himself, having published his "Ball" analysis still had additional questions about some of the video record. He decided to conduct a deeper and more thorough analysis and boldly attempted to "map" as many of the flight 175 plane crash videos as he could onto/into his 3D-model of Manhattan. This analysis was published on 21 May 2012[134]**Error! Bookmark not defined.** and revealed that 26 clips of the flight 175 crash did indeed appear to match the Radar Data supplied by the NTSB (but there was a discrepancy of about 1400 feet/430 metres with the 84RADES Radar Data). This tended to rule out the idea of "simple video fakery" – which is what most other "no planers" argue. It seemed to bring us to the point of realisation that "another" technology had been used – one which created the image of planes in the sky – which *really could be filmed/ video'd.* This also explains one of the fundamental difficulties with the "only video fakery" position – some witnesses *did* report seeing a plane – though there were sufficient variations in their accounts to suggest that there *could* have been issues with viewing the projected image from certain locations. One of the curious things is the "disappearing wings" observed in some clips [1[136]] [2[137]] – this should not happen with CGI!

Plane Sounds

Another problem with the video fakery is the *sound* – when I carried out my witness study, there were also considerable discrepancies as to the sounds reported – but this would make sense if it *was not a real plane* which struck the tower. The sound must have been generated somehow, or is it even possible that people "remembered" the sound after the event – having seen it on television?

Soap Opera

With repeated arguing, insulting and ridiculing, much energy gets absorbed[138] – which could otherwise be spent on finding the truth about 9/11. Speaking for myself, I try not to get engaged in such activities. Doubtless, some will accuse me of being a hypocrite – in "wasting time" composing articles such as this.

It has become clear to some of us that the truth about the events of 9/11 *can be discovered*. It also seems to be possible to discover unpalatable truths about how the 9/11 cover up continues – on internet forums populated by rude anonymous posters, and through people posing as evidence-based researchers – who then wilfully ignore certain evidence and attack others who have done the most to verify and analyse the most powerful evidence available.

Conclusions

Here again we have the pattern of a 9/11 researcher establishing himself in the "research community", completing some time-consuming and apparently very credible research. Yet, they then either ignore or just attack the most powerful, science-based and court-submitted evidence and research that is available. The forum they set up becomes another place where anonymous posters become abusive about the research and the person who has done the most with it. (The same has happened with forums at www.911researchers.com and http://forum.911movement.org/ both of which closed down after some months/years of operation.)

Instead of Simon Hytten saying "well, I am not quite sure how the towers were destroyed – I haven't studied the evidence enough yet" he states that he *believes in* "conventional demolition" and he posts supposed hate mail on his forum - which he suggests has come from Dr Judy Wood.

The record is now clear that Simon Hytten wilfully ignores evidence, implants information to encourage doubt and then expects someone like me to accept an invitation to his house in Italy!

> *[03/06/2011 21:36:02 | Edited 21:36:16] simon shack: Would you come over for the big 10-year celebration in my house over Rome?*

Each to their own, but to me having a "9/11 anniversary party" on 11 September 2011[139] is a strange idea – as is setting up a model of the twin towers for that party[140].

Messing with People's Minds

Simon Hytten's current position on 9/11 has become almost surreal – he states that *all* the photo and video record is fake, there were no victims and it was all a simulation. He has tried to persuade some people that basic observations (such as the towers turning to dust) may not actually be correct. Would anyone believe this? Apparently, they would – a friend of mine, who knows me personally - for a short time *began to believe* that Simon Hytten's view that one couldn't determine what happened to the WTC because *all* the videos were "fake." The conversation with my friend illustrated to me that "following" someone can mean that they can "lead you" in the wrong direction. However, as *evidence* is not *a person*, you are not subject to being influenced by a *personal agenda* if you stick with *analysing evidence*.

Since originally posting this article, Simon Shack has now made his views more than plain when, in a posting on his own forum on 25 June 2012, he said[141]:

> *I'll stop here for now. Please reply to this post of mine before you spam any other links to "Judy Wood's" blatant disinformation bullcrap on this forum. Thanks.*

Perhaps Simon Hytten's slow but sure "building up" of a following around September Clues can itself be seen as yet another "perception management" operation – perhaps this time made easier by the very convoluted nature of the video anomalies he originally set out to illustrate (i.e. it really does make you reconsider what is real and what is not).

Additionally, Simon Hytten's claim that some of the victims - and/or their relatives – are actors – without actually being able to *prove* this idea - can also be very upsetting for many people. This can divert them away from looking at the genuine anomalies which do indeed lay in the video record of 9/11 – and do, indeed, allow us to find out what really happened.

Perhaps Simon Hytten is himself an actor – hey, he (like most or all of the posters on his "Clues forum) decided to use a "stage name", didn't he? I leave the reader to decide.

9. Jeff Prager Nukes 9/11 Research
13th April 2012

The 9/11 Nuke Theory Explodes - Again!

Around 21st March 2012, links to a new, lengthy document first appeared on the internet – for example on the "Project Avalon" forum[142] and in an article which was posted on the "Veterans Today" Website[143]. The document entitled 9/11-America Nuked[144] is a total of 247 double-spread pages[145]. Its subtitle is "The Final Word On 9/11" – this statement is false, as you should realise when you have studied the evidence presented below.

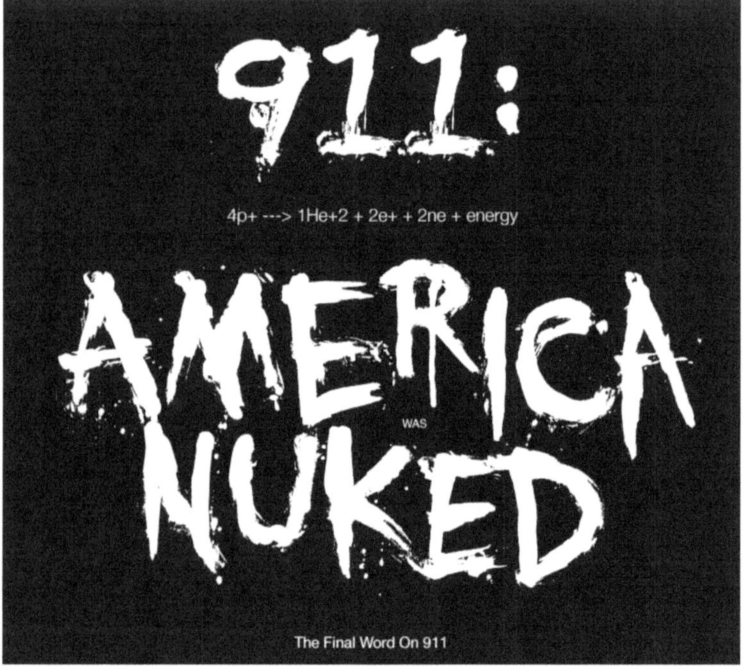

First Page of First Part…

The basic thrust of the document appears to be to promote the idea that some type of nuclear weapon was used to destroy the World Trade Centre.

PART FOUR

I think it's important to have a basic understanding of nano-technology and its history. The technology dates back to the 1950s and energetic compounds date back to the 1940s. Nuclear power and nuclear demolition also date to the early 1940s and the industries involved in the development of nuclear weapons are and always were active in experimenting with and developing new nuclear demolition technology. No less active, and in fact far more active, than those developing nano-energetic compounds. Nano-technology was started by the nuclear industry. The nuclear industry is, like the nano-tech industry, an industry involved in molecules. It only makes sense that nano-tech started in the nuclear industry and that's because it did. Yet the average person doesn't know this. Advances in nuclear technology are simply more difficult to fully understand because there is far less published material in that area of scientific development and improvements. Yet there's more than enough to be deeply concerned for our future.

UNDERSTANDING
MINIATURIZATION AND
NANO TECHNOLOGY

First Page of Second Part… (Fusion/Fission label highlight added).

This idea is not new – having been promulgated initially years ago by Ed Ward[146], Bill Deagle[147] (discussed in the first volume *9/11 Finding the Truth*) and others. If the "author" of this lengthy document (Jeff Prager) had not written to me, I would not even have bothered to post a new article about this - any idea that some type of hot nuclear explosion was used to destroy the WTC is simply not supported by a study of the available evidence.

I now reproduce a list I originally wrote in 2008. Hot nukes (whatever their size) could not have been used because:

1) There were no really bright flashes as the towers turned to dust.
2) There were no loud explosions as the towers turned to dust.
3) There was little or no heat in the dust cloud.
4) To my knowledge, there is no publicly viewable and verifiable research on small, concealable nuclear explosives (despite the claims being made).
5) Nuclear explosives cannot account for the 24-foot cylindrical holes seen in the buildings and in the street.
6) The use of a nuke or "large explosive/incendiary" does not explain the selectively flipped cars and vehicles.
7) The nuclear explosives created no seismic signature of any significant size (impossible).

Not only that, but consideration of nuclear explosive devices completely fails to address other evidence such as the presence and motion of Hurricane Erin in the days around the time of 9/11[106]Error! Bookmark not defined.

As I have said previously, this is NOT to say that some type of *nuclear process* was *not* involved. From our understanding of the Hutchison Effect (which is very relevant to how the towers were destroyed)[105]Error! Bookmark not defined., it appears to affect matter at an atomic, molecular and even a nuclear level, therefore it is possible that it could generate amounts of radiation under certain conditions. Dr Wood has addressed this in her book. She identified "magnetic-electrogravitic-nuclear reactions" as a more appropriate term for these processes. [Wood, J.D., *"Where Did the Towers Go?* Evidence of Directed Free-Energy Technology on 9/11"* (2010), p. 365.]

On 9th April 2012, Dr Judy Wood and I appeared on Deanna Spingola's RBN show[148], where we had asked to discuss the Jeff Prager "Nuked" document.[149]

Shortly following this interview, Mr Prager contacted me through my website. In the email exchange that followed (see below), he made several false statements, whilst failing to address some of the serious problems with his document.

Prager's Problems

On studying Mr Prager's document for some minutes, the following became apparent:

1) A lot of time went into producing it
2) It does not refer to John Hutchison, whose experimental results have produced evidence similar to that seen in the WTC evidence[105]Error! Bookmark not defined.

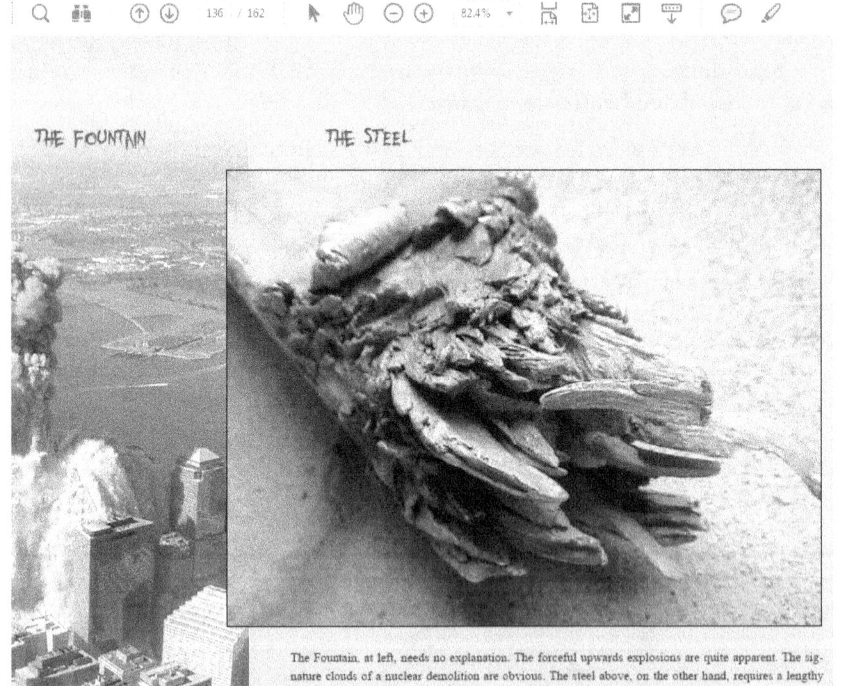

The Fountain, at left, needs no explanation. The forceful upwards explosions are quite apparent. The signature clouds of a nuclear demolition are obvious. The steel above, on the other hand, requires a lengthy

3) There are no references to Dr Judy Wood's website or book – and one particular instance where this is peculiar is the source for the image on page 136 of Prager's first file[150]. It looks identical to one of the images of Hutchison's aluminium bar[151] (yet the text refers to it as steel…) How could that get into the FEMA pictures of the WTC? Why is this shown there in Prager's document? Why is this in a section about "The Steel"? To muddle up the evidence? I'd really like to see the source for this image – one source of this image is Dr Judy Wood's site[152] (Figure 15). Perhaps folks can write to Mr Prager to ask him. Apparently, he's found the science involved here… But what are Prager's Science Qualifications? He does not furnish us with this information – only that he is a retired magazine founder/publisher (he states he retired a long time ago).

4) As mentioned above, his document does not include or address the Hurricane Erin Data[153]

5) The document makes repeated references to Jim Fetzer[154] and Leuren Moret[155] – please read the referenced articles to understand why this does not bode well for the validity of his 9/11 document.

6) On page 105, whole sections of text are copied from Dr Morgan Reynolds' article "Collapse of the Thermite Thesis[156]." This is plagiarism - as it is unreferenced and uncredited.

7) Many other sections copied without reference such as p. 100 (a[157],b[158]), p. 100-101[159], pp. 103-104[160], p.106[161], p.107 The reference to Gerard Holmgren's site appears on this webpage, but is out of date - he died in 2010. p. 108[162], p.109[159]**Error! Bookmark not defined.** (b[163]), (c[157]**Error! Bookmark not defined.**), (d[164]), (e[157]**Error! Bookmark not defined.**), p. 110[165] (copied reference list), p. 111a

8) Very few of the above links are to "science" sites and no one uses Wikipedia as a serious academic resource. Even Jim Fetzer knows Wikipedia censors important data[166]!

Most of the photos are unreferenced, so you can't check the source. In an interview[167] that Prager participated in with Mike Harris, someone phoned in and wanted to talk about the photo on page 84 ("The Pit") – they suggested it was proof that a nuclear device had been used.

The photo is unreferenced, and a claim is made that it has "never been published or shown in the United States" (this is just one example). A search reveals that what is shown in the photo is a 40-foot glacial pothole and this image above was published in the New York Times website on 22 Sep 2008[168]! It is odd to think this caller was "primed" with this information – very few people would be so bothered about this as to refer to a particular page. The same caller referred to Dimitri Khalezov[169] – who openly lied in his discussion of his[170] Nuclear Demolition idea.

It is interesting that Prager's document links to the Journal Of Nine-Eleven Studies (JONES) (Page 105 and Page 131) but nowhere does it link to any of Dr Wood's research – neither does it reference Dr Morgan Reynolds' site.

Arguing Specific Points of Evidence, Whilst Ignoring Others

In his e-mail exchange with me, Jeff Prager mentioned anomalous radiation readings

> *Please explain the 93 Bq/kg in the girder coating dust sample. Muon catalyzed fusion has nothing to do with 9/11 but was used to prove Jones is a LIAR and that thermite is IMPOSSIBLE.*

This is similar to what Ed Ward said in 2008[146]**Error! Bookmark not defined.** (Prager references Ward in his document):

> *Ten months ago - I published Update: Micro Nukes in the WTC - Main Evidence   -   See:*

> *Seven months ago - Prof. Jones Denied, Ignored and Misrepresented
> Proven Tritium Levels 55 Times Normal Background Levels. Why did he do
> so?*

Sadly, Ward and Prager both ignored the observed effects of thermonuclear
devices – and then in a similar cavalier fashion ignore most of the other
evidence too.

It is interesting they both reference Steven E Jones as being wrong – it is as if
they don't understand that we (myself and Dr Wood) know Jones' history and
we know he is wrong – for at least two of the same reasons Prager and Ward
are wrong (the heat issue and the lack of a seismic signature and so on). Why
do we have to *keep* repeating these basic, obvious pieces of data and
observations? What spell is being cast on people?

It should be asked of Mr. Prager why he has ignored and misrepresented the
tritium analysis in Dr Wood's book as well as on her website.

Additional Small Points

In the e-mails that Mr Prager sent to me, he claims I mischaracterised him in
the broadcast with Deanna Spingola, referenced above. However, if you listen
to the audio, you will find that I made no references to his character at all – I
didn't really know who he was! All that I pointed out were a few of the errors
and omissions in his document. This sort of accusation was rather reminiscent
of that made against me by Ace Baker, regarding me sending "hate mail" to
him[172].

Mr Prager also stated in email exchanges that I "claimed a degree in Physics"
this is also incorrect – I have a degree in Computer Science *and* Physics
(Physics being a minor part). Why would a founder and publisher of a
magazine make these basic errors?[173]

Possible Motivation Behind Producing The "America Nuked" Document

Again, the motivation can only be guessed at, and if you listened to the
broadcast above, you will already have heard my thoughts about this.
Suggested motivation includes:

1) Bringing in the idea of nuclear fusion to confuse what has already
   been established about the relationship between cold fusion effects
   and the Hutchison Effect – and 9/11.
2) Though Prager clearly stated he has original copies of the WTC
   images used in his document, not only is he telling people that he has
   pictures no one else has, *he is also associating many of the same images (that
   are on Dr Judy Wood's site and in her research, including high-resolution original*

images) with a different - and provably false conclusion. This again is therefore apparently to create confusion. In his email, he implies that Dr Wood's site does not contain high resolution images, which is false. But in making this statement, he implies he has indeed been to Dr Wood's site – or is simply denigrating Dr Wood's site.

3)   Giving this work away as a free download could make Dr Wood's research in the form of a book seem less attractive to get hold of – people could think "Prager's document has all the answers – in an easy-to-understand, clear format – and it's free!" What they will not realise is that it is heavily plagiarised in at least some places, incorrect, omits evidence and therefore is grossly misleading as shown above.

4)   He refers to Dr Wood as "Judy" in his emails, yet has never met her or exchanged emails with her. Also, in a recent radio interview, Mr. Prager referred to Dr Niels Harrit, Dr Jones, and "Judy Wood." Does he wish to present the false impression about her qualifications? Dr Wood has degrees in Structural Engineering, Applied Physics, and Materials Engineering Science, including a Ph.D., and has over 35 years of experience in the field of forensic engineering and science.

In his e-mail to me Mr Prager stated:

I have no desire to submit anything to a court. I know what happened.

This is very odd. If he knows what happened, doesn't he want to help prosecute the perpetrators? Why does he have no interest in trying to expose the criminals? This is what Dr Judy Wood tried to do[39]**Error! Bookmark not defined.|**

Andrew Johnson - "known on the internet as the moron of morons"

In a follow up email Jeff Prager wrote to me:

From: jeff prager

Sent: 03 May 2012 02:38

To: ad.johnson@ntlworld.com

Subject: Hi Andrew

You're a blithering, brainless, molecularly and neurologically challenged idiot. You're known to the detectives and the police force in your community as a complete idiot. You're known on the internet as the moron of morons, the Mans Moron. For goodness sakes, uranium at 93 Bq/kg with strontium, barium and thorium equally off the charts spells fission you twit.

Peace,

Why would Jeff Prager write such things? Perhaps we can find the answer on another 9/11 disinformer's website (Chris Bollyn), assuming the information is accurate – Prager was apparently Wanted by the Child Support Agency in Maricopa County (Arizona) who issued a warrant for his arrest on 25 Apr 2007.

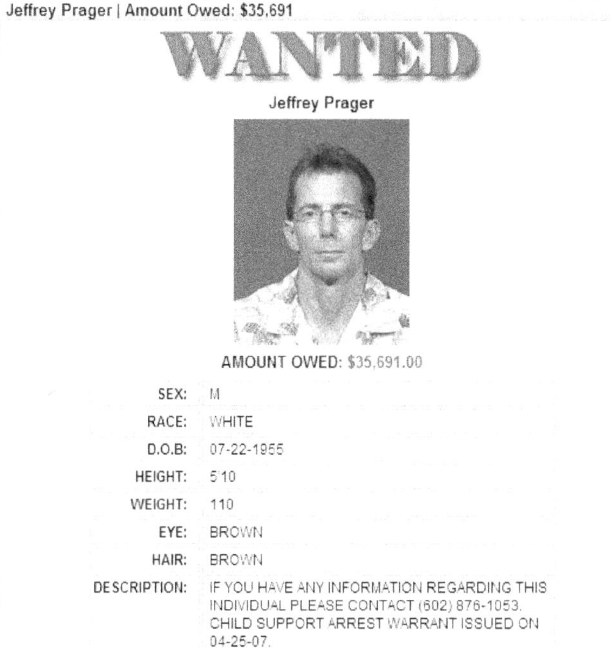

Assuming this is correct, it might explain Prager's peculiar and irrelevant references in the email to me about me being "known to the detectives and the police force in your community as a complete idiot." That is, he is *projecting* his own situation onto me.

You can read all the email exchanges with Jeff Prager on my website[174].

Conclusion

Here we have yet another attempt to subvert the truth about the events of 9/11 – whilst claiming to be disseminating the truth of what happened. It indicates yet again how important Dr Wood's research is. How many more attempts will we see to suppress, confuse, marginalise, cover up and ridicule the only publicly available, truly scientific and forensic investigation into the destruction of the WTC?

10. The Vancouver 9/11 "Hearings" Encouraging Conjecture, Discouraging Certainty, Obscuring Known Truths

06 June 2012

In a "re-run" of the 2011 Toronto Hearings, a similar event was organised in Vancouver, but this time, Dr Judy Wood was invited… why didn't she attend…?

"Conspiracy Culture"

People who have a more "fixed" mindset, believing (more or less) that what they have been presented with by mainstream news and "academic" sources is true, often scoff arrogantly at people like me. I have scratched through the "surface reality" to reveal the murky layer underneath. Perhaps the principle reason why they scoff is that they assume there is no evidence to back up or prove the things they just cannot accept are true – and it's not worth their time to look.

Sometimes, as I work through and review this material, I can forgive them for thinking "there is nothing to see here." Numerous false assumptions are being made in many areas of "conspiracy culture." This means that what is presented as being true is sometimes not provable – at least, not to the extent that is being claimed.

One good example of this is the chemtrail phenomenon – which I have studied in some detail and written quite a bit about[175]. A number of groups have whipped themselves up, almost into a frenzy, because they assume that all the trails they see in the sky are toxic spray – which is constantly raining down on them and poisoning them. However, carefully reviewing the evidence seems to show that the toxic spraying cannot be as widespread as people are claiming. I do not want to write too much about this here, because it is not the thrust of this article. For the moment, I will say that we have evidence that *some* toxic spraying has taken place and we do have some very, very strange videos[176] and photos which clearly show weather, cloud and contrail anomalies which cannot be explained in conventional terms. To leap from there to a conclusion that "constant toxic spraying" is taking place is not currently supported by the available evidence. Also, I think it is worth considering the tendency for groups of people coming to an unsupported conclusion can be utilised by those keeping secrets to help ensure that those secrets are *still* covered up. Such is the power of disinformation…

Encouraging Uncertainty

With so much uncertainty in the "conspiracy" or "alternative knowledge" culture, is it any wonder that some people scoff arrogantly? When one reviews all of the information available, how much of it is "open to debate"? Stop and consider how the language used within the culture is peppered with phrases relating to uncertainty. For example, common terms are "conspiracy theory", "hypothesis", "truth seeking" (implying that the truth has not been found), "the truth is out there" (not "in here"). Radio talk shows often have titles such as "out there", "the unknown" or "planet X." When one becomes involved more deeply in the alternative culture, it often seems like all certainties "melt away" and the whole of reality becomes more fluid. Do we then become "conditioned" that certainty is no longer available? What truth can we "truly establish"?

We can establish truth and certainty when we have available evidence – and the more evidence we have available, the more certain we can be about our conclusions. Unfortunately, in "conspiracy culture", it sometimes seems "unfashionable" to establish anything with certainty – it almost seems like establishing truth and certainty is *discouraged* – due to the level of conjecture and the amount of information which is interpreted in so many different ways. People seem to look to "leaders" and there even seems to be a kind of "hero worship" – which can, at times, mean that people don't think for themselves enough.

Discouraging Certainty

I would like the reader to consider that a culture of *discouraging certainty* is actively used and promoted by those wishing to keep important secrets, which allow them to "stay in the driving seat" of affairs on planet earth at this time. An area where certainty can be established, if the reader *chooses* to review the available evidence, is in relation to what happened at the WTC on 9/11. For many, they simply cannot accept this could be the case – on the one hand, they assume that they already know the truth, as told by the mainstream media and "international experts" and so on. Then, on the other hand in "conspiracy culture", they sometimes assume the truth cannot be known – because there are "too many conflicting theories." Few consider, as I have suggested above, that "conspiracy culture" itself can be used as a cover up for truths that can be - and are already - known.

9/11 Certainties

Dr Judy Wood, through her meticulous research, has established some profound and detailed truths (not theories) about what happened to the WTC. So profound and world-changing are these truths, that many methods and techniques have been employed to keep people from seeing, realising and comprehending these truths. What is the reason for this? This is how a friend of mine recently put it:

> *[Dr Judy Wood] being victorious - in her message to the public - results in the entire overthrow of our ruling elite - I wonder if she knows that - and the consequent forces aligned against her.*

Over the last few years, I have tried to compile the evidence that shows certain people are working on behalf of those forces – wittingly and unwittingly - to keep people from being certain about what happened. Overall, these forces – the ones encouraging doubt and uncertainty - have been largely successful. However, thanks to the efforts of a small number of folks in the USA and in the UK (mainly), we have shown that these intensive and intricate psychological operations (psy-ops) aren't working on everyone. My own efforts at summarising, compiling and distributing all this evidence about what happened to the WTC and evidence about who is covering it up - have not been without success. There is no denying, however, that I am, all too often, "outgunned" by folks with collectively more time, money and expertise in disseminating attractive or authoritative-*looking* disinformation. Which brings me to the latest part of a psychological operation.

Vancouver "Hearings"

Some time ago, Jim Fetzer decided to organise a new conference about 9/11 research - to which he invited Dr Morgan Reynolds and Dr Judy Wood. Dr Morgan Reynolds declined to attend. Due to the way Fetzer has covered up and muddled up important aspects of Dr Judy Wood's research (see *9/11 Finding the Truth*[110]**Error! Bookmark not defined.**), she chose not to even respond to the invitation.

When I first heard about this event, I felt that this was being done in desperation. It also seemed reminiscent of the Toronto "Hearings" which were organised by another group in September 2011 (see chapter 7).

An obvious question comes to mind here – Jim Fetzer and many of the speakers from these two conferences are US based – yet they have chosen to hold both of these events up in Canada. Perhaps they are afraid of being prosecuted under the Smith-Mundt act[177], which was related to how propaganda is allowed to be used by the government in the USA. In 1985, an amendment to the act wanted to ensure

> *"no funds authorized to be appropriated to the United States Information Agency shall be used to influence public opinion in the United States, and no program material prepared by the United States Information Agency shall be distributed within the United States."*

I am sure that the Vancouver hearings are propaganda. For example, instead of Jim Fetzer being honest and saying "Dr Judy Wood has not responded to my invitation to the conference" he simply invited someone else to speak about her research[178]:

> * Clare Kuehn, "Were DEWs used to decimate the Twin Towers?" (40 minutes)
>
> *A University of Toronto graduate in history and student of philosophy, mathematics and the arts, she will discuss Judy Wood, WHERE DID THE TOWERS GO?, and will present evidence for the use of "DEWs" as "Directional Free or 'Low-Input' Energy Weapons."*

It must be realised that this person was *not* recommended by Dr Judy Wood, nor has she given this person permission to act as any kind of authority on her research, or a representative acting on her behalf. It seems from the information above that Ms. Keuhn is not even qualified to present the research with anything approaching the level of expertise that Dr Judy Wood possesses. It seems, therefore, that this conference is a very specifically *orchestrated opportunity* to *introduce doubt and uncertainty* into an area where this should not and need not be done. Why did Mr Fetzer invite Ms. Kuehn? Why did she accept his invitation? A copy of the presentation she used was posted online after the event and[179] I downloaded it. Here is the first slide:

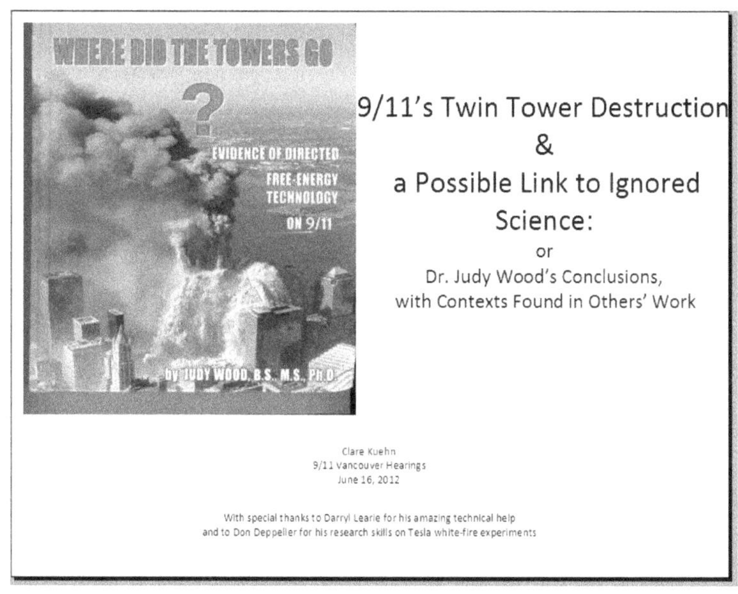

Most of the slides are poorly formatted and in places and some used blurred images. Here is a copy of Slide 66:

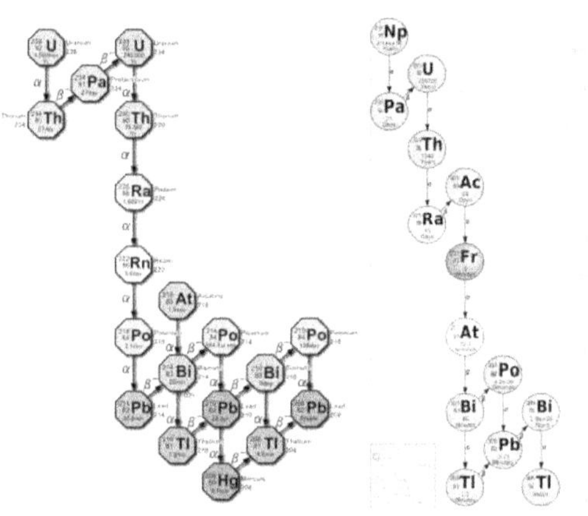

Slide 66 from Clare Kuehn's Vancouver Presentation – refers to Mini-nukes

Nukes are again discussed by Kuehn on Slide 79 – a scan from a nuclear physics text book:

Ir^{197} would then beta decay to platinum 197 (Pt^{197}), which would also beta decay to stable Au^{197} (natural gold is monoisotopic, and gold has only one stable isotope).

Figure 4-Uranium Decay Chain (left) and Neptunium Decay Chain (right)

Slide 79 from Kuehn's presentation

Here is a copy of the final slide:

Final comments

I hope you understand more about:
- Dr. Judy Wood's own findings
- the implications she mentions
- why other people might mention more about Tesla, torsion, and "new" physics

"New" physics and interference wave weapons:
- plausible
- already experimented on publicly
- possibly weaponized and even used on 9/11

MORE WORK TO BE DONE on:
- whether such weaponry would be used in conjunction with nukes

I personally believe the anomalies here mentioned are not properly covered by primary and secondary fission, and so on.

- This might not be a beam or from a space platform. (Dr Wood mentions the Star Wars program on her Website, but that is a PROGRAM of development, and this energy might be concentrated to areas but not "beams".)
- Maybe DEWs and field effects were studied even BEFORE that SDI program.
- And might well have been used, she seems to show, on 9/11.

We can therefore see that this was another "muddle up" to mix in speculation and things that Dr Wood has not presented in with the evidence that she *has* presented. Overall, Kuehn's presentation leaves a very confused picture of what happened to the WTC. This can only be to confuse and mislead people. As I wrote before, we were not consulted about the presentation and so they decided to go ahead and present this with errors. You can read my correspondence with Clare Kuehn on my website[180], where I point some of the errors.

Another of the speakers was Jeff Prager (see chapter 9):

** Jeff Prager, "Proof of Ternary Fission in New York City on 9/11" (40 minutes)*

Founder of an award-winning magazine for Senior Citizens, in 2002 he tried to prove 19 Muslims hijacked four planes and attacked us. By 2005, he realized this was false, sold his business, left the US and began to investigate 9/11 full-time. See 9/11 America Nuked.

Mr Prager simply cannot prove his claims and, therefore, is wittingly or unwittingly being used to introduce doubt, uncertainty and disinformation.

Mr Fetzer has therefore deliberately set up a conference which will not establish any truth – quite the reverse – it will encourage uncertainty and debate. Perhaps surprisingly, Mr. Fetzer essentially tells us that this is, indeed, the purpose of his conference[181]. On the relevant website, he wrote:

> *NOTE: None of these studies should be taken as conclusory but are instead being offered as exemplifying the kinds of issues that will be addressed during The Vancouver Hearings.*

Another speaker at the conference is Alfred Webre. He is one of the few people who has interviewed Dr Judy Wood *and* John Hutchison together, in person. It seems he, too, has since worked to introduce doubt and uncertainty even when he has claimed not to be doing this[155]**Error! Bookmark not defined.**. Alfred Webre was not too happy about my posting about this and wanted to sue me for libel[182]!

A Hearing Without a Judge

It becomes clear that the title of this event is a misnomer. It is not a hearing at all. On reading comments posted on the Amazon Books Website[183], in response to Mr Fetzer's review of Dr Judy Wood's book, one astute reader posted this:

> *The definition of a hearing is... " A proceeding before a judicial officer in which the officer must decide whether a crime was committed, whether the crime occurred within the territorial jurisdiction of the court, and whether there is Probable Cause to believe that the defendant committed the crime." BIG QUESTIONS ? 1. Will there be a judge from the United States present ? 2. Will there be territorial jurisdiction of the court in CANADA for a crime that occurred in the United States? 3. Who will be deciding the crime issues and definitions ? 4. Who is being tried ?*

Good questions.

Hypothesis, Theory, Feasibility and Possibility

From the conference posting above, and from previous postings by Mr Fetzer, such as those in relation to the Amazon review of Dr Judy Wood's conclusive study embodied in her book *Where Did the Towers Go?*[184], it becomes clear what his strategy is. It is to insert doubt, confuse, confound and encourage uncertainty – perhaps, almost, *engineering ignorance*. His actions would, in different circumstances, result in him being charged with something like "conspiracy to cover up a crime."

Other posts by Mr Fetzer characterise my writing of articles such as this as being "part of a cult"[185]. Is this because he has nothing to offer in order to refute this analysis and deconstruction of his actions? His writings are almost as desperate as those by Jeff Prager (who quotes Mr Fetzer in his own "9/11 Nuked" publication – see chapter 9).

Those attending Mr Fetzer's event will probably be somewhat bamboozled by his false authority and articulate but often meaningless "waffle." Let me attempt to mimic his strategy, by presenting a short hypothesis about why it's not safe to assume that 1 + 1 = 2. Here's how a philosopher (i.e. someone like Mr Fetzer) might attempt to persuade us that there is "room for doubt"…

"1 + 1 May Not Be Equal to 2"

In considering this most basic of problems, it has always been assumed that the "1 add 1 is 2." However, can we be sure this is always correct? Some have said that 1 + 1 = 3 and others have said 1 + 1 = 10. We need to study it further. Are there other ways of looking at this problem which may reveal important truths that have not been analysed closely enough before now? It is such an important issue, we need to be sure that we are correct – otherwise all other things which follow from this cannot be assumed to be true.

Let us start by considering the notion of interpretation of notation. For example, in the English language, the letter "I" has a similar notation to the digit "1" – therefore, it is possible that "1 + 1" may not be what it seems (it could be "I + 1" or "1 + I" or even "I + I"). Additionally, there are circumstances under which 1 + 1 may be equal to 10. One such "special case" is in the form of binary arithmetic – here, using base 2, the use of the digit 2 never occurs – it is represented as 10 (one "two" plus zero units).

Hence, we have to consider such issues as notation, representation and number base - it becomes clear that we cannot always be certain the 1 + 1 equals 2 and so care must be taken not to come to the wrong conclusion and we must establish the bounds of our hypothesis before coming to a conclusion.

"1 + 1 Equals 2"

Perhaps the above example is too simplistic – ridiculous almost, but hopefully, I have made a good enough job of the "argument" (waffle) to illustrate how doubt can be introduced in an area where it is wrong to introduce it. One thing I will point out is that, in the above "discussion", *I said nothing which was untrue.*

The evidence presented in Dr Wood's book and presentations about the destruction of the WTC can *only be explained by the use of* an unconventional directed energy weapon and it rules out *all* other "conventional" explanations – including *all* those being presented at the Vancouver event. It removes all doubt and makes debate pointless and worthless.

Importantly, what the study also shows is that the effects seen in the WTC evidence "left over" match closely with those produced in John Hutchison's experiments. This knowledge is very dangerous for the PTB precisely because it is established as being true and is not conjecture at all. It also directly implicates certain individuals and companies as having specific knowledge about 9/11 and how it was done.

Now, after a number of years, no one has been able to refute the evidence. Rather, individuals such as Mr Fetzer have singled themselves out more and more clearly as people who want to divert attention from what the evidence shows – and proves. They have become, and continue to be, accomplices to a criminal cover up.

An Energy Weapon WAS Used To Destroy the WTC – This is not a Theory

This is the truth – in the same way 1 + 1 = 2. Suggesting 1 + 1 does not equal 2 is dishonest. When the evidence has been openly and honestly and fully studied, suggesting the WTC was destroyed by something other than an energy weapon is dishonest. The destruction of the WTC and all the terrible, horrible things associated with that were a crime. Covering up a crime is itself a crime.

Characterising these discoveries – these truths as "a theory" is precisely how Fetzer and those doing similar things get away with continuing the cover up. He characterises it as a theory "which he supports." This is how he retains credibility and diverts attention away from the fact that he himself is an accomplice to the cover up. He can say things like "Oh yes, *most probably* an energy weapon - but I don't know the exact type." All the evidence is available now for anyone with the means and the motive to follow it where it leads - right into the heart of the Military Industrial Complex – through companies like SAIC and ARA. (Isn't it strange how we never hear these truths being spoken of by ex-US Marine Mr Fetzer and other military figures like Col. John Alexander – who is also familiar with the work of John Hutchison.)

The Towers Are Gone – Do You Care?

For those that are thinking about this, here is a Pop Quiz, suggested by Dr Judy Wood.

1. Were the towers once there? (yes or no)
2. Are the towers still there? (yes or no)
3. Did most (over 50%) of the towers turn to dust? (yes or no)
4. a) If your answer to question #3 was "no,"
   - Please review the empirical evidence more carefully or find someone who can.

   b) If your answer to question #3 was "yes,"

   - Does there exist a mechanism or technology capable of doing this? (yes or no)

   If your answer to question #4b was "yes," we are in agreement.

   If your answer to question #4b was "no," please explain your contradiction, claiming something occurred that could not have occurred.

So, if you're thinking of attending a conference where the truth of what happened on 9/11 is being "debated" or investigated, save yourself travel time and expenses and read Dr Wood's book. Request your local library find a copy for you through Inter Library Loan, borrow a copy from a friend, or buy your own copy. Watch the videos on my website or YouTube, or request DVDs and if demand is not too high, I will send them to you free of charge.

11.Steve De'Ak's "9/11 Crash Test"

(based heavily on comments sent to me by an astute reader/observer)

11 Sep 2012

It is ironic that I should find myself posting these "notes" on the 11th Anniversary of the event that changed the world we live in.

Quite recently, someone sent me a link to a new video which appeared entitled "Tired of War Without End" This was a well edited and well produced video which presented several key points which show that the plane crashes at the WTC were impossible. An associated website - http://911crashtest.org/ has also come online. The original video posting has been removed[186], but it was reposted[187] (and from memory, it looked to be about the same as the original).

An interesting idea about a "crash test" is presented – to fund an experiment to "prove" the official account of 9/11 is false. My first reaction was that just the video itself should give people a cause for re-thinking. It's a good, clear delivery of information, which should make people think about the issue more carefully. I therefore posted the following comment:

> *Excellent video - I do wonder if this video itself will have more effect than a crash test though!!*

However, due to my experiences over the last 5 years, I suppose I am a little sceptical of people setting up projects and attempting to raise $1000s for some cause like this. I can argue that it would be perhaps more effective if those dollars could be spent on equipping libraries with copies of Dr Judy Wood's book *Where Did the Towers Go?*[184]**Error! Bookmark not defined.**

On reviewing the "crash test" video, I found some interesting comments posted by Yankee451 (any relation to "Fahrenheit 451"?) such as:

> *"I disagree, and it was my idea so please stop making this a Judy Wood book tour. She is vehemently against the project. Steve De'ak"*

I thought that was an interesting statement partly because of how defensive he sounds, and also because of his assertion that Judy Wood is opposed to his project. Dr Judy Wood's stance is to say that it is very clear what happened to the buildings, once the evidence is studied, so whether they were hit by "real" or "fake" planes is not as important as studying the evidence of what happened to the buildings. This is not "opposition" to the project – nor is it vehement. Oddly, Steve De'Ak does not seem all that interested in what happened to the buildings.

> *"Stay focused please. This project is about the impact of the jets, not how the towers were destroyed."*

Or perhaps my criticism is too harsh, or my expectations are too biased or too unrealistic? Also, I note that he's claiming on the original home page[188]:

> *"What was shown on 9/11 is physically impossible in the real world, therefore the only logical conclusion is that the videos of the plane "impacts" are fraudulent."*

Why is he apparently not that interested in the physical impossibility of what happened to the WTC buildings? Further, he says:

> *This is not speculation; all images and videos which depict a 9/11 plane crash have since been exposed as having been tampered-with, meaning the media were a critical part of the operation."*

"All images and videos"? He doesn't offer any evidence for this statement and I would have thought it was impossible to make a convincing case for that now. Perhaps he has spent too much time reading Simon Shack's forum…[189] (See chapter 8.)

Could it be that he's alleging that there were no planes and nothing visible to an observer at the scene, in which case everyone who said they saw something must be lying? He does seem to imply in the video that people who said they saw planes are actors 'like extras in a movie', which could plant seeds of deep distrust in the minds of people who are undecided. On the other hand, this can also cause offence to those who did actually witness planes apparently crashing into the WTC towers. De'Ak is being rude to people who disagree with him, counter to the mild-mannered 'grandpa' demeanour he adopts in the video. When all the evidence is studied, the WTC plane stories do get rather convoluted and somewhat complicated[134]**Error! Bookmark not defined.**.

It perhaps fits in with a "second-tier cover up", because the people who still think the official version is true will see that some of his statements make no sense to them and so they will dismiss them entirely. Conversely, the people who question the official version will have the physical impossibility of the planes doing that damage to hang on to, and so support something that is still basically a lie. It's just going to stall the whole thing further in the manner we have all become accustomed to.

There was some interesting activity going on in the comments on the video - there are also users like "justin39641[190]," who apparently only uses YouTube to argue that the official story of 9/11 is entirely correct, judging from his activity feed on the channel. Is this an opportunity to watch the different tiers of the cover-up interacting with one another, perhaps? Again, we can perhaps observe the techniques of perception management in operation.

Steve De'Ak commented[191]:

> *"AE911Truth Wanted nothing to do with this test, the purpose of which is to raise awareness in the mainstream, making curious their refusal of an endorsement. I'll post their exact words on the Crash Test Website in the next few days. But this project isn't a pitch for Judy Wood either, far from it. It is what it is, and that's a Crash Test."*

On one hand he's taking an evidence-based approach, which is good, but then he's limiting that to one aspect of the whole thing that is largely insignificant given that it is apparent that those responsible for 9/11 never intended to hide their responsibility, but did intend to hide the *means* by which it was done. This video, focusing as it does on non-existent planes, only serves to demonstrate what so many people already know...that planes weren't responsible for what happened to the WTC complex. It's immune from the criticisms that Richard Gage suffers from due to his "scientifically unsound" arguments, because the arguments presented here are scientifically sound...they're just lacking in scope as they are too tightly focused, and this is perhaps suspicious - given the increasing awareness of Dr Judy Wood's research - which De'Ak admits he is aware of[192]:

> *"I am well aware of Judy Wood, and despite the fact I disagree with much of her work, she is more than welcome to partake in this project. We don't need to agree on anything beyond the test."*

It's extremely odd to encounter someone, who is apparently so sensible, finding little to agree with in Dr Wood's research. Wood's book, for example is a rigorous, totally comprehensive evidence-based study which proves most of the claims of the so-called truth movement false and impossible. It also presents some compelling new avenues for study.

On the other hand, De'Ak's "project" is suspicious – as suspicious as Steven Jones making basic physics errors[193], or Richard Gage not considering himself qualified to evaluate the seismic data[194], yet ostensibly being a San Francisco architect...

What does Steve De'ak think happened to the WTC Towers? If he thinks the means was conventional explosives or nuclear devices, his judgement must be called into question in a big way. He doesn't appear to want to actually consider any explanation overtly. He was challenged to discuss this issue in the comments on his video. He replied:

> *"Nukes? There are easier ways to explain it."*

When it was pointed out that we know how the WTC was destroyed, he also commented:

> *"Such certitude! The lack of debris and dust can be explained without relying on top-secret weapons that cannot be verified. If you have a genuine interest in learning the truth, you'll continue researching beyond Judy Wood."*

"Beyond Judy Wood" to... where, exactly? Back the way we've all come, to controlled demolition? As he himself says, you can't have it both ways. He can't be sensible about physics on one hand and totally wrong about physics on the other hand. Giving him the benefit of the doubt, it could just be too much for him to take in at this point... but if that's the case he is still quite wrong about the facts of the matter and this situation can be used to promote and promulgate disinformation - without his knowledge.

We also see hints of him wanting to embroil people in back and forth discussion – which achieves little or nothing. He comments:

"Once I get the crash test site forum up we can discuss it."

He is unwilling to be open and discuss this in an open forum. I wonder why? Could it be that, by making the discussion about the planes, it's about distracting people from the means by which 9/11 was achieved? He did indeed open a forum[195], though it appears to have been short lived, although this has since closed down.

It is usually interesting to find a bit of background information about these folks, but on his Website, Steve De'Ak reveals little. On his FAQ Page[196] in the "who" section, he states:

9/11 Crash Test can be blamed on Steve De'ak who can be reached at steve@yankee451.info.

But there is no additional information apart from him being a grandpa. However, on his "comments" page, he writes:

"for many years I was incognito, but I realized a while back that the only people I have a beef with have known who I am and where I live for quite some time, so no harm done. As far as I'm concerned, it's safer in the daylight."

Steve De'Ak posted additional comments on the David Icke Forum in Oct 2012[197]:

2. The media that published Dr Wood's book in defiance of the "establishment" will be able to continue flying their banner of faux independence and self-righteousness. With hurricane-powered energy weapons "dustifying" steel sky-scrapers and their contents, the media's role in this farce will be ignored. At the same time, the federal government, the FBI, the FDNY, the NYPD, the OEM, the Mayor's office and the PANYNJ won't need to explain how these buildings managed to be gutted and prepared with explosives since '93 while still maintaining the appearance of being fully-occupied "cities within the city". Furthermore, the ironically-named "truth movement" **will look like wild-eyed conspiracy nutcases thanks to the guilt by association one gets by being within spitting-distance of a Judywoodtard. All of the above considerations make the good doctor and her cult of followers highly suspect, at best.**

It seems Steve De'Ak revealed his "true colours." Talking about a "cult" and a "judywoodtard" reveals he is just another troll, out to distract and decoy. He never even bothered to find out that the WDTTG book was self-published – making his initial comment even more inappropriate.

And Finally...

Just for the sake of example, let us suppose the crash test experiment is successfully carried out, will it silence critics? I have to suggest that this is unlikely. Whatever method is used for the crash simulation, it will be criticised because it will not be a close enough reproduction of the original event. For example, a critic would say... "Oh, you didn't use 30-year old steel in your reconstruction...? Well then..." or "Oh, your wing went in vertically? That's totally different." or "Well, your wing wasn't actually attached to a plane and the rocket sled's mass - and the distribution of that mass is not the same as the original plane, so your test is not realistic." In other words, with such a limited set of evidence that you are presenting to people, it becomes easier for it to be cast aside.

Then, there is always the problem of comparison being drawn to existing videos online which seem similar to what De'Ak is proposing, such as the "Rocket Sled versus a car" done by "Mythbusters"[198] and an F4 Phantom Crash test, done by Sandia Labs[199]. De'Ak even references the "Mythbusters" video on his website…

12. Don't Tell the Truth About 9/11

As I have mentioned elsewhere, there seems to be a far-greater-than-expected resistance among alternative knowledge researchers to talking about the evidence contained in Dr Judy Wood's book and presentations. I have concluded, as I have also stated elsewhere, that this is not just due to ego, money, threats or similar reasons. "Something else" is going on. Informed and intelligent people - who have *already* "broken through" the mainstream indoctrination and programming - will not accurately report how the WTC was destroyed and what the destructive mechanism actually was.

In this chapter, we will examine what some prominent 9/11 and "Alternative Researchers" have said about 9/11. Also, we will consider what they *haven't* said, when presented with a suitable opportunity or a certain set of circumstances. The running theme is that they talk about controlled demolition, thermite and AE911 whilst ignoring most of the evidence and accomplishments of Dr Judy Wood. In some cases, as repeatedly documented in this book, they disparage Dr Wood and/or her research.

Dr David Ray Griffin

He was the person that decided to set up the "Scholars" group after he met Dr Judy Wood. He has written several books on 9/11 issues, the first of which was published in 2004.

On the Gianni Hayes radio show on 24 Sep 2008, Griffin was asked to comment on the size of the debris pile following the destruction of the WTC[200]. He claimed that the debris filled the basements – this is untrue, as shown in the WDTTG book and elsewhere in Dr Wood's presentations.

On the same programme, he was asked about the debris pile[201] and stated the towers "collapsed" into a pile "no more than four, five or six stories high." However, he acknowledges that much of the buildings contents were "pulverised" to dust, though the steel was "cut into pieces about the right length to be hauled away."

Another caller asked about the Scott Packs used by the firefighters (air tanks) exploding on the backs of trucks[202]. Griffin knew nothing about this. He was also asked about Hurricane Erin and said "there may be something to that, but I am not the one to talk to about it." He expressed no curiosity about this. This is odd, as Griffin was later to write a book about climate change[203].

On the same programme, the host asked about the molten metal at the WTC site and Griffin reported that it was "very hot" and the responders working at the site would have "boots that burned through." However, he does not discuss any accounts of burned feet. Griffin also claimed that the ground was hot for "months" after the event. Again, Dr Wood covers all this and shows that this statement about "high heat" was not and is not true.

Further information about Griffin's statements is on Dr Wood's website.[204] She includes the following:

> *It appears that David Ray Griffin values the hearsay of those on the payroll more than physical facts. This is very troubling. The molten metal myth seems to have been created as part of the official cover-up story. The above chart which shows the maximum operating temperature for hydraulics supports what NYT reporter Jim Dwyer has said. However, Griffin insults Dwyer by stating he "fully displayed his ignorance of crucial facts." But the crucial facts support Dwyer, namely, that high temperatures would have indeed permanently damaged hydraulic equipment. The facts in this matter are well-established and are available in mechanical engineering handbooks as well as on the internet [link]. It appears that Griffin is actually the one who has "the tendency to favor a priori arguments over empirical evidence."*

Readers can further investigate Griffin's connections such as the one to Richard Falk - a CFR member - who wrote the foreword to one of Griffin's books. Griffin has also made comments about the need for "global governance."[205]

Joseph P Farrell

Farrell is the author of a number of books on "conspiracy" or "alternative knowledge" topics – he is quite prolific. Books he has authored include *Roswell and the Reich*, *The Cosmic War* and *Babylon's Banksters* . Whilst like other names mentioned here, he talks about some of the same topics that I do, he appears to have another agenda. For example, in his second presentation at the 2014 "Secret Space Program" conference, JP Farrell begins to talk, (at approximately the 30 minute mark) about Cold Fusion[206] - he talks of how Dr Ronald Richter was doing experiments in the late 1940s or early 1950s, [207] which may have been similar to those which Pons & Fleischmann probably came to regret doing, years later. However, at no time does he mention the documented connection of some of the effects seen in Cold Fusion experiments to the events of 9/11[208]. This is kind of ironic, seeing as this *was* discussed in Dr Judy Wood's presentation at the Global BEM Conference which took place some 18 months earlier (a conference that was organised by the same people).[209]

Mimicry?

In her 2011 presentation at a UK group "New Horizons," Dr Wood reports that the remains of some WTC core columns (dubbed "the spire") "peels away like a banana"[210].

Spire – "Peeling like a Banana"

In April 2017 in an interview with "Sage Monitor", Farrell was heard to mimic/copy the language of Dr Judy Wood's description of the destruction of the WTC.[211] He discusses how he witnessed the initial 9/11 events after returning home from a night shift (he worked as a casino floor manager in Tulsa Oklahoma). He claims that he was watching the events of 9/11 unfold, after his friend who was staying with him, had turned on the television. He then says:

> *Just as I looked, the North Tower of the World Trade Centre was on fire and just as I looked, the second tower, the south tower was struck and immediately I thought, ye know, we're under attack and so I stayed up and watched the towers come down...*

He talks about the fires being cool fires and the meme being put out by the media. He continues

> *...and then the towers came down and I deliberately made myself count – I used my hands to kind of physically count and I thought "gee, that's near free fall speed" so this is not a conventional collapse, this is some sort of controlled demolition. And the way it looked to me, Tim, watching, literally kind of watching the towers kind of be peeled like a banana...*

The reference to "count with his hands" also seems to mimic what Dr Wood has said a few times in relation to clapping your hands quickly to see if you can match the speed at which the floors of the building are turning to dust.

In the interview, he talks about various 9/11 hypotheses and claims that "the presence of nanothermite cannot be explained" by one hypothesis and so forth. He also talks of "high heat" in the area, after destruction. He knows better. A real muddle up. Even though he had worked with WDTTG manuscript (in 2008 and 2009), he does not mention this – instead, he promotes disinformation and physical impossibilities, whilst acting like some kind of authority.

So, to clarify the point, *JP Farrell worked with Dr Judy Wood*, for several months *with the material used in Where Did the Towers Go?* However, it seemed he then became involved in an operation to remove content from the book and to delay or prevent the publication of the book. (Farrell wanted to remove much of the material relating to John Hutchison's research and the Hurricane Erin data. Also see the article "Is Richard Hoagland on a Dark Mission" in *9/11 Finding the Truth*. I did not name Farrell in that article – but it was Farrell who was responsible for taking the WDTTG manuscript to Ferral House publishers.)

During the editing, Farrell wanted to remove photos of the "toasted cars" and he made several subtle changes to the text, which were unnecessary. He had detailed knowledge of the text – yet he rarely if ever talks about the details of what happened to the WTC, except, perhaps, to fit it in with his own "storytelling" about a possible "operation within an operation." Suffice it to say, that Farrell has not been honest about his dealings with the WDTTG material and has also tried to "muddle things up" in his presentations.

Nick Begich

Nick Begich[212] has "made a name for himself" in the alternative knowledge community through discussing the HAARP facility in Alaska – having written a book about it with Jean Manning called *Angels Don't Play This HAARP*. Essentially, he talks about the possible harmful effects of classified technology such as HAARP. Back in 2006, I thought he would be quite familiar with the evidence which showed the "official conspiracy theory of 9/11" could not be true. I was to be disappointed when, on 10 December 2006, on Art Bell's "Coast to Coast" programme, he said regarding the US occupation of Iraq[213]:

> *We're in a conflict in Iraq, as an example, and we're there to win the hearts and minds and spread democracy. But that's not what the people apparently want. They want a theocracy. And if that's what they want in their own right to self-determination, maybe we need to recognise individual sovereignty and as long as they keep it within the boundaries of their country and learn to leave people alone. We're the only country in the world with 800 bases and stations around the world to monitor and interfere with everyone else's politics. Maybe it's time to pull back a little bit towards our own borders. Allow some governments to function. If they violate another state – if they violate the United States,* **I say stomp them into the stone age as we did in Afghanistan. We said give those guys up and they didn't do it, I think we were fully justified.**

Mr Begich *supported* the bombing of Afghanistan in 2001! Mr Begich and I were both speakers at the BEM 2012 conference in Hilversum, Netherlands. He was present during Dr Judy Wood's presentation about the destruction of the WTC at this same conference. Therefore, when an opportunity arose for me to ask him about his support of the bombing of Afghanistan in 2006, I needed to ask him if he had changed his mind about what happened on 9/11[214]. He agreed that "a lot of information had been brought forward." The rest of his response is below.

> *I have a very different viewpoint of warfare, alright, and a lot of people find it very objectionable probably in this room. But this is my view of it. I didn't support either one of those wars as a way of solving the problem. But if a country is going to go to war - and we just spent trillions of dollars going into debt over these two wars - my view is, if you go to war and you really feel justified and that's the decision that's made - annihilate them, but don't rebuild them. I believe that - and I know a lot of people find that objectionable, but if we really feel that's justified teach them a lesson and don't do it twice. We're in debt up to our eyeballs. We're about to destroy the entire world's economy over two wars we probably shouldn't have been in in the first place. Because we spent trillions and trillions and way too much time interfering with people's sovereignty. [If] people want a theocracy, let them have it. If they want a democracy, let them have it. If they want socialism let em have it. Stay in your own boundaries self-determine your own government and let's all have enough respect to let people do that. And that's our problem we interfere with everybody's government and the right to self-determination and that's really what it's about. I may not agree with somebody doing something next door but if they're within their boundaries, let them have their own revolution. We had one - everybody else has too. But it's self-determination [that] I think is primary and staying within your boundaries is part of that right to self-determination, I don't care what government you choose.*

As you can hear, instead of answering my question about whether he had a new understanding of what really happened on 9/11, Mr Begich chose to go into a monologue about the US attitude to warfare and invasion. It would have been simpler if he had just answered my question by saying "no," which is what he meant.

James Corbett and Mark Gaffney

In an interview with 9/11 book author Mark Gaffney by James Corbett on 9 September 2012[215], Gaffney remarked that Building 6 had a "huge crater right in the centre of it" (17:32) and he mentioned the official explanation for it. He then states that (17:50) "early on there were photos" and (18:15) that there was "very little debris of any kind." He states that there was another explosion in the building and that it may have "been demolished during the collapse of building one or two and the dust cloud concealed it."

This makes me ask, how could a conventional demolition leave very little debris? When was the building wired for this demolition? For what purpose was building 6 demolished?

At no point do either of them reference the WDTTG book – which shows exactly what happened.

In a programme/podcast on 11 June 2011[216] (about 20 mins in), James Corbett dismisses Dr Judy Wood's research, using the term "Space Beams." The term "Space Beam" given that it's not a term that Dr Wood has used in her book, website or many presentations and radio interviews. Here is what he said:

Anthony writes "I have yet to hear you comment on the split in the 9/11 research movement between the ideas of Dr Judy wood and her energy weapon theory and Professor Stephen Jones who backs the thermite Theory. Do you lend any support to Dr Wood's ideas or research?"

...let me be as clear as I can. I do not support mini nukes. I do not support TV fakery. I do not support "no planes." I do not support vic-sims and I do not support the mystery magical energy beams from outer space and I don't know how much more clear I can get on that. And that's not to say... please don't take that as me saying that I 100% unequivocally believe that the thermite story is the correct story - in fact that I have my reservations about that as well - but personally ultimately on this question, I think there are a lot of really fascinating and interesting distractions out there from some of the real issues of 9/11 and it's something that I've been saying for years now. And continue to stress that I think that a lot of the physical anomalies of what happened on 9/11 are ways to keep people in these endless inviting arguments about this and that little part...

... so people can continue to send me links to all of these interesting ideas about the interesting ways that the Towers were brought down and I'll continue to look at them but I haven't seen the single thing that's convinced me out of any of these theories and I doubt that I am likely to, but then again keep sending it in and I'll take a look at it.

Mark Gaffney - Again

Author of the book "Black 9/11" does not know the difference between theory and evidence and does not accurately discuss the evidence in Dr Judy Wood's book[217]:

In an interview on Red Ice Radio[218] (see chapter 13), he states:

Palmgren: Could this technology have taken down the buildings as well in your opinion?

Gaffney: That's a good question. No, I would answer no on that. I think the directed energy weapon high powered microwave would be... I believe this technology... It's not exotic. The 9/11 US military had it pre 9/11 And it would be the sort of thing that you could fit one of the devices in a small suitcase and it could be battery powered and it would put out an electromagnetic signal that could be very damaging to computers, any kind of electrical equipment, any kind of electronics. Commercial aircraft would have no defence against this kind of weapon because they're not hardened against this type of energy like this... it would have a range of probably around 5 kilometres.

What Judy Woods talks about in her book is very different. It would have to be something - a space weapon based on a space platform - something like that. And although I found some of Judy Wood's research to be interesting and valid, I really don't take it seriously. I think that the evidence for… in 2007 an independent team of scientists led by Dr Steven Jones Found traces of… Nanothermite in World Trade Centre dust samples and they also found unexploded ordnance - little bits of nanothermite that had not exploded. And the other evidence for explosives is the large concentration - I say about 5 to 6% by weight of iron - little iron spherules … That were found in the dust and this was one of the first things they discovered. You just put a magnet up against the dust and all this iron comes out of it. You put this under a microscope and you have these little tiny spherules - spheres of iron and iron is the principal constituent of steel and this is hard evidence of steel that melted in large quantities. So I think that the evidence is very strong, very compelling the buildings were taken down in controlled demolition… those buildings were wired and fairly large amounts of explosives were involved and this was a major operation - they must have been working on this for months.

Ian R Crane

Left to right: David Griffin, Richard Dolan, Andrew Johnson, Lloyd Pye, Nick Pope, Ian Crane

It was in 2005 that I first encountered Ian R Crane in the UK 9/11 Truth Campaign (see chapter 21), when he was said to be its chairman. Since then he has talked about the events of 9/11 in many of his public presentations. However, he has never, to my knowledge, discussed the WDTTG book. Indeed in a presentation given by him on 25 September 2011, at Conway Hall, London[219], he stated[220]:

"Building 7 was indeed a perfect – perfectly executed controlled demolition - the building came down in its own footprint and the pile of rubble was 12.5% the original height of the building – exactly as per the controlled demolition

textbooks. Buildings 1 & 2 which are more than twice the height of building 7. Just to put it in perspective, building 7 was roughly the height of the tower at canary wharf... just to put it into perspective. **Buildings 1 & 2 collapsed into dust. The buildings totally disintegrated. There is no explanation as to what has caused that – it's a big question that's left open.** *Take a look at this for a second...*

Jan Irvin

Jan Irvin runs a website called "Gnostic Media[221]." One of the areas it focuses on is critical thinking and the "trivium" - in medieval schools, this was the group of liberal arts first studied, comprising grammar, rhetoric and logic.

He posts Podcasts and articles on his website and, in one posting made on 25 January 2010[222], entitled "Logical Fallacies: The Critical Thinking Meme," someone added the following comment:

He was asked...

> *"Have you seen Dr Judy Wood's work? It undoubtedly has merit. The thermite theory seems likely a disinformation effort – I recommend all to suspend judgement until you have spent some time looking at the evidence presented by Dr Wood. I am sure you will be interested and I would love to hear your opinion."*

His reply included the following words:

> *"This isn't the 9/11 discussion forum, this is the place to study fallacies. However, when I studied Woods, there were too many fallacies. The one I find most interesting is Dimitri Kalezav. "*

Again, Irvin didn't say what the fallacies were and has clearly not studied the evidence.

A friend of mine, Menna, wrote to Irvin in July 2015[223]. Had he, in the intervening years, discovered the truth about Dr Wood's research – and what happened on 9/11? Here is part of the thread of the conversation:

> *From: contact@gnosticmedia.com*
>
> *To: menna*
>
> *Subject: RE: Dr Judy Wood and Andrew Johnson*
>
> *Date: Wed, 13 Jul 2016 15:59:24 +0000*
>
> *Thanks, but I don't think Judy Wood would be a good fit, as she appears to be part of the controlled op you talk about with Andrew Johnson.*
>
> *Judy makes a lot of speculations, and right where she should be meeting the onus of proof, she falters and argues the arbitrary. Maybe her book is better than her awful presentations. She's also Jewish and most of the evidence points to Israel as being behind 9/11 - probably why she avoids discussing this and Zionism.*

I've had former friends, such as Richard Grove, who was totally dirty and peddled the lies about 9/11. But I've not read Johnson's book to know if he'd be a good guest.

Thanks for your interest. Much appreciated.

Jim Marrs

Jim Marrs passed away on 02 Aug 2017 at the age of 73. He was very well known and very well regarded in the alternative knowledge community, having published many books on various topics[224]. He was perhaps most well-known for his work on the John F. Kennedy Assassination and his book *Crossfire* was used as a basis for the 1991 Oliver Stone film "JFK."

It appears Jim Marrs rarely commented about the destruction of the WTC, but on 27th December 2009, Jim Marrs appeared on the Dave Hodges[225] show. A man called Sheldon Day phoned in to the show to get Jim Marrs' take on what destroyed the WTC and ask him whether he had studied the evidence for directed energy weapons.

In an audio clip from this interview[226], you will notice:

1) Jim Marrs states "there is no real substantial hard evidence" proving the use of directed energy weapons (this is not true)

2) He will explain how he had put the thermite study in his book – he doesn't seem to have looked anywhere else. He seems to think the paper is valid and peer-reviewed and he has not studied the chemical formula of thermite – it contains the same two materials that would have been found in large quantities in the WTC remains anyway (Iron Oxide – rust – and aluminium – from the exterior).

3) He agrees that though Thermite burns paper, there was a great deal of unburned paper in the WTC dust

4) He mentions the cars on FDR drive – but does not acknowledge that they are out of range of any thermite burning.

5) He acknowledges there may be a problem with the source of the thermite study.

6) He suggests a new investigation is needed, but he ignores the one that has been done by the most highly qualified independent scientist[121]**Error! Bookmark not defined.**, lodged in the US Supreme Court.

1:25	The problem with the directed energy weapons in the World Trade Centre thing is that while that might be the truth, there is no real substantial hard evidence to prove that that's the case, so that's why I shy away from it, not because of being called a name. Now, as opposed to… like David Ray Griffin and others and … including myself in my book "The Terror Conspiracy" – who talked about thermite and the fact that controlled

	explosives – I think undoubtedly were used, also in the destruction of those buildings. And of course then I was the nut for talking… siding with people who said "Oh there were controlled explosions…" ye know and we can't even mention that.
2:11	And yet today, there's now hard scientific proof that thermate – a nano technology form of thermite - has been found in the debris of [the] World Trade Centre materials – and that was confirmed in a peer reviewed scientific journal in Europe *[Reminder: This is an internet only journal,* which previously published a computer-generated gibberish paper[227]. *Also, we don't know who the peer reviewers were]* Now, what I want everybody to understand is I – as an old journalist – I think that constitutes news – that should be headlines all across the country. A military grade controlled explosive residue found in World Trade Centre rubble, OK? And yet we don't see a word about that – it just doesn't appear. Now I think that should convince any open-minded person that the so-called watchdog media is actually the lapdog to the corporate interests that are running this country and I think that's why there needs to be another investigation – a truthful investigation and to prove other things up, but if they do that then we might come up with the hard evidence to show that directed energy weapons – for example…
3:19 Dave Hodges (DH)	Jim, let me ask you a question before you go further with this – I think the thermite residue has been shown and proven [right] would there be any such trace signatures for energy-directed weapons?
3:29 Jim Marrs (JM)	Well, because that's such cutting-edge technology – see that's the beauty of it – if you use a technology – in a public event like this – that is generally not known to the public – then you can put out any cover story you want to and most of the public – including the so-called experts – are going to be hard-pressed to prove otherwise – because, as he [the caller] said, this technology has been held in intelligence and military communities – ye know – and it's not known in the public so… it's like – I try to tell people I think those airplanes – because they exceeded their design limitations – which is an impossibility – unless you can override the computer – and because the transponders all went off about the same time – which is an impossibility for 4 separate airliners being hijacked – ye know there would be a little bit of a time lag – or advance in all of that.

4:27	These, to me are the tell-tale signs that computer capture was used to take over those planes and guide them to wherever they wanted [them] to go. And yet when I try to tell people that in 2001 – it's like "What are you talking about!?" – ye know. And yet, when we invaded Iraq … we invaded Afghanistan – what went in first? Those global hawk, remote-controlled planes and now you see them in advertisements for the air force and in advertisements for the marines and they'll say "Oh yeah sure – we've got that technology!" But we didn't know that in 2001.
5:01 DH	OK – Sheldon – a follow up? (Quick one…)
Sheldon	Well, this could really turn into a long discussion because I .. the thermite thing – the military uses thermite to burn paper – well look at all the paper laying around after the towers went away…
5:15 JM	Exactly – very good point
5: 17 Sheldon	and the guy who spearheaded this whole campaign about thermite – Professor Steven Jones – was instrumental, back in the late 80s [in] covering up this cold fusion technology that these 2 renowned world chemists Pons and Fleischman were trying to put out to the public. We can't trust Steven Jones and the other thing I wanted to say was hey Dave have you ever heard of John Lear?
5:41 DH	Yes I have.
JM	I know John Lear
Sheldon:	Yeah well, he doesn't talk about it on the Coast to Coast show but if you listen to John Lear on other shows, you know he's got a lot of flight experience and he says there were no planes on 9/11 it was all TV fakery and/or scalar holographic imagery.
6:00 JM	Well, again, I'm certainly not ruling out anything just off-handedly but there's going to have to be more work – ye know, you have to be very careful of all these sources, just like you pointed out the problem with Griffin [I think he meant Jones] and the Cold Fusion. The thing that I can't help but look at is there are photographs of cars on the FDR that are burned and scorched and they were blocks away from the World Trade Centre…

On 22 June 2014, Jim Marrs made a presentation at the Bloor Cinema, in Toronto[20]**Error! Bookmark not defined.**, which was hosted by Richard Syrett and

organised by Patrick Whyte. (Dr Wood gave a presentation - organised by the same people – on 11 Sep 2016[228]). Approximately 1 hr and 26 mins into the recording of this presentation, Jim Marrs was asked if he was familiar with Dr Judy Wood's book and the presence of Hurricane Erin. In response to the question, he says he wrote about Dr Judy Wood in his book *9/11 Terror Conspiracy Revisited.* He went on:

> *I think Judy Wood is onto something. I think there was exotic technology that was being used on 9/11 – technology that the public was not aware of. I did mention the global hawk [computer control] technology to take over those aircraft…*

He then mentions that no one was aware of that technology in 2001 and he talks about conversations with an airline pilot and about *that* technology. He goes on to say:

> *The only place I would differ is that she thinks this "beam weapon" may have come from a satellite and while that's possible, I think there's an even closer explanation because I actually know that at Brookhaven National Laboratories on Long Island, for some years, they've been working on a particle beam weapon and the idea was to try to see if they could stop a missile flight – which has been the goal for many years…*

He then talks about TWA-800 and Boeing planes and never answers the question about Hurricane Erin.

So now let us briefly look at his 2011 *Terror Conspiracy Revisited* book[229] (published after WDTTG). In the chapter entitled "Firefighters Thought the Fires were Controllable" Marrs writes about a "prolific blogger", calling himself "The Anonymous Physicist" and how this blogger thinks an EMP pulse results in massive sparking of electrical cables and connectors leading to fires and explosions."

Marrs then does indeed mention Dr Wood, writing

> *Two well-known 9/11 researchers, Morgan Reynolds and Judy D. Wood, also noted the evidence of an EMP pulse, noting "electrical outage over a wide area with repairs taking over three months, suggesting EM pulses." To further support the idea of EMP use, it should be noted that there were reports of many cell phones becoming inoperative near the WTC buildings.*

This is hardly true – Dr Wood doesn't talk about EMP's – it is misrepresenting (again) what she said. Though Marrs correctly includes Dr Wood's biography and what he says about the WTC "bathtub" seems to be accurate, he does not go into enough detail. Nor does he openly suggest people read Dr Wood's book to get all the details. Next, he talks about the "toasted cars," reporting an quote from Dr Wood (from a press release I wrote in 2008[230]):

> *In 2003 [This date is incorrect – it should be 2008], Wood stated, "I have been collecting data over the last year and a half or so and I have found these distinct and unusual characteristics, which I have given names such as 'fuming' and 'toasted' cars—I have even noticed flipped cars in some*

pictures. In some cases, the flipped cars are sitting next to trees that are fully covered with leaves." This prompted the question, "If the flipping of the cars was caused by big explosions or "wind from the towers coming down, how did the leaves stay on the trees?"

Despite Marrs having written about black programmes, related to UFO technology etc, he again leaves this reference "hanging" and explores it no further. His book does not include any pictures of flipped cars – or any similarly relevant evidence.

Steve Bassett

From his website[231]:

Stephen Bassett is the executive director of Paradigm Research Group founded in 1996 to end a government imposed embargo on the truth behind the so called "UFO" phenomenon. Stephen has spoken to audiences around the world about the implications of formal "Disclosure" by world governments of an extra-terrestrial presence engaging the human race. He has given over 1000 radio and television interviews, and PRG's advocacy work has been extensively covered by national and international media. In 2013 PRG produced a "Citizen Hearing on Disclosure" at the National Press Club in Washington, DC. On November 5, 2014 PRG launched a Congressional Hearing/Political Initiative seeking the first hearings on Capitol Hill since 1968 regarding the extra-terrestrial presence issue and working to see that issue included in the ongoing presidential campaign.

In the context that we are discussing, we can draw close parallels between the activities of Steve Bassett and Dr Steven Greer (discussed in chapter 6). Though some people are uncomfortable connecting the UFO/ET/alien issue to 9/11, I speak about this publicly and expect researchers and knowledgeable people like Steve Bassett to point out such connections when they are obvious. Clearly, he is interested in the weaponisation of black technology. This came up in a round table discussion on Sat 28 June 2014, (at 21:40 in)[232] at the 2014 "Secret Space Conference" held in San Metino California[233]. He said

*One of the very possible reasons why the secrecy has been so profoundly maintained is that the power of the energy systems and technologies being worked on as well as the antigravitic technology – **if it gets in the wrong hands could be a serious problem**. I'd like to mention something you may have forgotten about. Back in 1991/92 there were articles which I read that the military kind of had a problem in that they had been developing a huge range of sophisticated weapons and were very frustrated that there wasn't a war they could use them in...*

He then mentions Saddam Hussein and Kuwait and he talks about the Gulf War and how it was shown on TV in graphic detail. Then at about 24:30 into the discussion, he says

Maybe the secrecy is because these weapons, if they get in the wrong hands, could be dangerous. I would like to make the suggestion that they are already in the wrong hands...

This is very similar to what Steven Greer said in his *Forbidden Knowledge book*. So, again, the same applies here. If Steve Bassett had referenced or described Dr Judy Wood's book at this point, he would have been able to illustrate that he was, indeed, correct! *He would have been making an <u>observation</u>, not a <u>suggestion</u>.* Would that not have increased his credibility – referring to a comprehensive, publicly available investigation by a scientist, part of which had been submitted in a court case[39]**Error! Bookmark not defined.**? This investigation (contained in *Where Did the Towers Go?*) even includes reference to certain antigravitic effects discovered by John Hutchison and inspected by Col John Alexander in 1983[234]. I mentioned Col John Alexander, because Steve Bassett should know about him as a UFO commentator – Alexander has strong military ties and knowledge[235].

In a similar manner to how Steven Greer was questioned, Steve Bassett was asked if he believed the official account of 9/11, at the UFO truth Southern Conference on 29 Apr 2017[236]. He replied:

> *Q: Steve, do you believe in any way the official version of [the events of] 9/11?*
>
> *A: Well the answer is… do I believe that the investigation of 9/11 – which they didn't want to do until they were forced to by the women victims … Which was an utter insult to the American People – unbelievable – the investigation is not full, is not adequate and there are major discrepancies. We do not know the full story. We have a 100 theories, all of which cannot be right. So essentially, one of the most important events in American History. And again, just like so many other things – left unresolved - because "you don't need disclosure" – you're just people. As far as what's going on and my principal focus here… **I know Richard Gage very well…** The number one problem for the government is Building 7…*

Why would Bassett highlight that he knows Richard Gage? To confirm that they are both members of the same "cover up crew?"

Conclusion

I am sure that having read this chapter, some people will be rather despondent or depressed. I have shown that a sample of people who should be saying "Yes, I have studied Dr Wood's book and the evidence in it proves that the towers were destroyed using some type of undisclosed technology. The towers turned to dust before they hit the ground. This is really important to understand." This statement would take less than 1 minute to read out. Instead, these researchers say no such thing. If they say anything at all, it is wildly inaccurate or woefully incomplete. Before you reach the end of this book, you will read about many more examples of this sort of activity – which is central to how the cover up of 9/11 evidence works.

13. Red Ice Radio joins the 9/11 Disinformation Promotion Brigade
May/June 2013

This article shows a deeply troubling example of a relatively well-known alternative knowledge researcher/show host objecting to being criticised for not knowing the truth of what happened to the WTC and instead characterising what he has been shown as "theory" or "conjecture" (which is the same as what mainstream commentators do).

Red Ice Radio[237] is a subscription-based Website service which provides regular downloadable interviews with "alternative knowledge" researchers. Some interviews are free to download and some are split into 2 or more parts with the second and later parts usually only available to paying subscribers for download.

Red Ice Radio provides a very interesting and varied set of audio content – and the interviews are normally of good quality, as Henrik Palmgren is an informed researcher who is not afraid to explore the various "rabbit holes" that present themselves to us.

I was interviewed on Red Ice Radio in 2010, to talk about the subjects of Chemtrails and 9/11[238]. I met Henrik Palmgren at the 2010 Arc Convention in Bath[239] which was organised by Karen Sawyer[240]. In the interview with Henrik, we talked about the 9/11 "Truth" Movement's cover up of 9/11 Truth – especially the cover up of the "energy connection," which is indicated by the involvement of people such as Steven E Jones in both "Cold Fusion" (LENR) research and the bogus "thermite" theory that he initiated in 2005[241].

Dr Judy Wood[2**Error! Bookmark not defined.**], has, of course also been on with Henrik[242] at least twice[243] to explain what really happened to the WTC. She went to some trouble to provide Henrik with an electronic copy of her book *"Where Did the Towers Go?*[3**Error! Bookmark not defined.**]," to enable Henrik to study this before the interview, which took place before the first batch of printed copies became available. (Henrik was also sent a hard copy before the 10-year anniversary - which was when Henrik's second interview with Dr Wood took place). Almost everyone who reads this book will understand what happened to the WTC on 9/11. It is not a theory nor a hypothesis. It is not an "idea" and it is not speculation – it is a collection of diverse evidence, along with a scientific analysis of that evidence. Some of the evidence in the book was included in Court Submissions in 2007 – 2009[39**Error! Bookmark not defined.**].

A Danish chemist named Niels Harrit[244] had just been featured on Red Ice Radio. Harrit is one of many who is keen to ignore and ridicule 9/11 evidence. In 2008, I corresponded with Harrit just before writing an article[245] about the cover up of Dr Judy Wood's court case, but I did not name him in the article. Harrit makes ridiculous suggestions about "tons" of thermite being used to destroy the WTC[246]. Mr Harrit seemed to "come on to the scene" soon after

Dr Judy Wood's court submissions were made. He has continued to talk about thermite and nanothermite ever since, even though it can be proved from basic observation that thermite had nothing to do with the destruction of the WTC (Dr Wood has addressed this evidence – or lack thereof - in her presentations[247]). Harrit did contribute an affidavit to April Gallop's court case[248], but again all his statements were based on the use of thermite or some variant of it – which cannot explain the available evidence – or the observed WTC phenomena.

Red Ice Radio had around the same time featured Kevin Barrett[249], who has admitted a "professional interest" in 9/11 research[250]. I mention this because Kevin Barrett apparently does not understand Newton's 3rd law and therefore "does not really know" what happened on 9/11[251]. Kevin Barrett also does not seem to understand what bombs do to materials[252].

Henrik Palmgren has also in recent months featured Mark Gaffney[218]**Error! Bookmark not defined.** and Jeremy "Alien Scientist" Rys[253] who we have mentioned in previous chapters because again, they only seem to want to talk about what thermite and hot explosives and incendiaries do to materials. They both refuse to acknowledge the effects documented in *Where Did the Towers Go?*[3]**Error! Bookmark not defined.** and instead resort to either ridicule or mischaracterisation or blatant lies about what has been stated in Dr Judy Wood's research.

Back to the Red Ice interview with Mr Harrit. Near the end, Henrik Palmgren does bring up Dr Wood's research[254]. However, like so many other people, Henrik mis-characterises the content of Dr Wood's book as "ideas" or "theories" - this is not what I would expect of an honest alternative knowledge host/researcher who has had time to study the evidence. It is yet again worth re-iterating that some of this evidence was submitted to court[39]**Error! Bookmark not defined.**, unlike the thermite "evidence"[255]. Harrit also starts lying by saying he was not aware of the evidence in Dr Wood's research – I made him aware of it approximately 5 years ago. So, are Henrik and Harrit both suffering from amnesia?

What is the point of things like Red Ice Radio? For many of the topics covered, there are large swathes of speculation, where things are not proved – and opinions are essentially the main points of discussion (which is fine). However, Dr Judy Wood's research does not revolve around opinion – as I have repeated many, many times. The WDTTG book is a presentation of two sets of evidence which, in parallel, prove what happened to the WTC. This is quite clear to most people who study this evidence for long enough. Dr Wood and myself told Henrik the essentials of this over 3 years ago. I am therefore pointing this out to suggest that to let Harrit, Barrett, Mark Gaffney[217]**Error! Bookmark not defined.** and Jeremy "Alien Scientist" Rys spread disinformation without properly calling them out strongly indicates to me that Henrik is no longer interested in the truth of what happened on 9/11 – he is more interested in the Red Ice "vehicle" than stating clearly where lies are being broadcast. I know I might sound too harsh or judgemental, but we do *know* what happened to the WTC now - so to characterise knowledge as "theory" is dishonest. Henrik should know better.

Perhaps, as far as Red Ice goes, this shows that being immersed in "conspiracy culture" affects your memory or your ability to reason and you can end up not knowing up from down...? When I posted comments on my Facebook Page, people thought I was being unfair to Red Ice/Henrik. They seemed to think that Niels Harrit (and essentially Henrik) were "expressing an opinion." Of course, this is true – to an extent – but let us make sure we distinguish between *opinion, evidence* and *fact* – and note where a cover up or censorship is occurring. After all, if Henrik is letting these folks on for 2 hours to express opinions, why doesn't he invite someone like George Monbiot on to talk about how Al Qaida did 9/11[256] and how CO_2 is a global threat[257]? After all, it's folks just expressing an opinion - so what's wrong with that?

Some people may wonder why I go to the trouble of writing articles such as this. The reasons are:

1) We know what happened to the WTC on 9/11 and that knowledge is crucial in looking at the future and understanding the current state of our world – weaponised free energy technology, held by a hidden group, was used to destroy the WTC - and this should be disclosed to everyone. There is no issue that is not affected by this knowledge.

2) To effectively disclose this information, I feel compelled to make sure everyone realises how the cover up of the information proving point (1) is done. I hope to show how people are easily persuaded that evidence is "opinion" and that conclusive analysis is "speculation." People like Harrit and Henrik Palmgren have – wittingly or unwittingly – helped to confuse speculation with proof and they have also allowed the presentation of speculation as if it is proof.

Following my posting of the text above on my website, Henrik Palmgren recorded a 1-hour long tirade pointing out how wrong I was…[258]

Unfortunately, Palmgren was apparently unwilling to study what I had previously uncovered about some of his guests and use that to challenge these people for being dishonest. Instead, Henrik Palmgren chose to be dishonest himself.

9/11 Evidence and Theory – Is Andrew Johnson A 'Truth Fascist'?

I posted a response to Henrik Palmgren's "tirade" on 6 June 2013[259] and include the salient points of that response below, including some additional clarification of certain points.

I do not consider Red Ice, as a whole, is spreading disinformation. It would be stupid to claim such a thing because I couldn't possibly know everything about all the topics that have been covered on Red Ice Radio. The title of my article was "Red Ice Radio joins the **9/11** Disinformation Promotion Brigade" (notice the 9/11 in there?). Earlier chapters in this book show what the disinformation is and who is putting it out. Hence, I am now certain about what I am saying in this area. That is to say, my article is specifically about 9/11 – and what *we know* – Henrik does not seem to like me stating that *certain things* are known (and yes, there are other areas of 9/11 research – and other topics that shows such as Red Ice cover - where things *are not known*).

It is dishonest to characterise evidence as theory (and vice versa). This is what Henrik did in his interview with Harrit. He could have kept everything else the same – done almost everything else the same – but my main objection is that he did this. In relation to the crime of 9/11 – and its investigation this, to me, is the most important thing – he needed to make sure he differentiated evidence and speculation, theory and knowledge.

Henrik's overall thrust in his tirade is in line with the email I received from Red Ice Radio a day or two after I posted my article. They did not respond to the questions I then asked in my follow up email.

The Red Ice posting does not link to my original article[260]. My website is not mentioned (fair enough, folks can use Google – but I deliberately linked to *all* the important sources of information when I am writing articles like this). In his tirade, Henrik does not read out my article in full. I included <u>opening complimentary and explanatory remarks about the nature of his programmes</u> (which Henrik repeatedly stated "I did not understand").

One other issue that came up was when I expressed my concern that Henrik did not know the truth of what happened to the WTC. Henrik was among the first people in the world to receive an electronic draft version of the WDTTG book. At the end of 2010, a PDF version was prepared specially for Henrik's interview. It is a 500-page book with 800 images (he does not mention this). We thought he had the same philosophy about knowing the truth as we do – so he would need the evidence to decide what the truth was. Henrik, however, apparently wants to remain "neutral" about what the 9/11 evidence shows (at least, on his programme). In doing this, in the Niels Harrit interview, he characterised evidence as theory and analysis as "ideas" or "opinion." Hence, it seems we were mistaken about "how his programme would work," <u>in this case</u>.

Again, my specific reaction to the Harrit programme was because it was about 9/11. I am also interested in many of the topics that Red Ice covers and for many, <u>we cannot know as much of the truth</u> as we can about <u>what happened to the WTC</u>. (This basically boils down to the amount of available evidence which can be studied carefully.) I do, by the way, understand Henrik's philosophy about the programme, but **I don't agree that is appropriate to apply this same philosophy to the study of <u>what happened at the WTC</u>**. 9/11 was a huge <u>crime</u> – and it employed black technology. It has probably affected the world more than any other topic discussed on Red Ice. Dr Wood has investigated a large part of this crime (at the WTC site), worked out what happened and she has taken action by submitting the evidence in a fraud case. I tried to help[110]**Error! Bookmark not defined.**. This is one key thing that Henrik did not really bring out in the tirade or posting (he mentions a phrase from my article about Wood's Qui Tam case, but no details). This is very important.

In his tirade Henrik suggested several times such things as "Red Ice Radio should be run the way Andrew Johnson says" (he doesn't say this exactly – I am paraphrasing). This is *not* what I am saying. In this area, I appreciate some of the points Henrik makes - and this is why I wrote, above "I know I might sound too harsh or judgemental, but…" However, Henrik <u>did not read out this sentence from my article</u>.

Henrik implies that I asked him to represent Dr Judy Wood (or me) – but this is not the case. I can appreciate that what I wrote above can be interpreted as *suggesting* that – but <u>it does not say that</u>! What I wrote above states that <u>we can know the truth</u> and <u>speak the truth</u> – and we <u>can challenge</u> those who are lying – as <u>I am challenging lies here</u>!

Henrik also implies that he should ask me for a "stamp of approval" for his guests. That is misrepresenting what I wrote – what I would rather see happen is that he would come to know the truth for himself and correct his guests when they make incorrect, false or untrue statements. This is actually a more general problem in that show hosts aren't knowledgeable or diligent enough to correct guests on anything but the most obvious mistakes.

Henrik also implies that I asked them to censor or remove people from the "debate" or "discussion" – where did I suggest that? I expected Henrik to state that thermite could not turn the towers to dust. (Anyone can know this from simple observation!) I see now that this was an unrealistic hope or expectation. Also, I <u>did not suggest</u> we should "not allow them a voice" As I said above, I suggested he could use his own voice to <u>challenge them</u> when they are <u>not telling the truth</u>. Again, I am clearly expecting too much – and, as Henrik more or less says himself, this is where we disagree on our approach to things – and perhaps why I don't or couldn't do a regular series of podcasts like he does – because, I would quickly become unpopular. (I didn't write and post this article to become popular, but to point out where people are <u>not telling the truth</u> about <u>what happened to the WTC</u>.)

One observation is that it seems that many people turn to services like Red Ice Radio because they feel the mainstream media is not telling them the whole truth. Therefore, should it not be important for Red Ice (and similar services) to present the truth or refer to the truth when you can <u>prove</u> what it is?

Some people think this is all "infighting" or "squabbling." However, what should we all expect to see when the truth and lies are set against one another? When you know the truth, debates about what it might be are pointless. Just imagine maths lessons which debated the answer to a calculation, or what the third angle in a triangle was when the other two are known.

So what are the options when we know liars are receiving airtime? To "keep quiet"? Heck, all I did was post an article on my website. And, according to Henrik's philosophy about things, "it's just my opinion." Right? So why is Henrik so bothered about what I have written here? He should let people make their own minds up about it, according to his way of doing things? Instead, he spends good portions of an hour attacking and insulting my character, whilst omitting important elements of my original posting. Also, Henrik says that I do not know him as a person – and neither does he know me, yet he makes generalisations about my thinking and my knowledge.

Henrik discusses "the other side talking to us." The truth doesn't have "sides" and in any case, I have repeatedly communicated with members of the cover up crew in the past, and confirmed that their statements are, either intentionally or unintentionally helping to keep the truth covered up. Some of these conversations are documented in my previous book (and yet more are documented here).

Sadly, Henrik does not reference this in his posting or his spiel. He does not say "I did not realise Andrew had contacted Niels Harrit in 2008." Henrik makes a number of more emotive remarks, trying to suggest I have said things I have not said. For example, he says

> **When I read Andrew's material it's like other people should not be allowed to express opinions."**

This is not true! What I asked for in my article was for people to understand the difference between opinion and evidence! Also, when I was referring to George Monbiot, I was specifically referring to what we now know about 9/11 (and climate change). We know that Monbiot is wrong about 9/11! (That is to say, it isn't just that Monbiot has "another view.")

In his tirade, Henrik swears a few times and then, around the 30 minute mark, says I (Andrew Johnson) "toot this religiously?" Does Henrik think I should <u>not</u> tell people <u>what I know is true</u>? I should <u>not</u> tell them that the WTC turned mostly to dust? Instead, I should say "well, it might've been thermite, but if I don't include the thermite in my discussion, I would be being religious." What nonsense.

Henrik later called me "childish" and then compares me to the Official Group that investigated 9/11. Wow – I must be powerful! He then later calls me a "truth fascist." Maybe that's accurate. I suppose I'd rather be called a "truth fascist" than a "lying fascist"! Perhaps I should even take this as a compliment… as it means I am uncompromising when it comes to the truth…? (And, might I suppose that Henrik Palmgren is not that concerned about what the truth is.)

Henrik, at one point in his tirade, read out my email address and invited his listeners to write to me. Was he encouraging them to send me hate mail? Whatever his meaning was, I did receive some unpleasant messages saying I was "a bad man," but most if not all of the few people that wrote to me *did not even read the article to which Henrik was over-reacting*. They just took Henrik's tirade at face value and they didn't even check what I had actually written on my website!

Henrik, did read out the conclusion to my original article – but then implied that I was wrong to be confident that I/we do know about 9/11. He then mentioned Richard Andrew Grove! *He is not mentioned in my article and I have not referenced Grove's work anywhere on the site*! I actually found Richard Andrew Grove's interview very interesting – but couldn't really make any useful comments about it, as I have not studied it in depth. I <u>never</u> said what I wrote about the WTC disqualified Grove's work! Why did Henrik include this? In referencing the other speakers, I linked to <u>specific information and evidence about what they said and why I considered it to be disinformation</u>. Henrik did not specifically mention Rys defacing images of our books and using them in the videos. However, Henrik <u>did</u> make some mention of how myself and Dr Wood have been attacked.

To respond to another point Henrik made, let me say that I am not afraid of my conclusions or that I will be discredited – I post them because I consider these conclusions and these pieces of evidence are important to our future. Henrik clearly disagrees – as there aren't any conclusions that he thinks are worth taking these sorts of actions over.

Now that I have stated certain things and shown them to be true, according to Henrik, "Andrew is the enemy." Henrik spent a whole hour, attacking my character and my approach, whilst missing out important parts of what I actually wrote above.

I later had some further correspondence with someone at Red Ice, which is shown on my website[259]Error! Bookmark not defined.. Here is some of it. They said:

> ***So what Henrik called Judy's work a theory because at the end of the day, it is to us.*** *Have you seen the energy weapon with your own eyes? Yet you become high strung like a little neurotic puppy, peeing on the floor when something doesn't fit in line with your belief or threatens it.* ***Most of life on this planet IS speculation, ideas, theories.*** *You lack the ability to be a rational human being, let alone kind to your fellow truth seekers. Instead you are quick to judge and slandor. That speaks volumes about who you are.*

I repeated that to characterise knowledge as "theory" is dishonest. Henrik should know better." The "most life on this planet" statement is like something Jim Fetzer would say – try to put a "philosophical" spin on it, so that the truth can be marginalised and ignored.

> *Oh so we all know what happened with all certainty now, hu?*

> *Wow, what arrogance. You do not even know Henrik, other than the kindness he showed you…not to mention years and years of his hard work making it possible to interview researchers. **In fact, Henrik was the first to interview Judy!** Yet you the enlightened one, trash a kind man you do not know personally telling him who is disinfo and who is not. You accuse Henrik of being disinfo. You are so far gone while you accuse us of not being able to reason.*

There is a false claim here by Red Ice Radio – Henrik was *not* the first person to interview Dr Judy Wood – one of her earliest radio interviews about her 9/11 Research was with Ambrose Lane in September 2006[261]. Additionally, Mel Fabregas interviewed Dr Wood in Nov 2009…[262]

I pointed out that "Perhaps, as far as Red Ice goes, this shows that being immersed in "conspiracy culture" affects your memory or your ability to reason and you can end up not knowing up from down…?" In their response:

> *Of course people thought that because you are being out of line completely but you cannot even see yourself! You say "immersed in conspiracy culture" (after years and years of programs on a variety of topics) yet you yourself behave like a religious zealot in your remarks, gone beyond the point of being able to see up from down.*

> *Instead of being an arrogant truth fascist telling other people what they should do or what they should think, look at your own self Andrew. Learn to be a big man and let others make up their own minds and live their own lives. It is YOU who is spreading disinfo about a man (and others who help that man) who you do not know. Your words will have consequences by your own doing.*

This is just personal accusations against me – there is no acknowledgement of the truth of what happened on 9/11, nor is there acknowledgement of the difference between "theory" and "evidence" etc. I therefore made a final attempt to get them to see the issue clearly.

> Do you know the difference between "a view" and "truth"? Is it "a view" that your name is ---- and my name is Andrew? (Pick an example of this sort of thing to see if it helps).

> On 9/11 did the towers turn to dust or did they not? (Watch some of the videos)

> ----, has Niels Harrit submitted a court case based on evidence he has collected?

> Do you care more about what I have written about Red Ice Radio than what happened on 9/11? Why have you reacted this way to my knowledge of WHAT happened on 9/11? Do you care about the cover up of what happened on 9/11 and those who are assisting in it? (It's something I care about deeply, which is why I have gone through the painful task of documenting it over the last 6-7 years or so.)

> To me, your message is extremely telling. Perhaps you will consider what I have written above and in my article more carefully - or perhaps you won't. Perhaps you will consider it arrogant of me to state that today is Monday and tomorrow is Tuesday.

Best Wishes

Andrew Johnson

I received no response to this message.

Please remember that the important thing here is not Andrew Johnson or Red Ice Radio – it is the evidence of what happened on 9/11 – and what it means to our future.

14. The Weakness of "The Power Hour"
Posted 10 Sep 2013 – Originally Written in Late 2010

This was originally posted following Dr Judy Wood receiving an invite to speak on a popular radio show, with a large audience, called "The Power Hour" which was hosted by Joyce Riley. The interview would have taken place on 11 September 2013. Dr Wood declined the invitation, because of what is documented below. Joyce Riley passed on 25 June 2015. I hope she has found the truth now.

This is, of course, not the first time such an interview request has been declined by Dr Judy Wood. An interview with the BBC was declined by Dr Judy Wood in 2008. That was a good decision, it seems, (and was re-affirmed as such, with the airing of another BBC 9/11 criminal propaganda piece by the same producer – Mike Rudin).

Introduction

This article will attempt to analyse a previous interview conducted by Joyce Riley of "The Power Hour" and indicate why Dr Wood declined a request for an interview by her in relation to Dr Wood's fundamentally important 500-page tome *Where Did the Towers Go?*

On 23rd March 2010, Joyce Riley interviewed Dr Judy Wood in relation to her research into the destruction of the WTC complex, and resulting Qui Tam Case[263].

Sadly, it has become necessary to post this article to lay out the facts about what happened in 2010, so that information and analysis is available for those that wish to read it. Time and again we find ourselves having to work to correct misconceptions, misrepresentations and clarify the context in which evidence has been discussed. Again, it has become necessary to point out where psychological tactics seem to have been used, rather than relevant and logical questions being asked and answered.

I have become ever more wary about having to post articles like this and at times, feel that I have turned into some kind of "watcher" or even "policeman" (which is not what I intended). Overall, the evidence I have gathered over the last 6-7 years, shows that the cover up relating to Dr Judy Wood's research into the destruction of the WTC is so powerful and comprehensive – and it is often quite subtle.

In all of this, my overall objective and agenda is to make information available so that *those that want to learn the truth can learn the truth*. It is not an easy task – because of the mesh of forces which works to keep the truth from being known.

I was therefore saddened by Joyce Riley's response when I wrote to her on Dr Judy Wood's behalf to decline an interview that she had requested, around the time of the 10th anniversary (and the same has happened near the 12th anniversary). In short, it seems that Joyce Riley was not particularly interested in the truth of what happened on 9/11. It seems she would rather fill an hour or two of her radio show and then continue to suggest that the truth about what happened on 9/11 was not – and could not – be known.

We will now analyse parts of the interview.

Dr Wood Interviewed by Joyce Riley – 22 Mar 2010

Dr Judy Wood was invited, along with myself, to discuss her research on "The Power Hour" and the show took place on schedule[264].

Initially, there were no serious problems with the interview, although Joyce Riley started off reminding people about thermite being accepted by a number of people in the "truth movement." At about 13:04, when discussing whether large pieces of the building fell to the ground, she does say, however, that all she saw was "dust in the air." This theme is repeated several times over the next few minutes, and Joyce Riley seemed to understand.

At about 11:50 into the interview, Joyce Riley talks about the building being brought down by thermite charges.

At about 29:00 Hurricane Erin is brought up and Joyce Riley states that she had "never heard about this." A few seconds later she says that "people are emailing her because they do not believe what they're hearing." She makes no other comment and expresses no surprise.

The first caller appears around 31:30 and brings up the subjects of UFOs and molten metal!

However, when Dr Wood started to discuss her court case, some problems began to occur. At about 37:00 Dr Wood was talking about the contractors she had sued but she does not get chance to name them. Joyce Riley then abruptly cuts in saying:

> *OK let me just say to Larry in Texas we're gonna get to what she believes to be the err the reason…*

Dr Wood then says:

> *No, this isn't about **belief**.*

Riley continues

> *Alright – what she says her **belief** is… Larry did you want to say anything else?*

So, Joyce Riley is either not appreciating or deliberately putting the wrong emphasis on the word "belief." Perhaps she is even deliberately mischaracterising what Dr Judy Wood did with her research?

The caller then asks about WTC 7 and then there is a break after which Joyce Riley then says:

> *We're having a bit of a contentious discussion between some people who believe and don't believe what Dr Judy Wood says – now I'm open. I don't have a dog in this fight – other than I want the truth – I'm just like her. I want to know what the evidence shows – what the documentation shows…*

Joyce Riley seems to be muddling things around here – she claims to want to know the truth, but she put things in terms of "belief" and kept interrupting - when Dr Judy Wood was discussing some of the details of the court case. She then suddenly switches to talking to a caller, just when the discussion was beginning to cover who might know who "did" 9/11 (i.e. the military contractors who helped cover up what happened).

Joyce Riley then talks about "buildings coming down" and Dr Wood then goes on to say the buildings "went away." She then states that "Building 7 didn't come down" and points out the lack of a seismic signal for its demise. Joyce Riley says

> *"I think this is where people are gonna lose you right now…"*

Dr Wood goes on to explain what actually happened with the ongoing and voluminous "fuming" which lasted for about 7 hours. …

> *Well I don't know about that. Here again you're asking us to deal with a fact I am not aware of."*

Joyce Riley does not let Dr Wood elaborate on the evidence and present the truth about what happened to WTC 7. Rather, she then takes a phone call which turns out to be "Steve from Florida." He asks if he is "loud and clear" and then launches into a tirade[265]

> *"Judy you have misrepresented the facts concerning Hurricane Erin. I live here in Hurricane Country – Florida, I track all the Hurricanes. Erin hit Corpus Christy Texas, 15 August 2007. Your opinion[s] concerning 9/11 are not consistent with the facts provided. 9/11 Ripple Effect, Last Man Out, Richard Gage's Blue Print for 9/11 Truth , Loose Change Final Cut, Zero and Investigation into 9/11 and many other documentaries.*
>
> *I don't know what planet you've come from…"*

Joyce Riley then interrupts and then says

> *"We don't need to go quite that far. The point is we are listening to information here and trying to come to a conclusion. Give her 1 statement at a time that you'd like her to address."*

The question then is, according to Joyce Riley, "how far do we need to go"? How should we characterise the guest (Dr Judy Wood)? "Strange", "weird", or just plain "wacky"?

We then hear some background noises and Steve is "gone." Dr Judy Wood's voice is then heard saying *"as for Hurricane Erin, they did not retire that name."*

As it turned out, Dr Wood's *audio had been muted* while the caller was "ranting" and she was pointing out (but it did not go on air), that the facts can easily be checked at the Hurricane Data Centre. Dr Wood did give some facts about the Hurricane but seemed to have been surprised and put off balance by the caller's rant and Joyce Riley's lack of response to it.

Once again, we can think of what the caller said – **he asked if he "was loud and clear."** Note, he did not say "can you hear me"? Which is what most people would have said.

But Joyce Riley carries on reading e-mails and does not bother to correct the caller's false statement and then there is a break. After the break, Joyce Riley, says that "a lot of people have asked to have Dr Judy Wood on", but she then feels it is necessary to *defend herself* for having Dr Wood on. Joyce Riley asks that she not be "berated" if listeners do not agree with Dr Wood. She then says Steve is a "wonderful person and she loves him very much", but says "let's just try to get down to what the fact is."

The problem with this statement and its sentiment is that Joyce Riley, *prior to the interview*, had a 90-minute telephone conversation with Dr Wood and the Hurricane *was discussed*. Why would she not say "no, sorry Steve, you're wrong – I checked the hurricane and it really was there."

After a discussion of the conclusion about the buildings being destroyed with the use of an energy weapon, Joyce Riley then goes to a call from "George in Canada" – (it is actually George Freund).

At about 47:10, he then discusses "burning metals" - metals that can burn underwater (which is true) and he gives the example of divers welding under water and phosphorus bombs.

Dr Wood points out she talked about "molten metals" not burning metals and she said that you don't *store* molten metal at the bottom of a swimming pool. After the break Joyce Riley then says, "she doesn't know the answers" and goes back to George Freund who again talks about metals burning under water and how they have to be extinguished differently to "ordinary" fires. (He seems to know quite a bit about it). George Freund then goes on to talk about nanothermite and an MIT publication called Technology Review. He also mentions mini-nuke technology and goes on about various other "nanothermite-related" items. (I have already talked about this extensively in *9/11 Finding the Truth* and earlier in this book. Further information can be found on a blog I compiled called "9/11 Thermite Free".)[266]

Freund then goes on to question the issue of the Hurricane saying:

"I do recall almost every picture – in fact in every picture I've seen of New York on that day – the sky was blue – pure blue – not a cloud in the sky."

Joyce Riley interrupts and says

> *"this is hurting the situation because we can't verify some of your so-called evidence here. I mean, I'm trying to – I want to."*

Dr Judy Wood advises her to go to http://drjudywood.com/wtc and points out that the hurricane is documented at the National Hurricane Centre. I must therefore question, at this point, Joyce Riley's motives. We are 54 minutes in – now 17 minutes after the first caller has essentially accused Dr Judy Wood of lying about Hurricane Erin – and there have been 2 breaks! No one has checked.

She then goes back to George Freund – who continues to talk about demolition and he does not ask Dr Wood a further question. The discussion goes on to what William Rodriguez (see chapter 21) said about a sealed off area in the WTC and Joyce Riley says she "happens to believe him." This makes her on-air doubt about the presence of Hurricane Erin - already discussed with her prior to the interview – even more inappropriate.

We then have another caller talking about molten metal and melting boots (but not burned feet). He (inevitably) mentions Steven E Jones and the so-called "peer-reviewed" papers. He openly accuses Dr Wood of being a "disinfo agent" but she replies discussing how the thermite evidence has never been submitted in a legal framework, whereas her own research has.

Joyce Riley then *agrees* that these other people haven't filed a Qui Tam case based on their evidence, but then returns to the caller and enthusiastically seems to agree with him when he suggests "a combination of things" were used. She says

> *"Good point! Excellent point."*

Now, one hour into this broadcast (considerably longer in real time, due to the breaks), Joyce Riley finally announces that her computer is "fixed" and she has "confirmed" that Hurricane Erin was indeed the longest [lasting] hurricane in the 2001 season. The time frame was Sept 1st to the 15th (though she doesn't name the Hurricane at this point) and Dr Judy Wood continues to explain its relevance, but is again cut short as another caller is taken. However, this caller seems to understand the basis of the evidence and what it shows, and is complimentary.

Joyce Riley talks about people's reaction to the evidence and how the Power Hour is about "empowering people with facts and evidence." She then says:

> *Now I think there have been some statements made today that are probably inaccurate on both sides, but I think the idea though is that we are looking for the truth… if we are all looking for the truth, there shouldn't be this infighting…*

Following this, I also spoke for a time on the programme and after the programme, Joyce Riley did, indeed, ring me and compliment me on my presentation. (Only Jim Fetzer has done this same thing with me before now).

Joyce Riley seems quite open to what I said and even went on to ask Dr Wood to list the contractors that were named in her Qui Tam Case. However, this is not discussed for all that long.

Following a short summing up I offered, another couple of e-mails are read out, one of which says:

> *Judy is not the easiest person to follow, but when she said "Tesla" she got my attention. It may have been a sound weapon, as Tesla proved, as well as Thermite!*

Joyce Riley responds:

> *Bingo! What a good statement!*

A complimentary e-mail is read out asking for Dr Wood to be back on. She then closes with:

> *Listeners, it's all about being open-minded. We don't know the answers – we don't have the truth.*

Summary of Dr Wood's Interview

On 22nd March, the interview with Dr Wood is broken up, disjointed and the issue of doubt about the Hurricane is injected following a caller's (Steve's) false accusation.

A follow up call by George Freund then brings up thermite (but does not explain how it is supposed to have turned the towers to dust – a fact which is never challenged). Nor does the caller point out this evidence was not included in a legal challenge.

Whilst Joyce Riley appears to be supportive and complimentary at some points, she also injects doubt regularly, for example at one point she states: "we can't verify some of your so-called evidence here" – despite this same evidence having been discussed *before* the interview!

Joyce Riley, twice, gets enthusiastic when listeners suggest that a *mixture* of thermite and something else was used.

Joyce Riley states at the end

> *"we don't know the answers – we don't have the truth…"*

and she makes similar comments elsewhere in the broadcast.

Again, some people will consider I am being over critical here – because, after all, Joyce Riley offered a platform to Dr Judy Wood. And, because "The Power Hour" goes out on Short Wave, it has a large audience. However, details of the broadcast need to be studied to see that, at best, it was a muddle up and at worst it was an attempt to cast Dr Judy Wood in a bad light – primarily because her audio was muted when she needed to respond promptly to a point made and when she was not really given sufficient time to respond carefully to points raised.

Following the interview, Dr Wood contacted Joyce Riley and described how she was unhappy about how the caller who accused her of lying about Hurricane Erin was not handled. Joyce Riley was sent this e-mail from a listener who contacted Dr Wood and said stated,

> *"This hurricane existed well before 9/11-01. It was over 540 miles away from WTC location. ... I think she has been grossly mislead and is misleading others. I am surprised she was allowed to make such baseless claims on The Power Hour without opposition...I think she is out of her mind and I am quite literally disappointed that she was given the airwaves of The Power Hour to spout her nonsense."*

Andrew Johnson on the Power Hour for the 2nd Time – 31st Mar 2010

In a follow up interview with me on 31st March 2010,[267] Joyce Riley brought up the issue of Dr Wood's presentation and I addressed it by pointing out that Dr Wood was encouraging people to look at the evidence and think for themselves rather than be spoon fed with a conclusion – and how important that was. Regardless of what one might have thought of Dr Wood's presentation, the evidence is more important than the packaging. It is symptomatic of how the show progressed that this has to be pointed out to people. Similarly, a skilful host will, to some extent, adapt themselves to the guest's style of delivery and adapt their questioning to "get the best" out of their guest.

There were no real problems in the first hour of the show on 31st of March and I was able to present and make the points I wished. Joyce did not make any comments as I began to discuss the connection between the Cold Fusion phenomenon and the 9/11 evidence and cover up – except when I started to talk about Steven E Jones being involved with Cold Fusion. In the recording of the interview of 31st March, at around 26:45, Joyce Riley states

> *"That's quite a strong allegation to be making against err... Dr Jones."*

It is slightly interesting that she referred to Dr Jones, though maybe not significant – and this was the only time she commented in that part of the presentation.

After The Event - The Power Hour Shows Its Weaknesses

On her 24th March 2010 programme, Joyce Riley stated[268]:

> *JR: I am gonna be real honest with you all – that I don't think she presents herself well. I think there is a lot of... work that could be done on making her points understandable to people, um, interesting, easily... put them together so that you come from point A to point B to point C to point D and then you come to the conclusion. But I don't think that happened – and we talked*

about that because I don't want to think that that is going to limit her in her ability to do her production and her spreading of information.

Co Host: "Yeah it shouldn't discredit the message…"

But if you don't present well, you do discredit your message. I mean some people said she used terms like dustification – now that's not a PhD term.

Co Host: Sure

OK maybe so - but I think she's trying to bring it down to the level of a lot of people and the power hour people are not at a low level – they're really understanding what is going on – they don't need that kind of err limitation on the information. Aerosolisation I think would be more – I don't know – that to me – she didn't like that term but I thought would be the term that would be appropriate.

*Now what we did yesterday was talk about the idea… **that she says it is not just the thermite/thermate that brought the buildings down – possibly a combination of the two***

Co Host: I don't see why that's a problem – a lot of people are having a hard time about accepting new information

What is interesting is that they are still discussing how hard this is to accept – and they are also misquoting Dr Wood – as she does not say the building was "brought down" and she does not suggest it was a "combination" of "thermite and directed energy weapons."

Joyce Riley Makes Further Follow up Comments on 25th March 2010

Again, Joyce seemed moved to make further remarks[269], casting Dr Judy Wood in a bad light.

I don't have a problem with changing my mind. You know this issue with Dr Judy Wood – which I am gonna give you all the credit in the world – those of you who said she didn't present herself well – that is true – and she's very defensive on that issue also. She needs to have a better presentation of her material. I tend to think she's got some things there… that are actually on target. I tend to think that – I don't know how much though…

Couldn't Joyce look at the evidence and submitted court documents?

"These People Are Frauds"…

Shortly after my follow up interview (which was cut short, apparently due to technical problems), on 01 Apr 2010, Joyce Riley sent me the only e-mail I'd ever received from her (up to then). In this message was a "debunking" compilation of images by George Freund containing the statements:

DUST AT THE WTC A poor hoax

This email can be seen on my website[270]. Why was this the only e-mail I received from her? What did the photos Freund had compiled really show? (I would argue they just provided more evidence that Dr Wood was correct in her analysis.) George Freund phoned in to promote thermite – yet did not seem bothered that this evidence was not included in the RFC sent to NIST.

George Freund then went as far as to say:

"These people are frauds."

Wow. So, George Freund accuses us of being frauds and completely ignores all of the evidence – and that it had been submitted to court. Further, Joyce Riley *forwards* this, nonsense to myself and Dr Wood!

For these reasons, and the terrible handling of the issues in Dr Wood's original interview, when Joyce Riley contacted Dr Wood to ask for another interview, I sent her back a list of questions about these things.

I was not happy with her answers, so we declined the interview. Her responses were interesting. I won't even take the time to study and break down these messages in detail, as it is relatively clear that Joyce Riley does not address the issues I raised and seemingly tries to imply things "do not look good" for "our side." She also uses the word "ambush" - how interesting.

John Hutchison's Appearance on The Power Hour – 05 April 2010

John Hutchison was supposed to appear with me on the Power Hour on 31 March 2010, but it appeared there was some kind of power failure (so it became the "no power hour") and there was no broadcast. Joyce Riley therefore hosted an interview with him on 05 April 2010.

There were no real problems with this interview, I will just make one observation. Joyce Riley asked John Hutchison what he thought about 9/11.

I want to address 9/11. Now Dr Judy Wood has been on the programme, Andrew Johnson has been on the programme and of course, they refer to you heavily. Why is that when they talk about 9/11, they refer to the Hutchison Effect and to your work?

John Hutchison then states at 29:35:

Well, in Hangar 17 there's so many different strange metal samples that seem to resemble my samples as well as the buildings themselves, the central core [?] sort of just vaporises – when it falls down.

He then mentions a couple of times that he thinks Dr Wood is the expert and he expresses respect for her qualifications in engineering and her analysis of 9/11. At 30:59, John also brings up the thermite theory, saying:

I call them the "Welding Materials People." I mean there's no way that people put hundreds of tons of thermite in all those buildings.

John then discusses thermite is a welding material and that it was used for this purpose in World War One and World War Two.

Joyce Riley says:

Is Joyce Riley keen to suggest that thermite was used in some way? Why doesn't she ask John to go into more detail about the connection between the 9/11 evidence and the Hutchison Effect?

Conclusions

Again, on the surface, it looks as if Joyce Riley is helping to raise awareness of Dr Judy Wood's research – particularly as she also had John Hutchison on her programme – but she did not allow a sufficient discussion of the evidence. This is really quite straightforward, if a host takes time to listen or research for themselves – and, importantly, the host does not have an agenda to distract, muddle up, confuse or lead the discussion into a "dead end." Riley repeatedly mentioned thermite and I sensed there was a need for this bogus theory to be kept "in the frame" for the listening audience – rather than it being exposed as a fraudulent, misleading deception. Even if Joyce Riley felt she could not be confident about what the truth was, she could have exposed what it wasn't.

15. "Chilling Out" about 9/11 With Sterling D Allan and Steven E Jones

17 Sep 2013

In early November 2012, I was honoured to attend the Global Breakthrough Energy Movement (BEM) Conference in Hilversum, Netherlands, to give a presentation entitled "Infinite Energy, But Not For the Masses." A slightly different version of this talk was posted on my website sometime in 2010 or 2011[1]**Error! Bookmark not defined.**.

In the presentation, I discuss how free energy technologies have been and are being covered up, using various methods. One method involves the way in which certain groups or individuals function – in that they give the appearance they are interested in helping to bring out free energy technologies but when the evidence pertaining to their activities is studied carefully, it becomes clear there is "something missing." It seems that they are not helping people to understand the fullest picture of what has been discovered about free energy technology. It seems that in many cases, free energy researchers will not talk about the evidence that free energy technology has already been turned into a weapons system – and this weapons system was used on 9/11. Granted, some of these researchers are still not aware of Dr Judy Wood's research, which proves that free energy technology has been weaponised. The cover up of this research has been quite successful – which is why I have been writing about it since 2007.

Sterling Allan and pesn.com

Over the last few years, Allan has built up a large and interesting Website / WIKI about Free Energy Systems, researchers and Projects – it holds a considerable amount of information – in a well-organised structure. It is (or was) updated daily, or almost daily see http://pesn.com/. There is no doubt that this is a valuable resource - but I am afraid that due to recent developments, I have to raise serious questions about the integrity of the 9/11-related information on the site, which as readers will know, has been an area of special interest of mine over the last few years. Again, as with Steven Greer's "Free Energy" initiatives – Seaspower, Aero2012, The Orion Project and, lately, Sirius Technologies, (which I have analysed and written about before[271]), the intent seems good, but actual concrete results seem to be minimal or non-existent.

My concern about some pages on the site increased when I realised that initially, there was little reference to Dr Judy Wood's research – even though the site held articles about the research of John Hutchison. However, there *was*, at the time more reference to the research of Steven E. "thermite" Jones [272]. The PESN site mentions him on quite a number of pages. The site also references Alien Scientist videos[273] – describing one as "outstanding." See chapter 0 for more information about this "Alien Scientist[274]".

Sterling D Allan at Global BEM 2012

Sterling Allan was a speaker at the 2012 Conference. Curiously he did spend some time talking about 9/11 (which isn't talked about all that much in proportion to the amount of information on www.pesn.com) No prizes for guessing what particular part of 9/11 research he chose to discuss…[275] (Note: in the referenced video here, there are some problems with flashing images due to some issues with the video editing.)

Even though this is only a "preview" of the presentation, there is a section which is approximately 4 minutes long where he says he will be "going on a tangent" about something he has "never talked about" (presumably, in public). He then says he is reading a book – Dr Judy Wood's *Where Did the Towers Go?*[3]**Error! Bookmark not defined.** and he proceeds to present and discuss some of the details. However, in a manner similar to what Richard Hoagland did in 2011, Allan makes significant errors in his presentation. As was the case with Mr Hoagland's erroneous presentation, Dr Wood was not consulted about the content of this part of Allan's presentation, neither was she aware he was going to speak about this at the conference. Some errors in the presentation are discussed below.

- Initially when he starts discussing Dr Wood's research, at 8:37, Allan describes a "pillar of iron", though he then corrects himself to say "steel."

- 8:47: Sterling Allan says, "The is new technology based on a lot of energy, probably a free-energy technology."

- 9:22: The seismic signature was not that of an earthquake and therefore is not rated as a seismic signal, but can only be referred to as producing an equivalent magnitude with certain waves.

- 9:30: Sterling Allan claims it made the same seismic signature as "a superdome" that was 1/70th the size of (the towers)? Which "superdome"? In Dr Wood's presentation, she shows that WTC1 had about 30 times the potential energy of the Seattle Kingdome. In any case, it did not make "the same seismic signature." The Seattle Kingdome generated S waves, P waves, and surface waves. No S wave or P waves were generated during the destruction of WTC1,2,3,4,5,6,7. Only a surface wave was generated during the destruction of these buildings. So they did not leave "the same seismic signature."

- 9:55: Sterling Allan claims the signal lasted only six seconds. (It should be eight seconds for WTC1.)

- Sterling Allan claims "it would take 9 seconds for the things on the top to hit the bottom." Is Sterling Allan claiming the buildings would have collapsed in 9 seconds? Apparently, he has not developed any collapse models and done energy calculations for them. (It would take 9.22 seconds to drop a bowling ball from the roof to the ground in a vacuum.)

- 10:20: Sterling Allan claims "right next door, 200 feet from this, 12 firemen in a part of a stairwell that wasn't collapsed by the dust." Contrary to what Sterling Allan says, there were 14 people in Stairway B who survived [and two more who survived higher up in Stairway B, even though the Stairway didn't survive].

- 10:35: Sterling Allan implies a directed energy weapon would have to cut everything like a saw at one level and is surprised that this is not what happened, as if he is setting up to claim that therefore a directed energy weapon could not have been used.

- 10:45: Sterling Allan claims "This was new technology they deployed on that day." How does he know the age of the technology? Does he know who "they" are and has been given a tour through the facility where it was kept?

- 10:50: Sterling Allan claims that WTC7 was destroyed by classic controlled demolition. He obviously hasn't done his homework.

- 11:40: Sterling Allan discusses the height of the rubble pile of WTC7. Using the image Sterling Allan presents (albeit distorted), one can see that the "rubble pile" of WTC7 is not 6 or 7 stories tall. WTC6 was an 8-story building and the "rubble pile" of WTC7 is much lower down than that. And how does he know where "the energy weapon went in"?

It is interesting to note that Sterling Allan does not say anything similar to "well, Dr Wood will be presenting her research at this conference, so if you attend her presentation, you will get the full picture." Sterling Allan should have been well-aware that Dr Wood was scheduled to speak on the subject of 9/11 at the conference later that day.

Sterling Allan has made a gross misrepresentation of the evidence. Perhaps he will ask to be excused for his errors by claiming he is not a scientist? Yet he claims Dr Wood has "some holes in her logic and contradictions," yet has failed to identify any errors or even take responsibility for making unfounded accusations such as this. One must wonder why Sterling Allan, without a background in physics or structural engineering feels comfortable making claims that contradict physical evidence that has already been presented.

I'd like to suggest that the easiest way to convince the general and less-informed public that free-energy technology *does not exist* is to promote false information about what *does exist* so that it can simply be refuted by people with more knowledge and expertise in relevant fields. One can ask why Sterling Allan is presenting false information about someone else's work. Sterling Allan is not a scientist, so why is he pretending to present scientific work done by someone else where he makes many errors?

BEM Conference review by Sterling D Allan

Following the BEM Nov 2012 conference, Allan posted a review, in which he writes[276]:

> **Her premise** is that some kind of exotic technology was used to turn the buildings to dust, so that hardly any rubble was left (via a **combination of Tesla's Death Ray and Hutchison type effects**). She presents a wide range of compelling evidence; and in her three hours of lecture, she also showed video footage. Her PowerPoint presentation is well formatted to highlight things in such a way that they cannot be overlooked any more. **While there are some holes in her logic and contradictions**, overall, I'm convinced there is something to the premise, which the controlled demolition model doesn't satisfy.
>
> I'm working on a story about that, but it is not an easy subject. There are some strong points **on both sides of the argument**. But one thing they both agree on is that the government cover-up story is ridiculously erroneous and impossible -- that the buildings came down (in free-fall speed) because they were hit by jets.

This essentially repeats errors from his presentation, but goes further and states "there are some holes in her logic and contradictions." These "holes and contradictions" are not identified and discussed and therefore, for the casual reader of Allan's articles, doubt and uncertainty is introduced – possibly without the reader realising this. Additionally, in coming with others, Allan mis-characterises the evidence and research of Dr Wood as "a premise." Was this an intention of Allan's review? Mr. Allan introduces division by referring to "sides of the argument," but truth doesn't have sides. Either something is true, or it is not true.

Stephen E Jones and Cold Fusion and Tritium

As I have repeatedly stated in other chapters and articles, I first became aware of the connection between Steven E Jones and what is mis-known as Cold Fusion in 2006 or 2007. (Cold Fusion is better described as "Low Energy Nuclear Reactions" – LENR.) Jones also worked for Los Alamos National Laboratories[277]. I first joined Steven E Jones' and Jim Fetzer's "Scholars for 9/11 Truth" group in 2005/6 and I trusted Jones' research about "thermite."

In Feb 2007, I mentioned the Jones-Cold Fusion connection in the "New 9/11 Hijackers" article[94]**Error! Bookmark not defined.** that I had posted. Since then, more has become known about the connection between the evidence found in LENR research and evidence found at the World Trade Centre. This is to do with Tritium levels – a radioactive "sub-form" of Hydrogen. In LENR, anomalous levels of tritium were found in experiments carried out by many groups of researchers – one group being headed by Prof John Bockris at Texas A & M University[278]. Dr Wood (and myself) discussed this connection in our respective presentations at the BEM 2012 Conference[209]**Error! Bookmark not defined.** (November 9/11, 2012).

It was of great interest to me, then, when I found out that Sterling Allan had made a new posting[279] on his website less than 1 week after the conference. The posting included a letter from Steven E Jones – about LENR / Cold Fusion – which Steven E Jones had given a presentation on in Oct 2012.

From: Steven Jones

Sent: Saturday, November 17, 2012 4:15 PM [GMT-7]

Subject: Slides (with minor edits) from Seminar given at Univ of Missouri, 25 Oct 2012

Gents,

Scientists at the University of Missouri invited me to give a seminar and also provided a tour of their lab, where they are doing related experiments. I'm excited about this, and even if my hypothesis turns out to be incorrect, the research is proceeding well!

*I wish to re-emphasize that I find data for anomalous excess heat (without evidence for commensurate fusion products) to be compelling at this time. Back in 1989, **I tried repeatedly to get P&F to drop their claim that the "excess heat" was due to d-d fusion, to no avail at the time. In fact, my insistence on this point -- that it was NOT d-d fusion, earned me some enemies it seems.***

In recent years, many if not most researchers in the field have come to share this view (it's not d-d cold fusion, but something else!). Even Fleischman admitted it was not d-d fusion, before his passing.

Here I raise an hypothesis to account for the "anomalous excess heat" -- an idea that (evidently) none of the Univ of Missouri researchers had heard of before...

Best wishes,

Steven Jones

Emeritus etc

PS -- Slides from the Naval Research Lab which I cited are publicly available from the ICCF-17, Aug 2012, conference in Korea, here:

http://newenergytimes.com/v2/conferences/2012/ICCF17/ICCF-17-Papers.shtml

talk WEA1-2 (Dominguez et al.)

It is interesting to note that this was posted on Sterling Allan's website in the days immediately following Dr Wood's presentation at BEM – because Dr Wood's presentation included a discussion of a "vote" on Cold Fusion Research that Steven E Jones led in 1989[280]:

Jones leads the vote…

It has become clear to me that Steven E Jones has lied about Martin Fleischmann's work in the field of LENR – when he said:

Even Fleischman admitted it was not d-d fusion, before his passing.

He repeats this false statement in a 2012 interview with Charles Giuliani[281]. The truth is that Pons and Fleischmann soon revised their conclusion that nuclear fusion was involved[282]:

> *(Source: New Energy Times[283]) Within a year, Fleischmann and Pons backed off on their claim that their experiment showed evidence of fusion, but they did not retract their claim that their experiment revealed something new and inexplicable. They wrote the following in their 1990 paper:*

> *"The preliminary note was to have been published under the title 'Electrochemically Induced Fusion of Deuterium?' but the all-important question mark was omitted. It is our view that there can be little doubt that one must invoke nuclear processes to account for the magnitudes of the enthalpy releases, although the nature of these processes is an open question at this stage."*

Also, Jones himself admits that he coined the term "cold fusion[284]" to describe the process and research that he and a colleague, Paul Palmer, had been working on in the mid-1980s. Jones implies that Pons / Fleischmann then decided to adopt this term to label their own research[285] (which was in a completely different area than Jones' research). The truth seems to be that Pons and Fleischmann, in common with other researchers working in the same field, were not happy about ongoing use of the "Jones-coined" term "Cold Fusion."

One might ask – are both Sterling D Allan and Steven E Jones being deliberately careless in their description of important details – to divert people away from making connections between disparate sets of evidence?

Is Steven E Jones Worried?

A posting on 11 Jan 2014 on a site called "9/11 Blogger" [286] (a site which I rarely see referenced these days) states:

> *Many are aware that Judy Wood continues to attack Richard Gage, me, and Niels Harrit by name -- see for example her talk here: https://www.youtube.com/watch?v=T1NbBxDGSkI (especially towards the end).*
>
> *I should like to add that Wood's attack on me (in this talk) for a vote in 1989 regarding cold fusion claims is misleading and most unfair. The question I raised was -- did Pons and Fleischmann see deuteron-deuteron fusion as they claimed? My main argument then as now is that the observation of anomalous excess heat does not PROVE that d-d fusion is the cause, contrary to claims at the time. Even Fleischmann before his passing in 2012 finally admitted that he should not have called it "fusion."*

This, accusation again is untrue, Dr Wood's presentation, does not "attack" Steven E Jones or anyone in the manner Jones states (one might even say the reverse is actually true of Gage[96]**Error! Bookmark not defined.**, and of Jones if you listen to the clip above). Indeed, what he says above about Fleischmann and the vote being about d-d Fusion is also untrue[280]**Error! Bookmark not defined.**!

Steven E Jones - Remembering WTC Molten Metal and "Paint on Thermite"

I would now like to remind readers that Steven E Jones was one of the first researchers to talk about molten metal in relation to the events and aftermath of the WTC destruction. Indeed, Jones referred repeatedly to a video clip I helped him edit together in 2006[287] which he claimed showed molten metal flowing from one of the WTC towers, before its destruction. Jones falsely claimed that molten aluminium is silvery in appearance at all temperatures in daylight conditions[288]. As I have repeatedly noted, molten metal was spoken of frequently by Jones and later by Richard Gage of AE911, but Jones and his co-authors did *not* mention molten metal in their Request for Corrections (RFC) submission to NIST in 2007[255]**Error! Bookmark not defined.**. I contend that the molten metal "stories" were promulgated because some people really did see molten metal (firefighters apparently saw it) and Jones knew this. However, the metal was made to *melt and/or glow by a process other than heating* (i.e. some kind of process similar to what happens in some of John Hutchison's experiments).

In order to keep the hot molten metal myth alive, it seems Steven E Jones had to come up with some highly dubious suggestions – such as beams in the towers being "painted with thermite[102]**Error! Bookmark not defined.** or thermate"!

Keeping it in the Family?

Another curious thing which arose shortly before the BEM conference was that Sterling Allan's brother, Nathan Allan, posted a review of *Where Did the Towers Go?* on the Amazon page[289]. Apparently, it was Nathan Allan who described Dr Judy Wood's book to Sterling Allan and he became interested in it.

Though the review is favourable, he also wrote:

> *Her scholarship is so great in some areas, though unfortunately in parts she strays a bit far into tenuous tangents. For instance, even mentioning the "coral castle" and its surrounding hearsay unnecessarily discredits her efforts. The best nougats are tantalizingly hidden in subtle places throughout the book.*

He also claims "her math surrounding pancaking is incorrect" – a reference to Dr Wood's "Billiard Ball Example" (BBE) (this is not a model, it is a "thought experiment" to encourage people to re-evaluate, in a dispassionate way, the rapid demise of the towers). Nathan Allan has not fully understood this example, it seems – i.e. it is an "example" *not* "a model" or "a simulation." Note that Dr Wood's "Billiard Ball Example" (BBE) was accepted through peer review and presented at an international engineering conference in June 2006.

Nathan Allan also takes issue with the references to Coral Castle. In an article posted on his brother's site, he claims to have "busted" the idea that it is not well understood how it could have been built by one man. Nathan Allan makes a bold claim – Coral Castle has mystified engineers such as Chris Dunne. No one has been able to clearly show how all its features were built[290].

Certainly, from my own examination of Coral Castle[291], I have concluded that the man who built (and rebuilt) it – Ed Leedskalnin – seemed to have knowledge about how to move and carve rock that no one else in modern times seems to have.

Sterling D Allan "Reviews" Dr Wood's Book

On 9th December 2012 - one month after the BEM conference, Sterling Allan posted an article entitled "Part I: The Ambulance that Survived WTC1 on 9/11 = Best Evidence for Dustification and Free Energy Demo[292]." This article seems to be reasonably accurate in its description about some of what is covered in the book, although it repeats an earlier claim by Steven E Jones et al that "Active Thermitic Material [was] Discovered in Dust from the 9/11 World Trade Center Catastrophe." (And again, the claims of thermite do not explain the evidence shown in the book Allan claimed to be reviewing. These thermite claims were not submitted to NIST in 2007 by Jones, et al.). Allan included a number of images scanned directly from Dr Wood's book – and these were used without consultation or permission, but at this point, no action was taken. At the end of this article – seemingly out of sequence with what else is covered, Allan writes:

> *Steven Jones is not a "disinformation agent." He sincerely believes that controlled demolition, using nanothermite along with conventional explosives, was used to bring down the towers, based on the evidence he*

has personally witnessed and studied. (See my November 19, 2012 report about his reasons for saying that what people are calling "cold fusion" isn't "fusion.")

This statement implies that something to the contrary is stated in "Where Did The Towers Go," which is not the case.

Vote for the Evidence, Vote for the Truth!

The finalisation of this article/documentation was prompted by an anniversary posting about Dr Wood's book on Sterling D Allan's PESN Website.[293] Allan entitles this as being "Part II" of an earlier review of Dr Wood's book[292]**Error! Bookmark not defined.**. Again, Allan has included a number of images scanned directly from Dr Wood's book – and these were used without consultation or permission.

Whilst the thrust of what is written *seems* sincere and well-meant, there are again important errors which could have been avoided through prior consultation with Dr Wood (who is referred to as "Judy" in the article). Some of these errors will be discussed below.

First, however, I would like to discuss Sterling Allan's inclusion of "polling" in the article – is this to encourage doubt and uncertainty about what may or may not be in the book? As the article is *not* a full reproduction of what is in the book, then really, because of the importance of the evidence, I ask how can people make a fair judgement? Similarly, voting on whether the towers turned to dust is a ridiculous notion – especially when no images or video of this process are shown in the article! Additionally, voting on who committed this crime (i.e. "Inside job") is a ridiculous notion, considering that no evidence or discussion whatsoever is presented as to who committed these crimes. This appears to be an attempt to associate Dr Wood's work with opinions that are void of evidence.

Cold Fusion and Space Beams

Due to the concerns expressed above – especially Allan's connection to Steven E Jones, I finally decided to write and present these concerns to him. I also included audio clips of Steven E Jones mentioning "Space beams[294]", Pons/Fleischmann and fusion[281]**Error! Bookmark not defined.**, and Steven E Jones coining the term Cold Fusion[284]**Error! Bookmark not defined.**.

As has been the case in the past, for me at least, responses to the emails I have sent have been quite illuminating (you can read the full exchange on my website[295]).

The tone of his response is pleasant enough and, after all, he was not obliged to respond at all – but he did, and in some detail. I asked Sterling Allan why he had decided to use the pictures without permission. His response was:

> *I didn't finally decide to do this article until last night, and I wanted to have it as the 9/11 feature, hence I didn't have time to first get permission from Dr Wood.*

A lack of planning does not negate the need for permission. I asked Sterling Allan if he had used polls on any other articles and he kindly responded:

> *You can see a list of the polls I've done at http://www.99polls.com/profile_90262 You will see there that in the past few months I've done polls with other technology postings, including the Yildiz magnet motor demo and a feature on Geoffrey Miller,*
>
> *See http://pesn.com//2013/08/13/9602355_Interview_with_Geoffrey-Miller_Energybat-Labs/[296]*

I asked why he had gone to some trouble to use them in this article. He responded:

> *Just curiosity. I've actually been very pleased with the response so far. I had thought there was more hesitation in my audience regarding 9/11. However, a lot of this traffic is coming from Rense.com, which isn't my usual audience.*

I also asked him about a comment he made at the end of Dr Wood's BEM presentation where he stated he would discuss what he had seen in the presentation with his friend Steven E Jones[297] (Sterling Allan actually stated that what he had seen was "obvious"). I enquired if such a discussion had taken place and what the "outcome", if any, had been. Allan replied:

> *Yes, I met with him. He remains a good friend. I've gotten two emails and a phone call from him in the past week. I reported on my conversation with him following the Holland Global BEM conference at: http://pesn.com/2012/11/19/9602225_Steven_Jones_replica--Pons_and_Fleischmann_XS_Heat_not_from_fusion/*
>
> *and ever since that meeting, I've been driving home the point with my audience that "cold fusion" is probably not a proper terminology for what is happening. It's most likely not fusion but transmutation, if that. It is a high energy reaction, and most likely nuclear, but almost definitely not "fusion." That is the point that Steve was trying to make all those years ago, and it has taken this long for it to start catching on. Now, I bet if I were to take a poll of my audience (I should do this soon), I bet that around 70% would say it is "transmutation}, 10% would say "fusion", and 10% would say "anomalous heat", and 10% would say "nothing, bogus."*

This reply included nothing about Dr Wood's presentation – nor Allan's statement that following Dr Wood's presentation, certain things that happened on 9/11 became "obvious." Instead, he re-iterates Jones' position on Cold Fusion (which, as discussed above, is not accurate). This was not really what I had asked him.

In a subsequent e-mail I put it to Sterling Allan that Steven E Jones had lied – both about Pons and Fleischmann and the true nature of molten metal discovered at the WTC site. I suggested that Jones may, indeed, have some kind of knowledge about what really happened to the WTC and he was helping to keep this covered up – just as he had been helping to keep certain evidence, research and knowledge about LENR covered up. Allan responded:

> *Regarding Steve Jones, I don't find any problems in the audio files you attached. He's stating his position from how he sees things. Yes, he coined the term "cold fusion"; and yes, he admonished that the term "fusion" not be used where "fusion" was not indicated by the evidence. If he has a misunderstanding of Judy's presentation and mislabels it "space-based directed energy weaponry", chalk it up to misunderstanding and seek to set the record straight through cordial, not accusatory and inflammatory dialogue. Judy's portrayal of Steve is one of a crass conspirator, and I find it very offensive. She is very wrong on that, and will have to answer by karma; and perhaps part of that is the misportrayals of her work by others who are supposed to be on the same team.*
>
> *I have yet to find a case where Steve "lies" making a statement on something he knows not to be the case. He might portray something contrary to your believe on the matter, but that is not a lie, it is a difference of opinion or paradigm.*

I note that Mr. Allan refers to his good friend as "Steve Jones" but refers to Dr Wood as "Judy."

Allan is very keen to defend Jones – making excuses that he does not "understand" the evidence in Dr Wood's book and on her website. This is extremely odd – because Jones is a professor of Physics and Allan has no advanced degrees and openly states "he is not a scientist." Earlier, Allan stated that Dr Wood's evidence made it "obvious" what happened – but here we have Allan making excuses for Jones. Also, Jones used the term "Space Beams" not "space-based directed energy weaponry" – why did Allan "translate" this term? Dr Wood does not even discuss "space-based directed energy weaponry." Dr Wood does not discuss what the weapon was, much less where it was located. She only discusses the type of energy involved. She has ruled out thermal energy weaponry, kinetic energy weaponry, but has not ruled out directed-energy weaponry. Dr Wood has never stated where the weapon or weapons were located. This is even stated on the *conclusions page*[298] of her original article in 2006.

Also, Allan, criticises "Judy" – claiming she "castigated" Steven E Jones. Why does he make this claim, when it was Andrew Johnson that wrote to him about Jones lying – it was not "Judy" that made these statements? He diverts onto other issues, which I was not even aware of and had not questioned him about.

Allan characterises lies as "a difference of opinion." To me, this is the sort of language manipulation which is used to help a cover up stay in place.

Perhaps I should just "Chill Out"?

Again, there will be some who will chastise me for being over critical of Sterling Allan – perhaps suggesting he is giving "free publicity" to Dr Judy

Wood's book. However, the publicity is best when the coverage is accurate–indeed, accuracy is vital because of the importance of what we are dealing with here. I have found and documented that[110]Error! Bookmark not defined., on many occasions, the goal of quite a number of people has *not* been to fairly and accurately document, review or characterise what is in Dr Wood's book and on her website[2]Error! Bookmark not defined.. This has been true even though it seems, on the surface, like those people are trying to be "helpful."

In his email Sterling Allan says to me

> *Sorry this appears to be a hot-button issue for you. You're hyper sensitive to it. Chill out.*

And then

> *Judy really needs to chill in her castigation of the whole 9/11 Truth movement. She has a victim mentality that really sours the potential reach of her material. She, unfortunately, is her own worst enemy. She commits treason against her own mission in life.*

Amazing stuff. An ad hominem is a logical fallacy. Instead of addressing the questions posed to him, he insults someone else.

Lest, 12 years after the event, we are starting to forget something, let us remember what we are talking about:

1) The crime of 9/11 which killed 3000 people and set the stage for all the terrible things that have happened in "the war on terror."
2) The use and cover up of an advanced weapons system which operates by using some form of Directed Free Energy.

Sterling Allan wants us to "chill out"…?

"Under the Influence"?

I have written before about the evidence which indicates that (a) certain figure(s) in the alternative knowledge or "truth" movement seem to have the ability to influence others in subtle ways. Jim Fetzer is a prime example[299].

In reading through Sterling Allan's messages and postings, I got the sense that Sterling is "trying to do the right thing" and some of what he says in relation to 9/11 and Dr Wood's research is reasonably accurate. However…

- Why did he post these articles, using images without permission?
- Why did he talk about Wood's research at the BEM conference in the way he did?
- Why did he describe it as a "Tesla Death Ray"?
- Why does he not ask himself serious questions about the role of Steven E Jones in this whole matter? (Instead he chastises us and tells us to "chill out.")

The description "Tesla Death Ray" sounds, to me, similarly dismissive to the term "Space Beams." Sterling Allan tells us he is in "regular contact" with

Steven E Jones. Could it be the case that Steven E Jones is exerting some kind of influence over Sterling Allan – which blinds Allan to certain facts? I have only included this as I felt, especially at the end of the BEM presentation, he was "struggling internally" with conflicting emotions. This feeling of mine was only made stronger when I read some of his emails.

Here We Are Yet Again…

I have documented another example of Dr Wood's research being brought to someone's attention. They then:

- Characterise it as "just a theory"
- Say "Well, it's plausible"
- Say "Well, I think it was a mixture of things that was used to destroy the towers."
- Don't talk about the relationship to cold fusion.
- Behave as if to suggest we should "just be one big Happy Family, OK?"

Again, I can only present the evidence to you – because of what I have found and what I know. I cannot do things any other way. I hope it was worth it…

My email correspondence with Sterling D Allan can be read on my website[295]**Error! Bookmark not defined.**.

Sterling D Allan Sentenced to Minimum 15 Years in Prison in June 2016

A report from the Utah Newspaper "Daily Herald" describes that[300]

Sterling Allan was sentenced by Judge Darold McDade to 15 years to life in the Utah State Prison for two first-degree felony charges of attempted sodomy on a child.

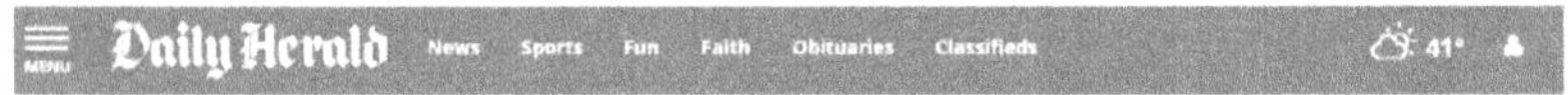

16. 9/11 and Cold Fusion – a Possible Attempt to Rewrite History?
03 Feb 2014

History

Since about 2007, I have been attempting to document and understand the 9/11 cover up – particularly in relation to the research of Dr Judy Wood[2]Error! Bookmark not defined.. To this end, in 2009, I self-published a book/compilation of articles which I called *9/11 Finding the Truth*. This compilation (now in its 3rd edition) can be obtained as a free download in various formats[110]Error! Bookmark not defined., or in a cost-price paperback[301]. I have continued to write articles on this subject, as attempts have continued to "keep the cover up / muddle up" going. The purpose has mainly been to document, with related evidence, how the cover up has continued to evolve - to include a number of related areas.

Recent correspondence I have received has lead me to wonder whether we might even be "ahead of the game" – at least to some extent – as I may have been witness to an attempt to re-write history. At this point, it is not quite clear if this is the case, but I wanted to document some things now and if it turns out I am wrong, then so be it.

Facts

Regardless of any conclusions I may make in this article, the facts about 9/11 and the facts about those involved in helping to cover up those facts will remain the same. Facts such as those stated by Dr Judy Wood following her comprehensive forensic investigation of what happened to the WTC will not change. "The WTC towers did not burn up nor did they slam to the ground - they mostly turned to dust in mid-air" will never change. The fact that Steven E Jones worked in a field of research that he and a colleague called "Cold Fusion" in the 1980s and he then worked in the field of 9/11 research from about 2005 onwards will not change.

Caroline Louise and Scholars for 9/11 Truth

On 13 Jan 2014, I received an email with the subject "Judy Wood/ Steven Jones and all the rest of it" from someone going by the name "Caroline Louise"[302]. She wrote:

> *I'm writing a piece about the confrontation that occurred 2006-7 between Judy Wood/Jim Fetzer/Morgan Reynolds and others on one hand and Steve Jones/Kevin Ryan et al on the other. I've talked to James Tracy of the Memory Hole blog about publishing it there.*
>
> *I want it to be a factual piece, as objective as possible, and I'm keen to talk to all **sides**. I've already made contact with Steve Jones who has agreed to*

talk, and I'm hoping to get input from Jim Fetzer, Judy Wood and Morgan Reynolds.

Would you be interested in talking to me about your perspective? As a non-US observer I think that would be valuable (I'm from the UK myself). I'm sure you're busy and I'll be happy to fit in to your schedule. We can talk on the phone or email as you prefer.

I had never heard of this person and immediately wondered about her surname – as I don't remember hearing anyone use a surname of "Louise." I was also curious about her referring to "sides" in the matters of what is true and what is untrue. I was therefore a little cautious / suspicious in my response to her, so I wrote back with the following:

A quick response, with some questions and answers.

1) Can you explain what your objective is with this exercise?

2) Where will said piece be published?

3) What is more important, writing a piece about an alleged confrontation, or establishing what happened on 9/11?

Here are a couple of facts for you:

A) Dr Judy Wood submitted a Qui Tam case in 2007

http://tinyurl.com/911qtam

B) Steven E Jones et al did not submit a Qui Tam case - indeed, they did not even submit the evidence that they claimed explained the destruction of the towers:

http://911thermitefree.blogspot.co.uk/2009/10/thermite-free-rfc.html

(some links out of date).

As "Caroline Louise" had talked about involving me in a "discussion" of some kind, I also wrote:

So really, there's not much point in involving me in discussion - the evidence is all posted really - so you can just reference that. If you want to quote me, you can say:

"There are a number of folks that I have come into contact with over the years, in relation to 9/11 research. I've written about the interactions I've had - and have published them in my free e-book '9/11 Finding the Truth'. I have collected considerable amounts of evidence that Steven E Jones, Jim Fetzer and others have taken actions or said things to help keep the truth of what happened to the World Trade Centre, as established in Dr Judy Wood's definitive research, covered up. I encourage people to study Dr Wood's research and then read my free eBook. I will send people free DVD's if they are of use, although all the evidence is posted on my website, http://www.checktheevidence.com/."

Caroline Louise responded a few days later, describing my email as "helpful" and she answered my questions as follows (please note her stated objective):

*1. **My objective is to try and tell the story of what actually happened to 9/11 Truth in the summer-winter of 2006-7**. It was momentous for the movement and, concomitantly, for humanity, and yet it's never really been examined, in fact a lot of people in the movement are not really aware of what happened at all. But when you begin to piece everything together - as I've been doing lately - a quite amazing story unfolds. It's a human story as well as a massive debate on what science is, how investigation should be done, what telling the truth really means.*

2. As regards where it will appear. I've talked to James Tracy of Memory Hole blog and he's expressed interest in hosting an article there.

*3. **I don't think you can separate the struggle to establish the truth of 9/11 from what happened in 2006**. Everyone concerned in that event alleged that they were fighting for this truth, but in the end the "truth" was the first casualty. Examining how and why that happened is important.*

I certainly did not agree with Caroline Louise's statement in (3) – it is quite easy to separate what happened on 9/11 from the statements made by various people in 2006 about it. Simply ask yourself the question "did the towers turn mostly to dust?" This is a starting point – the truth of which can be established by observation which has nothing to do with what anyone may have said since it actually happened. That's what the truth is – and "other talk" has often proved to be a distraction from that truth. Caroline Louise's statement about "truth being a casualty" in 2006 happened because Steven E Jones and Jim Fetzer did not want to talk about it, not because Dr Judy Wood presented the evidence she had been collecting!

I decided to respond thus, as I felt she had ignored the evidence I sent:

Dear Caroline,

Thanks for your response. However, you didn't refer to the evidence I posted. If people are interested in the truth, they have to study the evidence - and talk about their conclusions. Although you gave me some general answers and comments, you didn't comment specifically on the other evidence I presented you with. This is one way in which the truth gets covered up - by not talking about it.

You wrote:

>Examining how and why that happened is important.

This is exactly what myself and Dr Judy Wood have [done] in our respective research. It resulted in Court Action in 2007. How important do you think that is?

You said:

> But when you begin to piece everything together - as I've been doing lately - a quite amazing story unfolds.

Yes, and I started to do this in 2006 as well - and I have been writing about it ever since. It is very clear from the evidence that Steven E Jones and Jim Fetzer are part of the cover up of what happened on 9/11. What else would you expect me to say? "Oh it's all just an intellectual disagreement?"

I am not sure you have fully grasped what Jones and Fetzer are part of - and why they would say the things they have said or implied, at different times, about the sorts of things we have shown to the public.

*So, everything else is already on my website - but if you have *specific* questions, or you find any errors or omissions in what I have posted, please do write and tell me.*

Best Wishes

Andrew Johnson

Caroline Louise then responded:

*I do appreciate your **POV**, and I'm entirely open to your being correct. It's not that I don't believe this or that person is a disinfo agent, it's that I am trying to map out how the accusations came to be made and how communication broke down as completely as it did. If you like it's more of a meta approach. Looking at the drama engendered by the conflicting **beliefs** rather than the **beliefs** themselves. The thing is, at the moment *your* **POV** appears on your website, Fetzer's appears on his, Jones' appears wherever his considerable fan base gather, and that is fine. I'm not proposing **to take one side** or to even examine in detail the claims themselves. What I want to do is examine the history of how they came to be made. Thanks for being open to answer any questions I might have. I do appreciate that.*

Do you have an email address for Judy Wood?

The thing I must emphasise strongly is that I was not expressing a "point of view" – I was showing evidence (as I am here – just as I have been doing, in similar ways, for over 7 years). "Evidence" is not a "point of view." Another oddity was that she had asked for Dr Wood's email address (dropping the title). I therefore responded thus:

Dear Caroline,

That Fetzer and Jones have lied in relation to 9/11 research is not a "POV", it is a fact - which can be established from studying the evidence. It is fact in the same way that the towers turned mostly to dust (which they have tried to cover up or cover up the method by which this was achieved).

I am concerned that you do not have Dr Judy Wood's email address, as this would indicate you have not visited her website: http://www.drjudywood.com/ - the email address is given in the top right-hand corner. Does this mean you have not studied the available evidence of what happened [to] the WTC on 9/11? To emphasize, this is not a "Point of View." It isn't a theory, nor is it a hypothesis.

Regards

Andrew Johnson

Caroline Louise then responded:

*Actually **I have read pretty much everything on Judy Wood's website,** and did email her at the address provided, but haven't yet received a reply, so I was wondering if it might be a discontinued address. If it's still operational I'll email her again.*

Dr Wood advised me that a search of her email archive showed that up to this point, she had never received an email from a "Caroline Louise" although she had received a similar email from a "Hilary Swinton" a few days earlier. (See end of file on this link[302]**Error! Bookmark not defined.**)

Note that Caroline Louise said she has read everything on [Dr] Judy Wood's website. Oddly, Caroline Louise then asked.

> *Can you tell me more about the alleged threats made to Judy by Fetzer and Jones at different times? I understand Jones sent her an email after Michael Zebuhr's tragic murder, implying the same thing might happen again? I've seen a one-sentence quote from that email. A longer quote, putting the threat in context would be helpful, if poss.*

I replied:

> *I did not refer to the threat from Mr Fetzer, but it is discussed in an article I wrote.*
>
> *http://www.checktheevidence.com/cms/index.php?option=content&task=view&id=170*
>
> *I did not refer to threats by Steven E Jones, so I am not sure what you are referring to.*

I have not written about any threats by Steven E Jones on my website. I did wonder why she had immediately "zoned in" on matters relating to threats by Jones and Fetzer. In any case, the threat by Fetzer "appeared" in 2008, not 2006-7, which was the period Caroline Louise stated she was going to write about. She responded:

> *As I've said several times now, I HAVE read pretty much everything to do with this question on your website and on Judy Wood's, Morgan Reynold's and Jim Fetzer's. I've read every paper I can find, watched countless hours of video, read endless debates on various websites. I am very familiar with the claims to fact made by all **sides, but what I am trying to do is record the history and development of the schism, which means I have to document rather than editorialise**, do you see?*

With the emboldened quote above, Caroline Louise is again talking about "sides" and she completely fails to acknowledge that I had already recorded history – over a 2-3-year period, as it happened, and it is already published – as referenced documentation (including audio recordings) not in editorial. Therefore, there is no debate. It is a true and accurate record. So why doesn't she "get it"? Why can't she see that what I have said above is *true* - it is *not an opinion* nor is it a theory, etc. After I had read her message, I began to wonder if Caroline Louise was attempting to re-write history. At this point, therefore, I chose not to respond.

Steven E Jones - "Read My Lips" on Cold Fusion

A few days later, I received a rather specific message from Caroline Louise, thus:

> *Hi Andrew - trying to trace a quote you attribute to Jones/Koonin on this page:*
>
> *http://www.checktheevidence.com/articles/Jones%20Grabbe%20Koonin%20Timeline2.htm[303]*
>
> *Namely that cold fusion was "crazy, impossible" - you source it to pp. 140-45 of Mallove's book "Fire From Ice", but I have searched the book and can't find that quote anywhere.*
>
> *Can you remember where you found it?*

This immediately raised two questions in my mind. Firstly, Caroline Louise had stated her objective was "to try and tell the story of what actually happened to 9/11 Truth in the summer-winter of 2006-7" – and yet, this question pertained to something which happened back in 1989 and involved, you've guessed it – Steven E Jones. Secondly, I wondered why she had incorrectly stated that I had attributed a quote to Jones/Koonin (a fellow physicist) when the author of this posting is clearly given as Russ Gerst (who has helped Dr Wood and myself on many occasions and specifically with the publication and distribution of the *Where Did the Towers Go?* book). I quickly wrote back to Caroline Louise, saying

> *What problem are you trying to solve? Are you trying to say there is no connection between Steven E Jones, Cold Fusion, and what happened to the towers...?*

I said I would check the posting/timeline when I had time (as I had not written the posting, I wasn't sure exactly what the issue was). Having checked Dr Mallove's "Fire From Ice" book, I wrote back to her thus:

> *The date of 05 March 2007 on the above page was incorrect and should have been 05 March 2008. I have checked the references, and the summary that Russ did is perhaps slightly inaccurate in the entry you highlighted. I have now updated the text thus:*
>
> *5/1-3/1989*
>
> *Koonin implies Pons and Fleishmann are "delusional" at APES Meetings May 1-3, 1989.*
>
> *Jones says "Is it a shortcut to Fusion Energy? Read my lips... 'No'*
>
> *Eugene Mallove, "Fire from Ice", 1991, p. 143, p145*
>
> *FYI, this page is also included in "the main site" here:*
>
> *http://www.checktheevidence.co.uk/cms/index.php?option=com_content&task=view&id=162&Itemid=6 (this had the correct date of 05 March 2008 at the top).*

I again asked her what problem she was trying to solve? I asked her if she wanted to debate the difference between the adjectives "crazy" and "delusional." I then asked her who she was (I had no idea who she really was) and sent her additional links, holding evidence about Steven E Jones, similar to what I have referenced above. Her next response[302]Error! Bookmark not defined. was the most illuminating:

*What problem am I trying to solve? Fair question. I'm trying to document the rift in Scholars for 9/11 Truth 2006-7 which (whatever "**side**" one takes) was bad news for the movement and for the momentum gathering around the call for a new enquiry.*

Am I trying to say there's no connection between Steve Jones, cold fusion and what happened to the towers? No, I'm trying to ascertain to my own satisfaction whether there was a connection or not.

Andrew - Do you think Mallove's book documents Jones trying to discredit or cover up cold fusion? Do you think he intended this to be the message of his book?

I got your latest reply just as I was writing this - I'll look into that a bit later and check out all the links.

BTW - this is me http://en.wikipedia.org/wiki/Karoline_Leach

Caroline Louise was again repeating the "side"/division meme. Hence, I now knew that:

a)   Caroline Louise was not her real name
b)   She seemed to be focussing more specifically on Steven E Jones and Cold Fusion rather than matters related to 9/11 or what happened in the period 2006-7 within the Scholars Group. (Her stated objective was to write about the break-up of the Scholars group).

The signs were not good. Reading Karoline Leach's Wikipedia page (referenced above) I noted that she is

a British playwright and author and she wrote a book in 1999 called "In the Shadow of the Dreamchild"

Her book was about the life of Lewis Carroll (author of "Alice's Adventures in Wonderland"). The Wikipedia page also notes:

An article in the Times Literary Supplement labeled Leach and her supporters as 'revisionists' attempting to rewrite history

How odd that someone would use the phrase which had "popped into my mind" early on in the correspondence with Caroline Louise – sorry – Karoline Leach. In a later email[302]Error! Bookmark not defined., I asked her

Is it moral, just or right to cover up the knowledge of advanced energy production technology and then turn it into some kind of weapon?

She replied:

No, it isn't. But have we actually established this is what Jones was doing? Don't we need to do that first before rushing to condemnation?

I had been researching these topics for several years – arguably as many as 10, so I certainly wasn't "rushing to judgement." Here, she had either not bothered to check the dates on the evidence I sent her, or she was getting ready to mischaracterise what I had written.

In another email where I was asking the reasons for her writing to me she said:

*Atm I'm just trying to get a clear picture of the events. My personal **POV** is that the less we resort to **polarised thinking in any situation,** the better. I find it hard to think of any time in history when "you're either with us or against us" has produced anything positive.*

Again, she refers to a "point of view." However, it is not a "point of view" that the truth and lies will always be polarised. I would then also like to observe how her Wikipedia page says:

This book and her subsequent work on what she terms the "Carroll Myth" have been major sources of upheaval and controversy in recent years and she has produced very polarized responses from Carroll scholars and lay enthusiasts.

She sent me a few more emails and in them, it became clearer that she was specifically focused on trying to re-characterise or re-package the evidence of Jones' role in Cold Fusion. For example, she queries what I wrote in earlier email:

Mallove didn't just NOT say "Jones covered up cold fusion", he praised him for his work on cold fusion and predicted he would be a "hero" to the cause. Was he deluded in your view? Was Jones not really a cold fusion pioneer? Not really a potential "hero"? How so?

What I have been telling people are the facts. Jones "appeared" in 9/11 research in Aug/Sep 2005. Mallove was murdered in May 2004. Of course, you could say "there is no connection between these things." Unfortunately, due to the weight of evidence I have compiled, I no longer have that luxury.

And this weight of evidence would all be on your website? Is there anything you know that isn't on there?

The last statement I found very interesting. I leave the reader to work out why. Again, what becomes clear is that she has not actually read what is on Dr Judy Wood's website – especially the postings about Steven E. Jones email to Greg Jenkins, Recruiting a Hit Piece[93]**Error! Bookmark not defined.** nor the posting where even more evidence about "Cold Fusion" (LENR) and Steven E Jones is collected[304]. This latter page references a quote by Mallove in his "New Energy Times", from February 2001"[305] :

Dr Steven Jones in his skeletal three-page commentary confirms that he still trusts his sparse cold fusion neutron measurements—fair enough. But Jones, the egocentric denier of excess heat claims from day one, apparently has learned nothing and still knows nothing about the process of science. He is an example of the kind of scientist identified in the Bockris quote above. Jones writes disingenuously, "It is high time to strongly question claims of cold fusion based on crude techniques and to demand tests at a rigorous scientific-proof level. . .I have not seen any compelling evidence of any 'cold fusion' effects to date."

It seemed that Karoline Leach had *not* "pretty much read everything on [Dr] Judy Wood's Website." Caroline Louise's focus on Steven E Jones seems to be additionally confirmed in comments on a Willy Loman Blog[306] posted in 2011. Additionally, a comment made by a YouTube user with the name Caroline Louise[307] on 08 Jan 2014 (five days before a Caroline Louise initially contacted me) on a YouTube video entitled Steven E. Jones Cold Fusion Cover-Up[308] incorrectly states:

As I understand it Jones et al had been working on "cold fusion" at BYU since 1986, long before P-F began their work.

Her understanding about Pons and Fleischmann is wrong - as is documented in Issue 5 of Infinite Energy Magazine. On page 105 states[309]:

Fleischmann and Pons spent over five years and $100,000 of their own money on cold fusion research prior to 1989. They conducted experiments in Pons' laboratory in the Henry Eyring Chemistry Building at the University of Utah.

In an earlier email to me, regarding the "timeline" Karoline Leach wrote[302]**Error! Bookmark not defined.**:

Do understand - I'm not defending Jones here, I'm just looking for accuracy. I'm pretty sure you are too, and neither of us want to be in the position of our sources being shown up as faulty or non-existent!

Well, it now seems like she does not mind about inaccurate remarks being made by her about Pons and Fleischmann (in her YouTube comment), but she *does* mind about possible inaccuracy about SE Jones in the "timeline" article I had on my website. This was the only page on my website which she specifically referenced and asked about.

Karoline Leach also stated that her article was to be for the "Memory Hole Blog," run by James Tracy. Curiously, there are additional posts on this blog where Dr Wood's research is brought up, and mischaracterised in one way or another. One posting was actually about Hurricane Erin [310]and another was originally started about Sandy Hook, but then someone using the name of "Hilary" posts many comments incorrectly describing Wood's research – for example, as a "high energy beam theory"[311]. Just for the record, James Tracy has been a guest on Jim Fetzer's "Real Deal" Pod Cast on January 14, 2013[312] and October 11, 2013[313]. Fetzer and Tracy have also "stirred the pot" quite vigorously in relation to the events at Sandy Hook (which are, like 9/11, not completely explained by the Official Narrative, but Fetzer and people like him have, again, circulated false information about Sandy Hook and changed their story.)

In the email to Dr Wood, Caroline Louise wrote:

I find three interesting things about this – firstly, it is inaccurate to say I suggested she write to Dr Wood – I merely asked Caroline Louise if she was not able to see the email address on the website when Caroline Louise had asked me for it. Secondly, it appears she was in communication with Jim Fetzer before writing to Dr Wood. Is this why she was reluctant to discuss the threat that Fetzer made in 2008? Is this why she was reluctant to discuss any of the content in *9/11 Finding the Truth*, but instead focused on a small detail in an article about Steven E Jones, which I had not written (but I had posted)? Thirdly, Dr Wood and Dr Reynolds resigned from the original "Scholars for 9/11 Truth" group on August 17, 2006, before Jones and Fetzer began fighting and split up. Wood and Reynolds proceeded to conduct independent research and investigation – which is what many were calling for.

"Want to hold NIST accountable?"

At this point, I would like to note a campaign posted on the Architects and Engineers for 9/11 "Truth" Website.

As can be seen, they have a "membership" drive – and ask participants to donate $2.50/month[314]. Their page states:

"AE911Truth will begin pursuing legal avenues to require correction of the NIST report and holding NIST investigators personally accountable."

I only need reference here that Steven E Jones and Richard Gage already submitted an RFC (Request for Correction) to NIST in 2007 – almost 7 years before this correspondence with Karoline Leach. They did *not* reference the "thermite" evidence they claimed was a "smoking gun" in the destruction of the WTC. Neither did they take further action. Dr Judy Wood also submitted an RFC – 3 weeks earlier, which resulted in a Qui Tam case[315]. Knowing these facts, can we imagine a connection between the "launch" of this new AE911 "membership drive" and attempts to publish new articles with a "different point of view" about what actually happened in 2006 and 2007 in relation to research into 9/11?

Summary / Conclusions

Here is a summary of the information I have collected here

1) Caroline Louise contacted me claiming to be interested in writing a piece about the "Scholars for 9/11 Truth" group.
2) For some reason, she did not use her real/full name.
3) She seemed much more interested in articles and evidence to do with Steven E Jones and Cold Fusion.
4) She was already researching the Steven E Jones/Cold Fusion issue *before* she first contacted me.
5) She was in communication with Jim Fetzer around the same time as she first wrote to me and Dr Judy Wood.
6) Her intent was to post on the "Memory Hole" blog.
7) As a playwright and author, she has previously written a book which was said to "rewrite" some of the history of Lewis Carroll.
8) A new AE911 membership and "NIST accountability" campaign has been launched.

So, can I conclude that Jim Fetzer had somehow contacted Karoline Leach and asked her to write a piece to help "defend" Steve E Jones? After all, it was Steven E Jones and Jim Fetzer who originally formed "Scholars for 9/11 Truth" in 2006." Perhaps because of the efforts of a number of people, including Dr Judy Wood and myself, there is something of a growing awareness of the parallels between 9/11 evidence and "Cold Fusion" (LENR) evidence - for example, the tritium data[316]. They are also beginning to see the obvious role of Steven E Jones in these two supposedly disconnected fields of research. It is a very, very "dangerous" (revealing) connection for people to be making. The importance of covering up this connection must be enormous. So, to keep it covered up, and with a new campaign to get money out of "truthers", history would urgently need to be re-written.

17. Richard Gage and Dane Wigington - Lying Together about 9/11 Evidence

30 Sep 2014

Dane Wigington, for several years now has been running the "Geoengineering Watch" website[317]. He has talked quite a bit about the chemtrailing issue, which is discussed at length on my website and in another book I have written and compiled called *Climate Change and Global Warming - Exposed: Hidden Evidence, Disguised Plans.*[318] You can study his website for more information, but my composition of this chapter was motivated following false information being stated in an interview Wigington recorded with the liar Richard Gage of "Architects and Engineers for 9/11 Truth"[319] (AE911) on 27 September 2014[320]. We will return to Dane Wigington presently, but before that, I need to cover some additional material about AE911 which has come to light since I finished *9/11 Finding the Truth.*

Architects and Engineers for 9/11 Cover Up

Organisations like AE911 use our humanity and good will against us - and people don't figure this out until it's too late. In a book called Nanomanagement: The Disintegration of a Non-Profit Corporation,[321] Michael Armenia documents his experience with AE911. It's quite an interesting read - and seemingly exposes the AE911 "truth" group as some kind of "brainwashing" operation. Even though the author documents how the group operates, he is either unhappy about revealing why it has been run a certain way, or he does not realise what the reason is (i.e. to keep a cover up in place). I think there is an enormous clue on (PDF) page 238 of the book, where the author publishes a document of AE911's volunteer "vetting" guidelines. This particular page is reproduced below.

TECHNIQUES

The primary source for information is the Internet. (If necessary, contacting personal references may be considered.) Therefore, it is assumed that the vetter is competent in using the Internet for research, particularly with regard to using search engines and their respective advanced search criteria.

It is important to remember that the search results are not necessarily to be used as exclusionary criteria. A context needs to be established whereby the vetter can come to a reasonable conclusion.

A primary goal in the overall search is to find alternate identities (aliases) or usernames. The web searches should be performed with all usernames found to be associated with the candidate.

A. **General Search** (using Google.com)
Cross-reference search results to confirm identity. Attempt to find at least one photograph.

1. Google complete email address (username@domain.xyz)
2. Google 'username'.
3. Google phone number.

B. **9/11 Related Site Search**

1. Search the JREF Forum (http://randi.org)
2. Search 911blogger.com (http://911blogger.com)
3. Search 9/11 Meet-Up (http://9-11.meetup.com)

C. **Refined Searches** (using Google.com)
If not already found through Items A and B above, refine Google searches to determine any correlation to questionable ideologies using combinations of "username" and a search term, as well as "full name" and a search term. Among the search terms to be considered are: "no planes", "dew", "nukes", "harp", "ufo", "judy wood", "jews", "holocaust", "Zionism".

D. **Social Networking Site Search**
Search for social sites profiles using full name and primary email address.

1. MySpace (http://www.myspace.com)
2. FaceBook (http://www.facebook.com)
3. LinkedIn, etc. (http://www.linkedin.com)

AE911Truth - Volunteer Vetting Procedures – DRAFT – 09C312
Page 3/11

Pay particular attention to the search terms suggested - which include only one person's name in the whole of history.

C. **Refined Searches** (using Google.com)
If not already found through Items A and B above, refine Google searches to determine any correlation to questionable ideologies using combinations of "username" and a search term, as well as "full name" and a search term. Among the search terms to be considered are: "no planes", "dew", "nukes", "harp", "ufo", "judy wood", "jews", "holocaust", "Zionism".

I wonder who wrote these procedures... Let us know inspect AE911's 2012 return of income tax:

efile GRAPHIC print - DO NOT PROCESS	As Filed Data -	DLN: 93493319111043

Form 990

Return of Organization Exempt From Income Tax

Under section 501(c), 527, or 4947(a)(1) of the Internal Revenue Code (except black lung benefit trust or private foundation)

OMB No 1545-0047

2012

Department of the Treasury
Internal Revenue Service

► The organization may have to use a copy of this return to satisfy state reporting requirements

Open to Public Inspection

A For the 2012 calendar year, or tax year beginning 01-01-2012 , 2012, and ending 12-31-2012

B Check if applicable	**C** Name of organization ARCHITECTS & ENGINEERS FOR 911 TRUTH	**D** Employer Identification number
☐ Address change		26-1532493
☐ Name change	Doing Business As	
☐ Initial return	Number and street (or P O box if mail is not delivered to street address) Room/suite 2342 SHATTUCK AVE PMB 189	**E** Telephone number
☐ Terminated		
☐ Amended return	City or town, state or country, and ZIP + 4 BERKELEY, CA 94704-1517	
☐ Application pending		**G** Gross receipts $ 549,038

F Name and address of principal officer

H(a) Is this a group return for affiliates? ☐ Yes ☑ No

H(b) Are all affiliates included? ☐ Yes ☐ No
If "No," attach a list (see instructions)

I Tax-exempt status ☑ 501(c)(3) ☐ 501(c) ( ) ◄ (insert no) ☐ 4947(a)(1) or ☐ 527

H(c) Group exemption number ►

J Website: ► WWW AE911TRUTH ORG

K Form of organization ☑ Corporation ☐ Trust ☐ Association ☐ Other ► **L** Year of formation 2007 **M** State of legal domicile CA

Part I — Summary

1 Briefly describe the organization's mission or most significant activities
OUR MISSION IS TO RESEARCH, COMPILE AND DISSEMINATE EVIDENCE RELATIVE TO THE DESTRUCTION OF THE THREE WORLD TRADE CENTER SKYSCRAPERS, CALLING FOR A TRULY OPEN AND INDEPENDENT INVESTIGATION AND SUPPRTING OTHERS IN THE PURSUIT OF JUSTICE

2 Check this box ►☐ if the organization discontinued its operations or disposed of more than 25% of its net assets

3 Number of voting members of the governing body (Part VI, line 1a)	**3**	5
4 Number of independent voting members of the governing body (Part VI, line 1b)	**4**	4
5 Total number of individuals employed in calendar year 2012 (Part V, line 2a)	**5**	2
6 Total number of volunteers (estimate if necessary)	**6**	
7a Total unrelated business revenue from Part VIII, column (C), line 12	**7a**	0
b Net unrelated business taxable income from Form 990-T, line 34	**7b**	0

		Prior Year	Current Year
8	Contributions and grants (Part VIII, line 1h)	288,893	350,425
9	Program service revenue (Part VIII, line 2g)	180,464	198,613
10	Investment income (Part VIII, column (A), lines 3, 4, and 7d)	5	0
11	Other revenue (Part VIII, column (A), lines 5, 6d, 8c, 9c, 10c, and 11e)		0
12	Total revenue—add lines 8 through 11 (must equal Part VIII, column (A), line 12)	469,362	549,038
13	Grants and similar amounts paid (Part IX, column (A), lines 1-3)		2,430
14	Benefits paid to or for members (Part IX, column (A), line 4)		0
15	Salaries, other compensation, employee benefits (Part IX, column (A), lines 5-10)	155,269	158,145
16a	Professional fundraising fees (Part IX, column (A), line 11e)	1,788	944
b	Total fundraising expenses (Part IX, column (D), line 25) ►29,489		
17	Other expenses (Part IX, column (A), lines 11a-11d, 11f-24e)	334,979	389,376
18	Total expenses Add lines 13-17 (must equal Part IX, column (A), line 25)	492,036	550,895
19	Revenue less expenses Subtract line 18 from line 12	-22,674	-1,857

		Beginning of Current Year	End of Year
20	Total assets (Part X, line 16)	87,336	99,803
21	Total liabilities (Part X, line 26)	79,080	93,404
22	Net assets or fund balances Subtract line 21 from line 20	8,256	6,399

Part II — Signature Block

Under penalties of perjury, I declare that I have examined this return, including accompanying schedules and statements, and to the best of my knowledge and belief, it is true, correct, and complete Declaration of preparer (other than officer) is based on all information of which preparer has any knowledge

Sign Here	****** Signature of officer	2013-11-12 Date
	RICHARD GAGE PRESIDENT Type or print name and title	

Paid Preparer Use Only	Print/Type preparer's name Patrick McDermott	Preparer's signature	Date 2013-11-15	Check ☑ if self-employed	PTIN P00402645
	Firm's name ► Patrick A McDermott CPA			Firm's EIN ► 08-0386750	
	Firm's address ► 1442A Walnut St PMB 28 Berkeley, CA 947091405			Phone no (510) 841-9901	

May the IRS discuss this return with the preparer shown above? (see instructions) ☑ Yes ☐ No

For Paperwork Reduction Act Notice, see the separate instructions. Cat No 11282Y Form **990** (2012)

Let's see those figures more closely…

. . . .	**6**	
. . . .	**7a**	0
. . . .	**7b**	0

	Prior Year	Current Year
. . . .	288,893	350,425
. . .	180,464	198,613
. . .	5	0
11e)		0
ın (A), lıne .	469,362	549,038
. . .		2,430
. . .		0
A), lınes	155,269	158,145
. . .	1,798	944
. . .	334,979	389,376
lıne 25)	492,036	550,895
. . .	-22,674	-1,857

	Beginning of Current Year	End of Year
. . .	87,336	99,803
. . .	79,080	93,404
. . .	8,256	6,399

It is also worth noting from 2008 to 2012 AE911 Truth's income was $1.365 million!!! I think it's time for a tax audit...Just a thought...

Where does this amount of money come from? At least we know how Gage manages to do 30-date tours in the US and Canada![322]

Richard Gage Lies about the Contents of the WDTTG Book

Now let us return to the lies of Richard Gage. On 08 May 2011, Ralph Winterrowd, on his RBN show, asked Mr Richard Gage – leader of AE911 "truth" - about the evidence on Dr Wood's website etc. Mr Gage has continued to claim that Dr Judy Wood ignores the 9/11 evidence he focuses on. This is an outright lie.

"…now when Judy Wood is not going to acknowledge any of that evidence and just hand wave it away, then she's not practicing science, she's practicing witchcraft. Go ahead…"

Here is part of the contents page of the WDTTG book:

Where Did the Towers Go?

Table of Contents

ARCHITECTS & ENGINEERS FOR 9/11 TRUTH, INC.
AKA AE911TRUTH
OPERATING ACCOUNT
3527 MT. DIABLO BLVD., SUITE 370
LAFAYETTE, CA 94549-3815

4430

4/9/11
DATE

PAY TO THE ORDER OF _Mathew Naus_ $ 60.00

Sixty and no/100 ——— DOLLARS

Wells Fargo Bank, N.A.
California
wellsfargo.com

FOR _Judy Woods Book 75 + Jesse Ventura Book 20_   _Richard Gage_

Above is an image of the cheque which Richard Gage used to purchase a copy of WDTTG from Matt Naus, a long-time 9/11 truth campaigner who, in 2011, realised that Gage was part of the 9/11 cover up. "Ah but," you might say, "this cheque was written on 4 September 2011 and the Winterrowd interview was in May…" read on…

Now back to Dane Wigington on 27 September 2014, he interviewed Richard Gage for one of his Podcasts. The part of most interest to me is from about 55 minutes till the end of the recording. [323]

Not only does Dane Wigington not check his facts, he joins in with the lying. Here is a transcript of the relevant portion of the interview / discussion.

> *Wigington: The whole 9/11 issue bottom to top… there is really nothing that supports the official story and everything that supports the conclusions that your group... and again how could you have a stronger group than that - 2200 people... I know there's a lot of disinformation - we talked about this off the air... a lot of people that want to grab at straws. And they grab at, you know I've seen mentioned the laser beams from space and all this sort of stuff... It's been designed to make people reject the actual facts.*

> *Gage: Regarding Judy Wood and her theory of directed energy weapons... what she does is look at the site around the towers and tries to find unusual evidence to try to support an unusual theory - that she doesn't even know what evidence would support that theory because we don't know anything about directed energy weapons or how they work. We don't even know if they exist. We know there are experimental programmes... But in the process what Judy Wood does is deny the scientific forensic evidence that we do have for nanothermite... (bla bla) she also denies the evidence for explosives... (bla)*

> *Wigington: We have one person - Dr Judy Wood - ignoring evidence and disputing literally not just 2200 experts but many more when you **count all these other first responders** that heard the explosions. One person denying who knows how many - 2500, 3000 experts from various fields. Which would people be reasonable in believing? Obviously, you guys are standing on solid ground. Nobody else is.*

I can first point out that Dr Wood actually *quotes* first responders and their accounts of explosive sounds in the WDTTG book, so Dane Wigington has lied. I can then observe that Wigington did not mention the very likely case of Geoengineering that took place around the time of 9/11[106]**Error! Bookmark not defined.**, i.e. that seen in the movements of Hurricane Erin.

Aside from 9/11 evidence itself, Wigington talked about how many members Gage's group had. He claimed that the size of the group was a validation that they were correct – i.e. that what they said was true. This is ridiculous logic - hundreds of thousands of "experts" are "signed up" with the official story of 9/11 (and geoengineering issues). By Wigington's logic, they must be correct - and everyone else (including Gage and himself) must be wrong.

Perhaps at this point we should note Wigington's connection to[317]**Error! Bookmark not defined.**Bechtel[324] and note the sorts of projects that large corporation undertakes and who its customers are.

If people who claim to be revealing truths about geoengineering don't want to talk about Hurricane Erin and the events of 9/11, I cannot help but think this is strange. Similar experience of "this sort of talk" up to now has shown me that this again, is part of an ongoing cover up.

It seems that several people have written to Dane Wigington about 9/11, having listened to the comments he made above. So, does he "fess up"? Does he say "I need to study this more…" Here's what he said in a later Podcast on 02 June 2015[325]…

> One point I want to make – a picture of – the six story high digital billboard in Times' Square – Richard Gage – and his group Architects and Engineers for [9/11] Truth paid for … to show Building 7 collapsing… **I am tired of the Judy Wood argument – I don't care what happened, OK?** And I'm tired of people throwing that at me, ye know. 2200 architects and engineers for truth compared to one single person that has an opinion. I lean towards the architects and engineers but whatever the case, I think we all agree on this – building 7 didn't fall down from the fires on the first floor. We all agree on that. That showed in Times Square for over a month. Did the population do anything?

Readers who are not now familiar with what Dane Wigington is "about" can research his dealings with G Edward Griffin and Michael Murphy.

18. Methodical Creation of a Methodical Illusion

March/April 2015 (Posted 30 April 2015)

Novel Research?

In late 2014, a new 9/11 related novel appeared called "Methodical Illusion." The novel was primarily about the movement of planes and the alleged hijackings which took place on 9/11. I first heard about the book in a YouTube video interview[326] and found there was an associated website - http://www.methodicalillusion.com/. The YouTube video itself seemed slightly peculiar because it was stated as being an interview with "The Writing Room" – which seemed like a radio programme or podcast. However, I could not find a podcast or programme with this name. Nor could I find the name of the host, or when the recording was made. In this interview, Rebekah Roth - the author of "Methodical Illusion," – was introduced as "renowned." However, I had never heard of her before.

Her story is that she was a flight attendant for quite a number of years, and so she was suspicious about the events of 9/11. She described how she has done a lot of research and she is presented as "an expert" on 9/11. This was also peculiar, because I have been researching into the events of 9/11 for over 10 years (see other articles and my free eBook[110]Error! Bookmark not defined. about all of that). Roth said that she decided to write a novel "encapsulating" some of her research - from the perspective of a fictional flight attendant named Vera.

I bought and downloaded the Kindle version of her eBook[327] and read it. I also posted a review on the Amazon US and UK websites for the Kindle version. This review is reproduced below.

The idea of writing a fictional novel about the events of 9/11 is not new – another such effort was "The Shell Game" by Steve Alten[328] (2008). Little of what actually happened on 9/11 is discussed in "Methodical Illusion."

Old News

In interviews, Roth makes little or no mention of other 9/11 research or researchers. However, almost inevitably, her expertise is called into question when she starts talking about thermite and nanothermite in relation to the destruction of the WTC buildings. It has been known, clearly, for 7 to 8 years that this story is bogus and those promoting this story are liars[329]. If Rebekah Roth really had "done her homework", then she would know this too – and she would be pointing this out to other people – as I have been doing for … 7 to 8 years[330]!

Roth also talks about the problems with Planes and Hijackers accounts as if it's new information. However, I must point out that, thanks to others, I became familiar with the "surviving hijackers" story almost 10 years ago. For example, a BBC "surviving hijackers" story was posted on 23 Sep 2001[331]! It was included in "Loose Change 2" (LC2) which was released in 2005[332] - as was information about the story that 2 planes landed at Cleveland Airport (this information was taken out of later LC films). Additionally, it is said that two of the named flights weren't even scheduled to fly that day. All of this information is included in a 15 minute section of LC2[333], which I don't think Roth has mentioned in her book or any of her interviews. She claims to be an "expert" on 9/11 - why would she not mention this - and that the information has been available for years? Roth doesn't "follow through" with this evidence - she doesn't "take you to the end of the road." It's "limited hangout" again – she does not point out that none of the plane crashes were real – which means that the plane crashes were illusions.

Bait and Switch?

Roth makes the claim that they would use a hijacking codeword if this ever happened to a flight they were on. However, is this true? A flight attendant called J. Moore posted this comment on an Amazon review of Roth's book[334]:

> *I was a flight attendant with United Airlines for ten years from 1997. Neither was there a Methodical code word, nor a hijack switch in the main cabin. Utterly false.*

Promotion

In March 2015, there was an apparent sudden increase in promotion of the Rebekah Roth and "Methodical Illusion" with her being interviewed on Coast to Coast[335], Red Ice Radio[336], Veritas Radio[337] (now deleted) in fairly quick succession. Curiously, a 9/11 Facebook group that I help administer was also "visited" by someone who was quite keen for people to listen to these interviews.[338] When I asked this person "why"? He was rather sketchy about the reason and would not discuss Roth's failure to acknowledge the bogosity of the thermite story. He was not deterred from saying "listen to the interviews." It didn't give me a good feeling…

Coincidentally, the increase in exposure for Roth and her novel was around the time of the Germanwings Air crash – where, in the official story it was alleged that the co-pilot had become suicidal and deliberately crashed the plane[339].

Around the time of Roth's refreshed promotion, a new video entitled "Could This Be the Next False Flag Attack?" appeared on her YouTube channel[340]. It sounds like a radio interview, but the interviewer is not named and the programme is not stated either. To me, it was quite reminiscent of a talk between Dr Steven E Jones and Dr Bill Deagle which took place in 2007. I wrote about this in *9/11 Finding the Truth*.[341] Roth also seemed keen to talk about this in her various other interviews. Why was Roth talking about Al Qaida? Is she trying to scare people? Doesn't she know that Al Qaida is, essentially, irrelevant when one considers what happened to the WTC towers? Who is the host of this interview? Is Roth being presented as something she is not? After all, we really don't know much about her beyond a brief biography on her website[342]... At least, we know she's not a scientist – though she does claim a more varied career in at least one of the interviews (I haven't listened to all of them.)

Also on the subject of her website, she shows pictures of the destruction of the WTC[343] but this really isn't discussed in any detail in her book - and where it is discussed, it is wrong anyway! There are no pictures of planes or related things to do with flight attendants etc. Also, there is no reference to Elias Davidsson's research which is quite relevant to what Roth talks about[344]. Is Rebekah Roth trying to encourage people only to think about what she is suggesting to them, and not consider how what she says fits into a larger picture?

And we haven't even discussed her preponderance for wanting to bring Israel into the issue! I think the Roth promotion is relying on folks forgetting things - they try and reveal her research as "new information", when it isn't really.

Scripted Promotions?

A video made by Betsy McGee (aka Conspiracy Theorista) documents the strangely sycophantic nature of introductions given by several radio / podcast hosts such as Jeff Rense, Pete Santilli and others[345]. Roth is lauded as "one of the most knowledgeable people that I think I've come across" (Santilli) and "one of the, right now pre-eminent researchers on the scene" (host name unknown), "the worthiest of dames" (John B Wells). Kevin Barrett said "she may have won the prize for getting the most hard core 9/11 information into a novel." As the saying goes, "who writes this stuff?"

"Keeping Mum"

Can I suggest that the perpetrators are willing to let most aspects of the plane stories "go" - i.e. reveal the plane stories are fake. However, they don't want their technology revealed - that is, the energy weapon and image projection technology. It therefore makes sense that they create distractions about fake hijacker stories and what happened to the passengers etc - it distracts from the key evidence which proves that even bigger secrets have been and are being kept – secrets which affect the whole of our civilisation.

"Wood" or "Woods" - I don't know…"

In August 2015, Rebecca Roth appeared on Truth Frequency Radio in an "exclusive" with Kev Baker[346]. She started to discuss the Tianjin explosion in China[347], which had occurred a few days before the broadcast. She said

> *… What's going on with China and the devaluation and their money… All of these things are interconnected – a lot of people don't realise how connected we are – and when I say how connected we are I mean if they start devaluating (devaluing?) money then we start to see things happening like crazy weird explosions that look like a nuclear blast. And if you look at that Chinese explosion you will see… And if you're not familiar with Doctor Judy Wood… "Wood" or "Woods" - I don't know… I'm not sure what her name is but… whether there is an 's' on the end or not… Because I was really concerned about her name as much as I was the pictures I saw on her website… And this was a long time ago… I don't remember the exact spelling of the name. But she showed these cars - she called them "toasted." If you look at the pictures of the cars in China - very much like the cars around the World Trade Center… Which tells us they are using some type of weaponry or something exploded in China and of course that was all done around the same time as an economic hit as well, so… everything is connected.*

In the past, Roth has claimed to be a "9/11 Expert" – yet she couldn't remember Dr Wood's name? She didn't know about the 2007 Qui Tam Case? And so, she muddles up all this with explosions in China. But hey, it's all "good conspiracy fodder" now, isn't it…? If Rebekah Roth had actually done the research she claims to have done, she would have found the video of showing three successively more powerful explosions in Tianjin[348]. Videos are now (since late 2015) available showing the blast crater and damage following the explosions.

The 9/11 Expert Speaks Again…

A call-in to the Coast to Coast talk show during Roth's interview on 19 Mar 2015 is revealing[349] (thanks to Bill Ryan for the transcript!)

> *George Noory: International caller, Leah, in Ottawa, Canada — welcome to the program. Leah, you're on the air with us.*

> *Leah: Thanks for taking my call. Remember, George, you had a woman saying that it was Tesla technology that took down the towers?*

> *George Noory: That was Dr Judy Wood.*

> *Leah: Yes. I'm wondering, Rebekah, if you entertain those ideas at all, because it would even work in with your theory, because your concentration isn't so much the buildings.*
>
> *Rebekah: Well, you know, it's interesting. I've actually been contacted by some scientists who are trying to give me a heads-up without losing their jobs and without, you know... **everything we do is monitored now, so almost some of our conversations almost in code**.*
>
> *And so getting to that, there is a technology that was used, I can almost guarantee you — even though I'm not a scientist, I am taking with one that was relating some information that... let me just put it to you this way, when... our military has established, and are actually using, things such as laser weapons.*
>
> *We don't know about it on the ground unless we're in Research and Development and a scientist, or in the higher-up part of the Pentagon, perhaps.*
>
> ***The amount of things that were used to bring those towers down, there could have been a dozen or more methodologies. There may not have just been nanothermite — they did find nanothermite — that may only have only been one of the techniques used. They just needed to make sure that they were absolutely turned to dust.***
>
> *And so I am not a building demolition expert, but I am open-minded to believe that... I know that ten years ago, if we would have said somebody had a laser weapon that could shoot through a tank, in five seconds or less, and burn through it in a hot-hot-hot... and that laser weapons, by the way, chemical lasers, actually do create a great deal of heat, and that's one thing that we see reported from the World Trade Center towers. The degree of heat was much more beyond kerosene fires from jet fuel.*
>
> *George Noory: Yes, there's no doubt about that, too.*

Here again, we see a muddle-up occurring — Roth just babbles her way through buzz words and makes no reference to weather, court cases etc. She makes sure she inserts the "talking points" of "nanothermite" and "high heat." I hope you can see the pattern by now…?

More Lying Ensues

In a video made by Betsy McGee/Conspiracy Theorista[350], Roth's lies about the official "hijackers" story are more clearly explained. "Betsy" carefully breaks down what Roth says, and what is actually in the official record regarding the alleged conversations between flight attendants and people on the ground. Roth claims transcripts have been edited and she also contradicts herself. "Betsy" concludes:

> *So among many other lies and distortions the main part of your entire "9/11-phone-calls-made-from-an airplane-hanger-theory" is based on a bunch of things that were never even said. Yet two books and over 120 interviews later, no one has called you on it. You've been allowed by the so-called truth movement to peddle your lies repeatedly and without question - by a bunch of people who are supposed to be the "smart" ones - the skeptical ones, the*

ones who supposedly understand the PsyOp that we're all under and are supposed to be working against.

Roth makes up a bogus story about a bogus story of hijacked planes and then the "truth movement" circuit heavily promotes all this. Is it any wonder we are "where we are?"

I will just add that over the time Rebekah Roth was promoting herself, quite a few people became suspicious of her motives and her actions. This led some people to suggest Rebekah Roth was a creation – an actor etc[351]. This would not surprise me in the least.

Closing Comments

It does not really matter whether Rebekah Roth is an actress/actor or whether some parts of her book are true. The effect of her implementation is clear – lies and misconceptions have been recycled and the "truth movement" was deceived – yet again.

In closing, I include comments I received from 2 different people about Rebekah Roth the author…

Apparently, an intelligent and questioning mind, seemingly capable of tasking themselves to author a highly revealing story on this profound event still, somehow or other, managed to completely overlook the most important factual work produced to date in the U.S[3Error! Bookmark not defined.]. Or, if they did read it, became strangely incapable of recognizing it as in anyway relevant to their fearless attempt to expose the 9.11 "plot" through their fiction?

And

I've been looking at all of this since 2007. Never heard of this woman.

Amazon Review

This is the book review I posted on Amazon[352].

Having heard Rebecca Roth's short interview with "The Writing Room" on YouTube, after I was sent a link by someone, I decided to buy the Kindle version of this book, which I have now read. It was an interesting book - covering a topic that I, too, have compiled a book about. In my own 10 years of research, I had not heard of Rebecca Roth, but I am familiar with many of the facts which are related in the narrative presented in the 2nd half of her book.

The book reads well, and initially builds a fairly engaging story, centred around Vera - a flight attendant of many years' experience. Vera has always had questions about the official story of 9/11 but following two terrifying aircraft/airline incidents which directly affect the fictional US president, Jim Sherman, she begins to re-investigate those events with the help of an old friend of her deceased husband.

The first half of the book (more or less), just introduces the main characters in the story and how they are and become connected. This is essentially a build up to the second half, where some of the anomalies in the 9/11 story are discussed by these characters as they share their research. Most of their exchange of details centres around the plane/passenger anomalies (which was what I wanted to read about) and the alleged theft of gold from the WTC just before the towers were destroyed (a story which I have heard about, but not studied the evidence for). The scenario presented regarding what happened to the planes is intriguing, but is largely based on the alleged cell phone conversations which, as the narrative rightly points out, were used to generate the "hijackers" fable and implant it into the public consciousness soon after the events took place. The narrative makes the argument that these conversations were "staged" while the planes had been landed. Again, the narrative rightly points out that the observed damage at all 4 crash sites does not indicate that planes crashed there.

One oddity in the story is where 2 of the characters pull a stunt with a wheelchair to demonstrate a "hole" in security procedures - yet the characters talk about the intrusive nature of TSA pat-downs and so on. So why advocate *further* security checks when they are uncovering a fraudulent story of hijackings?

However, regarding the plane stories, certain issues are overlooked in the narrative - such as "if the planes were landed somewhere, what did people in New York see crashing into the towers, and what was filmed there?" This is a question which I think can be answered by studying the research of Richard D Hall and his 3D Flight Analysis. Also, my article entitled "Going in Search of Planes in NYC" offers some clues to fit into this story.

Regarding the planes, the "what people really saw" issue is only covered in the narrative with the suggestion that missiles were fired - which may have been the case - though the evidence for this part of the theory isn't really covered in the narrative at all well. (It's mainly covered in a conversation between Vera and someone who worked at the Pentagon).

More troubling is the inclusion of a Physics Professor named Jonas and his "peer reviewed scientific paper" about thermite being used to destroy the towers. Similarly, the towers are described many times as having "collapsed." The research of Dr Judy Wood (not mentioned or referenced anywhere in the narrative) shows the towers did NOT collapse. They mostly turned to dust in mid-air. It seems the author is not familiar with my own research into this area of 9/11 evidence - that the thermite story was implanted to distract people away from the evidence which shows what happened to the towers. I have evidence in spades that this is true. Thermite is a bogus theory - and unlike Dr Wood's research, none of the thermite evidence was put into a court case (i.e. those like Jonas promoting this evidence actually *know* they are lying).

So overall, this is an interesting narrative and the president's speech at the end is perhaps one we would all like to hear. But in the end, and I don't mean this to sound cruel, insensitive or "wrong", the stories of what happened to the planes some may consider as just a distraction - from asking the question *"Where Did the Towers Go?"* [3]Error! Bookmark not defined.. So please read that book, and mine! *9/11 Finding the Truth*[6]Error! Bookmark not defined..

19. David Icke Backtracks on 9/11 Truth

It is quite likely that those reading this book will know of David Icke – a former BBC Sports Presenter/Anchor, who had a kind of spiritual awakening in the early 1990s. Since then, he has written many books and done hundreds of talks and interviews around the world. He has been an inspiration to many and therefore has many "fans." He has revealed much important and compelling information – for example, regarding the existence of a paedophile network which operates within power structures in the UK – and probably around the world. Icke was talking about this long before revelations in the mainstream media, which seem to have increased since 2010.

I met David Icke in April 2008, by arrangement of a mutual friend (Justin Walker) and I spoke "one to one" with David Icke for about 2 hours. This was around the time Dr Wood had first published the 9/11 related Hurricane Erin information. I showed David Icke an outline of this on my laptop. I then I explained the "energy" connection to the events of 9/11 and his eyes "lit up". In his is next book *Human Race Get off your Knees*, published in 2010, on page 132 he writes:

> *I demolish the official story of 9/11 in my book, "Alice in Wonderland and the World Trade Center Disaster - Why the Official Story Of 9/11 is a Monumental Lie," and there is a wealth of written and video information in the 9/11 research archive at my website: davidicke.com. The twin towers were brought down by controlled demolition to ensure a maximum impact on the collective human psyche, preparing it for the 'solutions' that were waiting to be unleashed. If anyone thinks none of this could happen they should look at the Operation Northwoods documents that came to light in 2001 (see The David Icke Guide to the Global Conspiracy).*

On page 135 he writes:

> *Silverstein also said that another World Trade Center tower, known as Building Seven, was 'pulled', which is demolition parlance for a 'controlled demolition'. Yet the official story is that the building fell because it was so damaged. Silverstein let the truth slip out, however, and has been desperately trying to explain away what he said ever since about how the WTC underwent controlled demolition.*

This is even more unusual, because in the earlier book he authored, i.e. *"Alice in Wonderland and* the *World Trade Center Disaster - Why the Official Story Of 9/11 is a Monumental Lie,"* (published in 2002) on page 365 he writes:

> *Beam weapons?*
>
> *It is possible that charges were placed in the buildings at crucial points and exploded by remote control, but we should remember that the illuminati are not - working only with the technology we see in the public domain. They have access to their secret science, and the development of weapons and other technology that is far in advance of anything we see. One example is the energy-particle or "beam" weapon that fires an invisible laser or sound*

> *wave so powerful it can turn a building to dust. It has been noted by a number of observers that debris was turning to dust as it fell through the air and not only when it struck the ground. The television evangelist Dr Robert Schuller said after visiting the site that there "was not a single block of concrete in that rubble" Some 425,000 cubic yards of concrete disintegrated, most of it into immense clouds of dust."*

This is much closer to what actually happened - although somewhat inaccurate. Crucially, Icke does not point out that steel and other materials turned to dust, not just the concrete that he mentions. On page 366-7, Icke continues:

> *An eyewitness to the collapse told the American Free Press that as he stood two blocks from the World Trade Center he had seen "a number of brief light sources being emitted from inside the building between floors 10 and 15". He saw about six of these brief flashes, accompanied by a "crackling sound" immediately before the tower collapsed. This may or may not be relevant. …The American Free Press interviewed a German physicist who believes a laser beam weapon could have caused the collapse of the twin towers using infrared technology that was first developed in the Soviet Union. The physicist, whom the American Free Press does not name, was described as a former East German physicist who studied Soviet infrared technology and plasmoids during the 1960s and 1970s, and was directly involved in the demonstration of a Soviet laser beam weapon for the US Air Force in Weimar in 1991. He was quoted as saying there is evidence that a directed-energy weapon using "deep infrared" radiation was used to bringdown— the World-Trade Center …*

> *He said that in 1991 the GRU demonstrated for the US Air Force Electronic Security Command (AFESC) the capabilities of its infrared beam weapon by reducing a ceramic plate to dust from a distance of one mile. He said the demonstration was designed to show the US "how a stealth bomber could be turned into dust in the same way". The plate had been turned into such fine dust, he said, that it was difficult to pick up with a vacuum cleaner. "The plate was not destroyed suddenly as if hit by a bullet, rather it disintegrated in a process taking about 15 minutes." The physicist said that one of the transmitters involved in striking the World Trade Center with a beam weapon could have been located in a high building nearby or on a satellite, plane, or ship.*

So why did David Icke not make the connection to Dr Wood's research more thoroughly? Why did he "go backwards" in 2010?

For more than a year, David Icke's website was the only other site in the UK, apart from Richard D Hall's[133]**Error! Bookmark not defined.**, and my site to list the WDTTG book for sale - yet he has never spoken (in sufficient detail) of the evidence the book contains in any of his lengthy public presentations.

Instead, it appears he has "muddled together" the data about changes in the earth's magnetic field, discussed by Dr Wood in the WDTTG book, with readings from the "REGS" which are part of the "Global Consciousness Project." For an explanation of the Global Consciousness Project 9/11 data, please see the article on their website "Formal Analysis, September 11

2001[353]." Also, a short news item in a YouTube video "Prediction of September 9/11" gives a good summary of the project[354].

In an interview on Alchemy Radio, dated 9 September 2013[355], approximately 21 minutes into the discussion Icke says:

> *In terms of meditation and coming together where consciousness connects across the world, you've only got to look at the graphs of what happened on 9/11 when... there is technology around the world that is measuring changes in the earth's energy field - the earth's magnetic field and at the time that 9/11 was happening and that global focus of attention - ... energy flows where attention goes there was this enormous spike in the earth's energetic field - in terms of something impacting upon it - and that was caused by the global attention - negative in this sense, shocking in this sense - emotional shock - that was actually focused on that time when the world was to becoming aware that 9/11 was unfolding...*

David Icke's "backward motion" on the truth about what happened on 9/11 seems to have continued, judging by what he said in an interview with his close associate Richie Allan on 21 Nov 2015[356]:

> *We've got to say okay, we agree this is happening, we might not agree on the depths of the rabbit hole from which it is happening and that "Icke seems to be a bit far out... In some of what he says." But let's come together on what we agree on. Which is I mean for instance... 9/11 all we need to agree on about 9/11 is that it was created on purpose to provide the excuse for what has followed. THAT'S ALL WE NEED TO AGREE ON. We don't need to agree on whether this substance brought the towers down or these energy weapons – that might be interesting, but we don't need to agree on that – we don't need to argue over it we don't need to come into conflict over it – like children. All we need to agree on is the obvious - 9/11 was created as an excuse for all that followed. Okay? Got there let's move on.*
>
> *And again seeing the picture and not getting caught in the dots and the bubbles because 9/11, Richie, in the alternative media has become for many people - a bubble - arguing about whether it's an energy weapon or whether it's this bloody substance which brought the towers down, whether the planes were this or whether it was a bloody holographic... all this stuff.. It's interesting but it doesn't matter what matters is that it was done as an excuse for what followed*

In his monologue, David Icke casts aside over 7 years of research into the events of 9/11 by a qualified scientist – summarised in a book which *he used to sell*. He fails to see the importance of the recognition of weaponised free energy technology and how the military industrial complex connects into the "bigger picture" of which he himself speaks. Of course, having listened to David's scientific expertise here, I must agree with him that people like me are just "childish..."

The People's Voice

In 2013, there was some excitement regarding a new initiative that David Icke was involved with - "The People's Voice" (TPV) - a web TV "channel." This crowd-funded project raised £300,000, but ended a few months later, after a period of considerable acrimony and back-biting. I don't think David Icke was solely to blame for this – I do think the project was derailed, though Icke's reputation was not improved by what happened.

I mention "The People's Voice" because one of his first shows on this new channel was about 9/11. Can you guess who appeared on it? Richard Gage, Jim Fetzer and Kevin Barrett[357], whose names should be familiar to those who have read other articles in this volume and the previous one.

In chapter 20, I will discuss how I *didn't* get invited to appear on TPV's first show to speak about 9/11.

Perhaps David Icke was getting ahead of the script on 9/11 research, back in 2002 and so he had to be reigned back in…? A further discussion of David Icke's research by Richard D Hall and myself can be found on the Richplanet Website[358].

20. Ken O'Keefe and Truth, Justice and Peace

In September 2016, alternative knowledge speaker and podcast host, Max Igan, posted an article about his "former friend" Ken O'Keefe (KO). Igan described his experience with KO and the proposed "World Citizen contract" initiative.[359] Igan also discusses this in an interview with Richie Allan, which was posted on 31 Aug 2016[360].

I have been unimpressed with KO since approximately December 2013, when he had failed to follow up on a commitment to discuss the truth about the destruction of the WTC on his short-lived "People's Voice" Programme entitled "Ken O'Keefe's Middle East[361]". I will explain the background to this below. It is just a shame that someone like KO - who seems to have taken an important and authoritative stance against the horrendous acts of violence, war crimes and occupation by western and Israeli armed forces in places such as Iraq, Afghanistan and Palestine - has now shown considerable dishonour. Many, many people have been cheering KO on in his strong, public, and fully justified stand against these evil groups of people.

How can it be, then, that Max Igan has now become convinced that KO is not who he first appeared to be and is, instead, a counter intelligence agent of some kind? Of course, if you read Max Igan's article, mentioned above and listen to his interview above, this will become very clear. (I also asked myself questions about KO, not too long after meeting him, but unlike Igan, I never expended any significant funds or energy supporting him.)

Ken O'Keefe – Awakened State – 11 May 2013

Both KO and myself were kindly invited to speak at the Awakened State Conference in Edinburgh in May 2013 – KO had filled in for Tony Farrell, who pulled out of the conference a few months before it was due to take place. Hence, this conference was where I first met KO and he sat through my presentation about the energy cover up, and how it links in to what happened to the WTC[362].

His talk, entitled "War of Terror: Iran, Palestine, Syria, False Flags and Banksters" was given on the same day as mine[363].

At some point over the weekend of the conference, I told him that I was aware that he had appeared on Press TV with Jim Fetzer and Kevin Barrett and that he should be wary of these characters, as I had documented their part in the criminal cover up of 9/11 events[110]**Error! Bookmark not defined.**. (Fetzer's role in the cover up is probably far more significant than Barrett's, however.)

Following the conference, we both travelled back down South and I spent over one hour with Ken O Keefe explaining personally to him, face to face (during the train journey) that the 9/11 thermite story was bogus. On my laptop, I showed him a PowerPoint presentation about the destruction of the

WTC and I went over the main points – showing him the photos and video clips. He said, "I think I can see what you mean" (or words similar to this). I gave him a free copy of Dr Judy Wood's "Where Did the Towers Go[3Error! Bookmark not defined.]" which proves the thermite story is false. When I gave him this tome, he seemed deeply appreciative, even bowing his head and seeming genuinely moved by this.

On 4th November 2013, we talked on Skype and, if you listen to an extract from this conversation, it seems he "got" what was in the book – and why it was so important[364]. He said to me:

> *I've started reading Judy's book and I've watched some videos and what not and I'm convinced. In fact, I have to say, I'm planning … admitting my own… wow even I was manipulated as well, because how did I not see this sooner… clearly the lack of debris… I had been meaning to look at Dr Judy's stuff, but I hadn't done it and who knows how much longer it would have been. But… it's obvious… it's clearly obvious… What I've come to love about Judy's position is that while it reveals this incredibly destructive technology, the flipside, as she makes very clear is that, this technology could be used in the most constructive of ways and literally liberate us on a massive scale. So this is the proverbial silver lining in the dark cloud, if we choose to see it… For me, this is where… one of the issues we need to confront… the very serious issue of all the infighting and the politics and the bullshit where we sit and argue over details and while I'm willing to accept that people are convinced that it's thermite and so on and so forth, I don't think it's so important as it is for people to see the truth about this issue.*

I really thought he "got it" – he even talked about the "silver lining" of free energy, which few people talk about.

He therefore invited me onto his first "Middle East" programme planned later in Nov 2013 and I agreed to go down to London on 24th November - but he never followed up with his invitation. Indeed, the last I heard from him then was when he was asking a question[365] about the Dr Greg Jenkins / Dr Judy Wood Ambush Interview[366].

Ken O'Keefe Promotes 9/11 Disinformation

A few months later, it became clear, however, that KO had decided to help to promote disinformation about 9/11. On a "9/11 Special" programme he did, neither Dr Wood nor myself were invited to discuss the evidence - and he did not mention her investigation and court case[121Error! Bookmark not defined.]. Instead, he allowed Chris Bollyn to lie about what happened to the WTC and what Dr Wood has said. I explained, in detail, to KO that the thermite story was a lie and in his Skype call to me, linked above, he seemed to understand this. So, then, it was now on record that Ken O'Keefe had not chosen the path of truth with regard to what happened on 9/11. In KO's 9/11 Special, Chris Bollyn gets quite a lot of time and talks about thermite[367].

I mention Bollyn because he is also part of the 9/11 cover up and has chosen to lie about Dr Wood's research[368]. Again, Bollyn has not taken evidence to court and he just repeats the Jones/Gage/AE911 talking points. Why is Bollyn lying about someone else's research, if he claims to be interested in the truth about 9/11? Why did KO give this liar air time? I explained all this to him and he agreed it was "a good investment of time."

Now, as KO discusses, there is evidence that Zionists played their part in orchestrating and covering up what happened on 9/11 - and it seems there are other powerful vested interests, connected with the Israeli and US/Israeli power structures that have their dirty fingerprints all over the 9/11 planning and its cover up. However, to miss out everything I told him - and instead include disinformation that I had already pointed out to him – was a huge disappointment to me, as I took him to be an honourable man.

In September 2015, I posted some of these remarks on a thread on Facebook[369] and KO replied to my comments – with some apparent humility. He argued that he had given Bollyn airtime because Bollyn was willing to talk about Mossad and 9/11. So why did he *also* include the 9/11 disinformation that Bollyn was coming out with? He could have just edited that out, and contacted me to discuss other aspects of 9/11. (After all, we'd already agreed he could/would do that.)

So, I commented to KO, on Facebook.

> *Ken -- I respect what you are trying to do. However, you wrote "you are feeding the very problem that is among our deepest of problems" - and I could say exactly the same to you - because you helped promote false information about 9/11. We know it is false scientifically and we also know it is false based on the actions (or lack thereof) of those promoting it. The reason I didn't reach out to you was because I thought you understood what I was trying to tell you. I thought you understood the scientific evidence and also about what people like Fetzer and Barrett were doing - muddling up the vastly important truth of what happened to the towers - the MOST important issue of our time - because it affects geopolitics, energy, the weather and all issues connected with those things. Of course, what I hope people will do is say "Oops - sorry I was wrong - and I can now see this." But unfortunately, most people "go along to get along" - because "that's politics". Myself and Dr Wood are not politicians and only concern ourselves with the evidence of what happened (I won't bother to address what you said about Dr Judy Wood as it's not relevant to the evidence I showed you in May 2013). I have also reverse engineered the cover up of 9/11 - and it's all in my free book. The fact that many people don't like what is in our books (or they don't like our personalities or the way we speak) doesn't make it untrue and it doesn't in any way reduce the importance of those truths. I hope you can understand this. Best Wishes, I hope you are successful in exposing the things you are working on - but be aware there are scoundrels around you try to convince you some things are not known or are not that important.*

I subsequently offered to do an interview with KO, so that we could "straighten it all out." We could then have talked to each other about the parts of 9/11 which interest us – and record it as an interview. I even offered to set it up and record it and edit it - at my own expense. I said I would seek his approval before posting it online. I also offered to buy him some lunch! He seemed to be amenable to this at first, but then backed out of the idea saying, "I cannot work with you."[370]

Former US Marine(s)

When Max Igan posted his comments, and I had read through his article, I was reminded that KO had apparently been a US Marine. Now that Max Igan had revealed evidence that he and others had been misled by KO, it reminded me how another former US Marine – Jim Fetzer – had misled me[371] – and many others, a few years ago. Fetzer has continued to mislead people ever since[372].)

A similar scenario unfolded with a man called Pete Santilli – who, became an "uber supporter" of Dr Judy Wood[373] and her research for several months. He heavily promoted the WDTTG book on his "Guerrilla Media Network" and I recorded an interview with him on more than one occasion.[374] Santilli got involved in various squabbles and even recorded and posted a conversation with another character called Gordon Duff where Duff admitted that Dr Wood was correct and disinformation had to be circulated[375]. Santilli even had an interview with Jim Fetzer which had Fetzer "effing and blinding" when Santilli grilled him[376]. Later, however, Santilli was caught up in the long running protest/stand-off at Bundy Ranch and allegations of him being an FBI informant began to circulate[377]. I don't know what the truth is about Pete Santilli, but he certainly "started a lot of fights" and the muck that got spattered around then had the potential to become attached to Dr Judy Wood and myself, perhaps. I mention all this because Pete Santilli was… a US Marine.

I then began to wonder what connection there might be to experiences disclosed almost 20 years ago by Kay Griggs – former wife of a US General[378]. Kay Griggs, who had terrible and violent experiences at the hands of her husband, was also treated badly by one or more US Marines that she knew.

Conclusions

Max Igan has come to a similar conclusion to myself in that KO is not being honest in his dealings with others. Igan raises additional important questions about exactly how KO has been able to travel freely around the world when people of less importance are on a "no fly" list. I feel sorry for Max that he trusted KO as much as he did. The result is yet another explosion of angst and ill-feeling and negative energy between prominent figures in the "truth" movement (for want of a better term) – all part of a successful and often imperceptible plan to "divide and rule" those that stand against the evil powers that control the world.

21. David Shayler, Annie Machon and The UK 9/11 Truth Movement 2005 – 2009
November 2017

In this chapter, I discuss, some of the activities of the UK 9/11 truth movement, which I became involved with in mid-2005. What's left of the UK 9/11 Truth Movement can mainly be found on the UK 9/11 Truth Forum[379]. This forum is now run by Tony Gosling (who runs www.bilderberg.org and has been featured on RT[380]). Jim Robinson and I helped Simon Aronowitz and others set up this forum in June and July 2005. A number of other UK 9/11 truth-related websites were in existence between about 2005 and 2010, with a number of local UK 9/11 groups (e.g. West Yorkshire, Bristol, Lewes and London.)

In parts of this chapter, I will be relating some of my personal experiences, which you will only have my word for. I don't have recordings or transcripts of the conversations themselves (which is what I have generally referenced everywhere else in this book.) You can therefore decide for yourself whether what I am saying is true.

Early Days - 2004

The beginnings of the UK campaign were probably in January 2004. Ian Neal had asked for a meeting with Simon Aronowitz, Nafeez Ahmed and Ian Henshall following Ian Neal becoming aware of Ian Henshall's website (http://www.911dossier.co.uk/). Several concerned individuals in London had meetings about the problems with the Official Story (termed "Official Conspiracy Theory" – OCT) of 9/11. Among this group were Ian Neal and Noel Glynn. (I think they had been involved with the "Stop the War" group/campaign.)

Ian Crane who had (somehow) been designated Chairman of the British 9/11 Truth Campaign, had been researching problems with the Official Story since 2002.

Justin Walker (a former Green Party Member) had also been working more in the "political paradigm" and, with Simon Aronowitz and others, he delivered a deposition to Tony Blair's house in Sedgefield in 2005.

Following a generous donation by Jimmy Walter, 17,000 copies of Walter's DVD presentation "Confronting the Evidence" were distributed to houses in the area.

The "Jimmy Walter Roadshow" – May/June 2005

With the Friends' Meeting House in Euston only about 1/3 filled, many of the campaigners mentioned above – and a good few others met for the 1st time as we listened to and watched Jimmy Walter, William Rodriguez (allegedly the last man to be pulled alive from the WTC rubble), Chris Bollyn (who is currently a died-in-the wool "thermite sniffer"), Thierry Meyssan and Eric Hufschmid. The event was introduced by Ian Henshall (more on Henshall later). There was also a well-attended evening of movies in the Prince Charles Cinema off Leicester Square.

An identical event in Manchester drew a larger attendance of about 500 people. These events were essentially a "scaled down replay" of those that Jimmy organised in the USA. Jimmy then went on to deliver similar presentations in a number of European Cities.

UK 9/11 Internet Forum and Tony Gosling

My involvement with the UK 9/11 forum lasted just over 2 years. On 12 Sep 2007, I resigned from moderating[381] the forum, though I continued to make occasional postings until 2011.

The main reason I resigned was because of the actions of Tony Gosling himself, who began editing and moving posts without my permission and he broke the moderation policy that we had loosely agreed.

I became unhappy with the number of anonymous posters who hardly revealed, anything about themselves and when asked, they often simply suggested they shouldn't be being asked. Their style of posting never really added much if anything to the debate and is typically framed in a sarcastic manner. Most of these posters used handles and a few used what appeared to be real names.

I was particularly surprised when I posted the news about the unsealing of Dr Morgan Reynolds Qui Tam suit against NIST (for fraud) when it was moved to the "Controversial" section[382] – then Tony Gosling said he would move the post back if I convinced enough people that Morgan Reynolds' analysis was valid! (How, exactly, would Tony judge the success of this? Would the almighty Tony Gosling have set up a poll and decided on a reasonable percentage of "people convinced" before he deigned to move my post back again? What gave Tony such authority? For example, what advanced degrees did he have, like Profs Wood and Reynolds?) The irony then became that as of 11 September 2007, the press release I wrote about the legal actions of Prof Judy Wood and Prof Morgan Reynolds made the Front Page of the now-defunct "Shoutwire" news service[383].

Another problem was the constant "trolling" on this forum – this can still (in Nov 2017) be observed on the thread I referenced above, about Dr Morgan Reynolds' Qui Tam case.

There were several other people who were quite active on threads discussing Dr Judy Wood's research – wanting to "shoot it down" in some way. They were John White, Calum Douglas (using a handle of "SnowyGrouch"), Andy Baker and "Stefan" (whose surname I cannot remember). Numerous other anonymous "trolls" also seemed devoted to the ways of ridicule, insult and derision.

Another person I was particularly disappointed with was Ian Neal, whom I counted as a friend. In a posting he made on 16 July 2009[384], he stated:

> *Secondly Judy Woods is a really bad public presenter of science. I've watched her DVD presentations and I guarantee that a vast majority of her academic peers would agree with me that the way she presents her arguments in a lecture format is very poor indeed (and that's being kind).*

I asked Ian Neal how he could *guarantee* this. Had he collected e-mail responses from a questionnaire sent to "Judy Wood's" peers?

I would therefore characterise Ian Neal's statement as a lie. This is because he can make no such guarantee. (You can see further responses on the thread referenced above, but it all becomes rather tiresome.) I have, time and again, discussed how statements like this do not actually analyse what happened on 9/11 – and rather they shift the reader's attention onto "Judy Wood." Making negative remarks like this does not address the truth of what happened, or how to convey that truth more effectively.

Following my "departure" from the UK 9/11 forum, I set up another forum at www.uk911.info, although this never became particularly active or useful. I tried to make the forum more "troll-resistant" by asking people to use their real names, but it became too time-consuming to try and establish the motives of people who wanted to post things. By that time, I had started to write articles about the cover up – which eventually became the *9/11 Finding the Truth* book. I had also begun to help out with Drs Reynolds and Wood's Qui Tam documentation.

David Shayler and Annie Machon

Two other more well-known people that got involved in the UK 9/11 Truth Movement were David Shayler and Annie Machon. As I write this chapter in November 2017, they are still active in the "truth seeking"/alternative knowledge scene.

In 1997, David Shayler became famous in the UK[385] following him blowing the whistle when he was working for MI5. He received nationwide media attention for an extended period when he stated, during conversations in MI5, he had discovered a plot in MI6 to kill the then Libyan Leader Colonel Gaddafi[386]. Shayler was charged with breaking the Official Secrets Act. After this, he and Annie Machon went "on the run" from the UK, but Shayler was arrested in France in 1998. He eventually made a staged return to the UK[387] and was arrested and then he served a short prison sentence.

This was all written up in their book Spies, Lies and Whistleblowers: MI5, MI6 and the Shayler Affair[388].

It seems that there was indeed a plot to kill Gaddafi – but maybe it could never be linked to MI6, I don't know. What I do know is that Gadaffi was killed in October 2011[389]. Some people suggest this was because Libya had a banking system which was not fully controlled by the global banking cartel and so the regime in power had to be toppled so that this could be changed. (Indeed, you can read quite a number of books and articles which strongly suggest that this is often the reason for regime change – i.e. to take control of their banking system, as well as any resources etc[390]).

During meetings in either 2004 or early 2005, David Shayler and Annie Machon came into contact with members of the then embryonic London 9/11 Truth Group and soon after, started to speak publicly about 9/11 Truth issues. Rather abruptly, David's involvement as a speaker for the *Stop the War Coalition* came to an end – they refused to give him a platform (despite the evidence) to talk about 9/11 Truth.

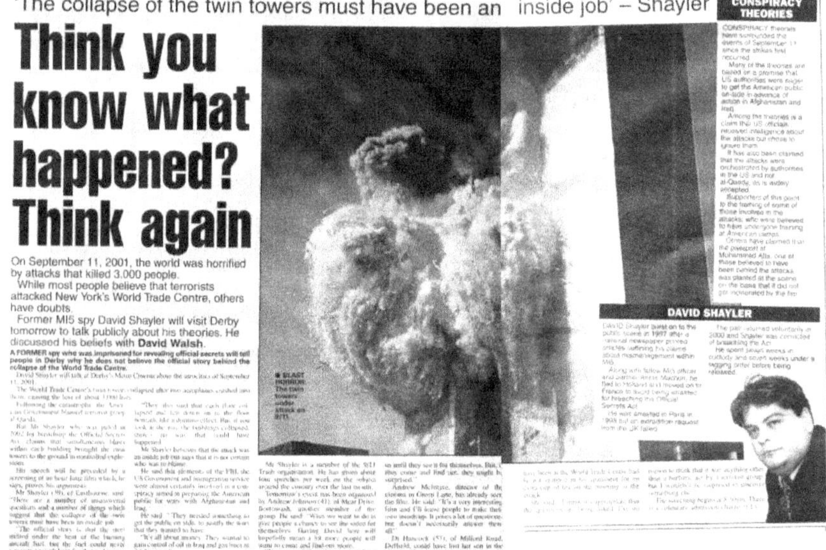

In late 2005, I got in touch with them and invited them to speak at an event I organised in Derby at the now-defunct Metro Cinema, where I showed the original "Loose Change" film and David and Annie made short presentations. About 130 people attended this presentation. (I also organised a venue in Nottingham for them to speak at, but had little chance to publicise this and so no one attended.)

After the event, they stayed at my house and I got time to speak to them. We seemed to get on very well. I paid their travel expenses, mainly out of my own pocket (I received some donations at the event).

In October 2006, I actually went to meet one-time cabinet minister Michael Meacher, (who had publicly expressed scepticism about the official narrative of 9/11)[391] in his Oldham Constituency – I was accompanied by Annie Machon and Justin Walker. I presented Meacher with a 200-page document summarising our activities as a group for the 2005-2006 period. Nothing obvious came of this meeting, though there were apparently several MPs who Meacher had spoken to who were also sceptical of the official 9/11 narrative and I remember, at one point, there being talk of a showing of the Loose Change film to a group of MPs in London.

William Rodriguez – "Last Man Out" Tour – February 2007

William Rodriguez had claimed, since at least 2005, that he was the "last man out" of the World Trade Centre on 9/11 and he was almost killed. You can read about his story online and watch videos of his presentations. He had spoken at many venues in the UK and Europe and had, for some time, toured with Jimmy Walter (as mentioned above). It is interesting to note that Rodriguez "split" from Walter[392] when Walter started to take the "No Planes" at the WTC issue seriously[393].

As part of his "Last Man Out" tour in February 2007, he stayed at my house when he was accompanied by Annie Machon. I organised two venues for them – to speak at - one in Spondon, Derbyshire (The Asterdale Club) and another at the Carrs Lane Church Centre in central Birmingham. The events took place on Friday 16th and Saturday 17th Feb 2007.

Also, on the Friday, I took Rodriguez for an interview on BBC Radio Derby with Shane O'Connor. O'Connor barely spoke to me but he had done his research on Rodriguez – and noted in conversation that Rodriguez had worked at one time with debunker Magician James Randi. I did not know this at the time, but Rodriguez verbally confirmed that this was true.

During the evening, at my house, I was also quite surprised at how well he was able to operate his laptop, connect to my wireless network and talk to his partner on Skype. I am quite familiar with how people who are confident with laptops, wi-fi and so forth are able to work with devices, compared to those that are not confident. My intuitive reaction was "this man is not just a janitor."

On the morning of Saturday 17th Feb 2007, we went to BBC Radio Birmingham (see photo). Whilst we were waiting at a coffee shop just outside, he was chatting and saying that he thought "the story of 9/11 was like the story of Jesus" and that "Annie Machon was like Mary Magdalene." He suggested that two other guys who were with us (Anthony Beckett and another chap called John who was making a film about Rodriguez) could be "the apostles" and then he said, "who can be Judas?" And he said "Morgan Reynolds can be Judas." Of course, you only have my word for this part - as I don't have a recording. I thought this was most peculiar as Morgan Reynolds was in the process of setting up a court cases against NIST contractors, for their part in committing a fraud in relation to their 9/11 technical reports.

I have archived the interview he did with Janice Long on 17 February 2007[394] (although I used the wrong date of the 18th of February on the filename).

I became more suspicious of Rodriguez when I heard a portion of his interview on Simon Mayo's popular Radio 5 Live program on 23 Feb 2007 (probably heard by over 1 million people in the UK)[395], when he said

> *…I agree that a lot of the conspiracies are wrong – I am not contending that. Remember, the idea here is to dispel… many people have come out and said there were no planes hitting the buildings – which is ridiculous because we have actually gone with cameras to interview people in the ground zero area and they have come along [and said], "We saw the planes, we saw the parts." Some people say that there were holograms to superimpose these on televisions. Other people say it was CGI other people came out and say… Morgan Reynolds for example and Judy Woods which were people that worked with the Bush Administration say that it was weaponry of exotic kind… that they have some kind of infra-red satellite … they have this technology that will bring the towers down. So, ye know… ridiculous thing after ridiculous thing.*

Only two people are named in this clip. These were the same two people I had begun to communicate with extensively around that time.

Though I cannot say I trust everything Nico Haupt came out with, he did seem to collect some useful information about Rodriguez on a forum posting on the now defunct 911researchers.com[396].

After his stay with us, Rodriguez never thanked me or my wife for putting him up and organising an event for him to speak at.

Look who Rodriguez likes to be seen with:

Willy Gump…?

Belinda McKenzie, David Shayler and Annie Machon

I got to know Belinda McKenzie in 2004 due to her support of Lloyd Pye and the Starchild skull[397]. In late 2004 or early 2005, it was probably me that first showed her a video about the disappearance of the towers (I was still calling it "freefall collapse" then, however).

She then supported Jimmy Walter when he came to London (with his "Confronting the Evidence" tour) and Belinda stored quite a few boxes of David Ray Griffin books in her lock up garage in Highgate. Three years later, I had realised Dr Judy Wood's research explained what happened to the WTC, but Belinda didn't quite seem to "get it".

If I had ever felt the need to directly ask for support in matters relating to the dissemination of 9/11 truth, Belinda McKenzie would have been one person I thought I could count on.

However, following the William Rodriguez tour in February 2007, I had a telephone conversation with Belinda in which I discussed a peculiar incident that happened between Annie Machon and Rodriguez. The nature of this incident caused me to be concerned that neither Rodriguez nor Machon were being totally honest and they lacked integrity. I discussed the details of this with Belinda and Belinda only. This was because, at the time, Annie was a lodger at Belinda's house. (Annie and David Shayler lived in Belinda's house for several months.) Shortly thereafter, Annie Machon was sending round an email to a list of about 10 people claiming that, though I was "reliable" in relation to dealings with her regarding 9/11 truth issues, I had been "spreading rumours about her." Note, Annie Machon did not privately address me in email, she included several other people in the list of recipients. So it was *she* that spread the rumour! I simply had a private telephone conversation with Belinda, expressing my concern! In other words, Annie

Machon attempted to smear me for "making up stories about her." However, I had a witness to the incident and so her attempts failed.

After a direct request from me, it was Annie Machon who refused to discuss Dr Wood's Qui Tam case in 2007 and 2008 – because she thought it was "speculation." Annie Machon is part of the cover up crew.

Shayler Talks "No Planes" and becomes the New Messiah

In August 2006, David Shayler appeared on Sky News and discussed details of why the official narratives of both 9/11 and 7/7 could not be true[398]. He talked about the lack of plane crash investigations on 9/11 as well as the (disinformation) evidence for controlled demolition of the buildings (I can forgive him for that, as I was still talking about the same things then.) Perhaps David Shayler had gone too far and, like David Icke in 2002, was "getting ahead of the script." Only a year after this Sky News broadcast, he was again in the news, claiming that he was "The New Messiah[399]." Again, this seems very similar to what happened to David Icke in 1991.

In an article in the Daily Mail in August 2007, Annie Machon stated[400]

> *He was in trouble. He was quick to anger if anyone questioned him. He became obsessive about little details, espoused wacky theories and shunned his family and old friends. His paranoia also escalated.*

Shayler and Machon separated around the same time.

In 2009, Shayler was reported to have adopted an alter ego, which involved him dressing as a woman and calling himself Delores[401]. David Shayler was no longer a problem for the establishment.

Belinda Hosts Fetzer

My trust in Belinda McKenzie essentially dropped to zero in 2010, when I was visiting Lloyd Pye again. He was staying at Belinda's while doing a few more talks. During my visit, who should I find staying in her house? Jim Fetzer and Kevin Barrett! (I'd told her repeatedly what they were up to - but she didn't seem that interested in what I had to say about them being part of the 9/11 cover up crew.) Please see the first volume of my book for more information about Jim Fetzer's "antics."

Belinda even attended a talk in London in 2012 (or perhaps 2011) by someone called Tracy Blevins (and she herself is yet another story) who was talking about Dr Wood's research. This talk was not widely advertised, I found out about it by accident. I mention this because Tracy Blevins had come over from the USA. Why didn't the group that organised the talk invite Dr Wood – or even myself - to talk about her research? This, in itself, is not the main issue – what was weird was to me was that Belinda had not contacted me at all about this event – for example, to obtain copies of Dr Wood's book *Where*

Did the Towers Go? (which was, apparently, the subject of Tracy Blevins' presentation.)

This is a rather long-winded way of saying that Belinda has, for me, failed the "9/11 litmus test." There are other factors, too, which made me conclude she was not totally "on the level" and she was either being manipulated, or she was choosing to ignore important things and thereby help the cover up crew.

Ian R Crane

It was in 2005 that I first encountered Ian R Crane in the UK 9/11 Truth Campaign, when he was said to be its chairman. Since then he has talked about the events of 9/11 in many of his public presentations. However, he has never, to my knowledge discussed the WDTTG book. In chapter 12, I already covered how Crane said there was "no explanation" for the WTC towers turning to dust. He avoids this topic.

In 2009, I was asked to give a presentation in the South of England, on the subject of "Chemtrails" (see *Climate Change and Global Warming: Exposed*) and I was happy to accept the invitation. I spent two nights in the area where the presentation was and enjoyed a very warm welcome and great hospitality. In conversation with one of the people (I will call him John) who had helped to organise the presentation, Ian Crane's name came up. John explained that he had approached Ian Crane to "sound him out" about being a speaker at a possible conference he was organising. John also mentioned the subject of 9/11 in relation to the conference. Ian Crane offered John some advice about organising the conference and then asked who else John was thinking of inviting to the conference. John replied to Ian Crane that he was thinking of inviting me. At this point, Ian crane said to John that he "wouldn't share a platform with Andrew Johnson on the subject of 9/11."

For the record, I would be quite happy to share a platform with Ian Crane and talk about 9/11 because I know that what I have been telling people in this book - and in my presentations - is true. Not only that, but I am happy to receive corrections or augmentations from anyone who has verifiable evidence to add to what I have talked about. I would be able to discuss anything Ian Crane didn't understand in relation to the truth. I was later to realise that Ian Crane probably wasn't interested in the truth about how the WTC was destroyed...

On 12 December 2009, Crane and myself, along with Tony Gosling and Brian Gerrish spoke at "The Wake Up Call" conference in Kirkcaldy Fife[402]. We were all staying at the same hotel (with some extremely noisy people in the room next to mine, as I recall). While we were sat in the hotel lounge/bar area, there were a couple of people, one of whom was Adrian Connock. I think it was Adrian who mentioned something about Tony Gosling's UK 9/11 forum activities and the "episode" where I had resigned from it, because Gosling had edited and moved posts. Ian Crane asked what we were talking about (as he had not been very active on the UK 9/11 forum at the time I resigned, though he posted fairly regularly during the 2005 – 2006 period, I recall). I explained to Ian Crane about Gosling's soft-censorship of my post about the Wood/Reynolds' Qui Tam cases (discussed earlier in this chapter). Ian Crane said *"Well, to be honest, I would have done the same…"* So, it seemed Ian Crane agreed with the soft-censorship Gosling had enacted. I therefore asked Ian Crane if, in his talks and presentations, he was presenting evidence to people to show them that what he was saying was true. I pointed out to him that this was exactly what Wood and Reynolds were doing – except that they had prepared the evidence to go to a court – where they could be subject to cross-examination and possible prosecution if they were found to be being frivolous or deceptive. To my surprise – dismay even – Ian Crane responded, *"You're pissing in the wind."*

At this point we can perhaps consider that Ian Crane used to work for Schlumberger – an Oil Industry service/consultancy company. Is this why he never talks about the obvious-once-studied connection between the events of 9/11 and the free energy cover up?

Conclusions

From my experience, then, the cover up of what really happened on 9/11 is operated on a global scale – with speakers and researchers in the UK working to insert doubt, mislead and misdirect other people – in just the same way as I documented in *9/11 Finding the Truth*. We will examine other UK-based cover-up activities in Chapter 23.

22. Honouring the Real Truth of Ground Zero

By Keith Mothersson

Keith Mothersson was the Scottish representative of the Muslim, Jewish, Christian Alliance for 9/11 Truth. He was a well-known Peace Activist. He died under somewhat mysterious circumstances[403] on 3rd July 2009[404].

I had the pleasure of meeting Keith on 1 or 2 occasions and he was one of the few in the UK that understood the truth of what happened to the WTC. This article is a slightly edited (to smooth out wording and punctuation errors) version of what was originally posted on Op Ed News[405] 20th Feb 2008. Keith also gave me permission to post it on my website.

Keith Mothersson in September 2006

September 11th, 2001 was so shocking that most people didn't notice how the Manhattan murders were instantly framed as an 'attack on America', i.e. something from outside requiring a military response, not good domestic policework occasionally bolstered by fake 'Bin Laden' videotapes and occasional show trials based on 'confessions' extracted under torture.

However, thanks to the 9/11 truth movement, more and more people have wised up to another sort of 'framing' that day as well; the framing up of Muslims from Oil-land as so-called 'hijackers', *despite a complete lack of evidence* (except from entirely unreliable sources) "Ye who are conscious of God - If a fasiq comes with alarming news, make sure to verify their word, lest you afflict people out of your ignorance, and regret your action." Holy Qur'an, Surah 49:6)

In October 2006, a CBS/New York Times poll found that only 16 percent of Americans continue to believe that their government has told the truth.

Unfortunately, the mainstream media blockade continues, so the official mythology is just about holding up.

Avoiding the swamp of 'fasiq' allegations about a supposed entity called 'Al-Qaeda', most 9/11 truth activists have increasingly homed in on unarguable physical phenomena from the day in question, such as the absence of any plane-sized hole at the Pentagon.

Of all the 9/11 events, few have spoken more powerfully than the neat 'collapse' (controlled demolition) in free-fall time of the 47-storey steel-framed World Trade Centre Building 7 at 5.20 in the afternoon.

If one, why not the twin towers too? They were also destroyed in the time equivalent to that which the top floor of these towers would have taken to reach the ground if they had been falling through air, and not through 109 other stories of steel-framed building!

For those whose heads begin to swim, at this point, let me just add: None of us need worry about our lack of degrees in Physics and Engineering! By the age of ten we had already figured out that apples dropped through a pile of apples would take longer to reach the floor than when dropped through air, likewise sticks through a pile of sticks, books through a pile of books, etc.

<u>So demolition it is then</u> - but ***have we looked carefully enough?***

After two years when most truth-activists accepted the Prof Steven Jones theory of the towers being demolished using thermate-enhanced military explosives, many of us are now realizing just how many weird physical phenomena can't be captured in Jones' hypothesis, not just in the towers but across the whole World Trade Centre site - and even up to seven blocks away!

Mechanical and materials engineer Dr Judy Wood has assembled an impressive website with extraordinary pictures of hundreds of

- 'toasted' or overturned cars
- huge vertical 'pastry cut-outs' which hollowed out Building 6
- beams shredding turning to jelly or with snakelike contortions
- 'meteorites' of fused steel and concrete
- flickering fires which didn't burn paper
- cold dust clouds, etc.

Many of these phenomena correlate closely with experimental effects created in directed energy experiments of Canadian inventor John Hutchison, whose work came to the attention of the Pentagon in the 1980s.

It has been shown in photographs Dr Wood has collected that the rubble pile from WTC 1 & 2 was very small - less than 3 stories high. A "cover story" says that the steel was all quickly shipped to China or Asia, but the pictures, taken before WTC 7 was destroyed, tell the truth. Videos, when examined closely, show steel and concrete from the towers turning to dust as the material fell. What technology can do that?

It looks so obvious now, but it seems that for six years we were so *spell*-bound by the WHO and the WHY and the HOW of 9/11 that we have mostly omitted to begin with a close forensic examination of WHAT happened! The bulk of the material in the twin towers *turned to fine dust and was spewed out upwards*, which is why Dr Wood has launched a formidable legal case against the National Institutes for Science and Technology for fraudulently speaking of building 'collapse'.

One huge implication is that once people realise that the Military-industrial complex and Big Oil have been hiding such amazing energy technology in so-called "Black Projects", what pressure might not build for enforcing accountability over these and over those secret fraternities, so that innumerable secret or bought-up discoveries concerning ecological alternatives to petrol engines might be brought into play at this time of accelerating climate havoc?

And 9/11 is still happening! - Not only in the sense that we all, Muslims especially, suffer the psychological strain and physical oppression of the aftermath of this global coup. But also in another sense which Dr Judy Wood attributes to the *'non-self-quenching' nature* of 'Hutchison effect' type technology.

It seems that some switch was turned on at the deep molecular level which leads to continuing slow motion molecular dissociation in buildings 'infected' in 2001, such as the Bankers Trust building which after fruitless repairs is now being dismantled, supposedly because of a "mould infection". Photos from the site, however, indicate levels of rusting in the steel far beyond anything that is normal.

From Day One the sorcerers of 9/11 have been struggling to manage their wayward apprentice, with scores of huge trucks bringing in top soil in a vain attempt to quench this phenomenon. And still today they come and return at the end of the week to ship it all out again!

Now that we've noticed, how can they hide these trucks, and how on earth will they explain them?

Now that you've noticed, who will you tell? Or, to put it another way, as the masthead of Judy Wood's website proclaims: 'A time comes when silence is betrayal' (Martin Luther King).

23. "Re-Investigate 9/11" and the BBC TV Licence Fee (UK)

This chapter is derived from two articles posted in September 2012 and April 2013.

I first encountered Ian Henshall in May 2005, when he helped to host Jimmy Walter's "Confronting the Evidence" event at the Friends' meeting house in London (see Chapter 21). At some point he set up a website called Re Investigate 9/11 (the domain name http://reinvestigate911.org/ was registered on 29 July 2008).

If you explore this website you will, predictably, find no reference to the evidence showing what happened to the WTC. For example, there is no reference to Dr Wood's forensic study on the "Books" page of Henshall's website[406].

In 2012, I noted how Ian Henshall's "Re-investigate 9/11" Initiative had continued to ignore and censor scientific research that has been published for years. In an email he sent around to his email list on 08 September 2012, this short paragraph is especially noteworthy:

> *There has been no detailed explanation for the unprecedented collapse of three multistorey steel frame buildings, World Trade Centre 1, 2, and 7 at near free fall speed, landing neatly in their own footprints. Most of the planes' jet fuel was burnt off in the initial impacts and Building 7 was not even hit by a plane. The buildings were explicitly designed to withstand a high speed jet impact.*

Ian Henshall knows who I am and the area of research I have been involved with. For example, following an email he sent to me in September 2012, I responded noting that he never talks about Dr Wood's research or the WDTTG Book – or the 2007/2008 Qui Tam court case. He wrote back and accused me of "attacking him." In his response he stated:

> *Just in case you don't realise, you were personally the biggest single cause of the collapse of the 9/11 truth campaign in the UK.*

You can see further details of this email on my website[407].

Tony Rooke and the BBC TV Licence Fee

In April 2013, and on several occasions since then, a "fuss" was made about a supposed victory by a man called Tony Rooke when he refused to pay his TV Licence Fee. Ian Henshall (discussed above) was involved with this pointless and mis-reported effort.

A posting was made on Facebook and elsewhere[408] which claimed that Tony Rooke's case against the BBC was a victory. Tony Rooke had previously refused to pay his TV licence because he had stated that the BBC was engaged in the act of supporting terrorism. He therefore refused to pay his TV Licence Fee because of the Terrorism Act (2000) - Section 15 Fund-raising. I agree with Tony Rooke on this idea – but I wondered if Tony Rooke was really interested in what happened on 9/11 and wanted to know the real truth.

Just before Tony Rooke's court hearing, Ian Henshall sent a message on 23 Feb 2013 to his email list entitled "Tony's Plea to Activists." In this message, Ian Henshall wrote:

> *At least one mainstream media crew will be present but Tony is asking activists not to talk to them and **not to hold up placards which do not represent his views**. Please go to bottom to see his message in full.*
>
> *The message to the mainstream media is that Tony will be making a statement after the hearing and they should wait for that.*
>
> *Campaigners are concerned that the media will seek out and interview whoever they can find pedalling a radical 9/11 theory and use them to attempt to discredit months of hard work. This has been a common tactic, for instance from the BBC in their Conspiracy Files programmes. To prevent this happening, organisers intend to physically obstruct interviews with mainstream media outside the court if necessary.*
>
> *Activists attending the hearing are asked to make sure any signs represent the message of this campaign: that the BBC has covered up the truth on 9/11. Those with signs saying anything that would appear speculative to a general audience (eg 9/11 was an inside job) will be seen as undermining the court case and Tony's campaign.*

The message goes on to say

> *On the factual side Tony is most concerned to highlight the symmetrical collapse of WTC Building 7, a large portion of which fell at free fall speed and which was announced by the BBC some half hour before it happened.*

Whilst the BBC did indeed prematurely report on the destruction of WTC 7, Tony Rooke was not the first to bring it to the Public's attention - the BBC was! This was, apparently, in order to "debunk" the story in their 2008 "Third Tower" programme[409] - which was meant to be a "documentary"[410] - but of course was just another piece of establishment propaganda to protect the real perpetrators of 9/11.

Tony Rooke made a film about 9/11[411]. I am not sure I like the title of his website – "Killing Auntie Films." (Interestingly, the title of this film was

"Incontrovertible." I mention this because, unknown to most people at that time was another film that was being developed privately, by a single individual, which was released in 2015 – the film was called "Irrefutable" and is about the WDTTG book. Note the similarity of the titles.)

I wrote an email to Tony Rooke and cc'd Ian Henshall and other people who are apparently involved in Rooke's proposed film[412]. The only person that responded was Ian Henshall, who again claimed I had attacked him. This, of course, is untrue – I have questioned him on several occasions in a very similar manner to what is shown in the e-mail referenced above.

> *Just to place on record that I do not agree with Andrew's science at all although I presume he is sincere.*
>
> *Sadly Andrew was a hugely divisive figure in the old 9/11 truth group in the UK because he insisted we should all agree with his questionable space beam science when most of us thought we were trying to persuade the public that the official 9/11 story was wrong in the hope of stopping the wars.*
>
> *The quotes he cites from me are highly selective and taken from private correspondence which followed on of his periodic attacks on me.*

Tony Rooke never replied and apparently wasn't interested in presenting irrefutable evidence in his court case. He did, however, pose for a photograph that ended up being published in the UK's Daily Mail Newspaper[413]. Danish 9/11 thermite-sniffer Niels Harrit was apparently on-hand to give evidence in court.

Fan base: Around 100 supporters of Tony Rooke arrived at Horsham Magistrates' Court in West Sussex to watch the court case - although only 40 could pack into the public gallery

It's nicely posed – and quite a bit of time surely went into producing this banner! Who produced it? Whose idea was it to display it for the Daily Mail photographer?

Richard D Hall wrote to Tony Rooke[414] to ask who it was that was holding up a banner mentioning "thermite", proudly displayed for the Daily Mail. Rooke stated he had "no idea" who it was – and neither did Ian Henshall.

As regards Tony Rooke's case, Ian Henshall described it as a "moral victory" – my understanding of the verdict was that Rooke had to pay £200 costs[413]**Error! Bookmark not defined.**, and he was given a 'conditional discharge'. That means that - if Rooke still refuses to pay he could be prosecuted at a later date. (I don't necessarily agree with the whole TV licencing arrangements in the UK – but I expect to see things accurately reported by a site concerning itself with the truth of 9/11.) What apparently did NOT happen was that the BBC were in any way censured (i.e. "The actual object of the exercise") Apparently Rooke was not allowed to show his pre-prepared video evidence in court because the District Judge said it was not relevant to the trial – and Niels Harrit and other witnesses never spoke at the hearing/trial.

24. Media Propaganda Exercises

This chapter is derived from three articles written in August 2006, May 2011 and Apr 2012. I hope they give something of an insight into the way media propaganda is developed and promulgated.

"Don't take them seriously…"

In August 2006, Duncan Gardham, of the UK Daily Telegraph, telephoned me. This was probably because he had received an e- mail which I had sent as part of a "campaign."[415] The email represented a rejection of the fake airline "shampoo bombers" terrorism story which had been pushed by all mainstream media outlets earlier in the summer of 2006. (In relation to this false narrative, it was reported in 2010[416] that the jury could not convict because "At the end of a £10 million investigation and trial lasting more than two years, jurors were unable to decide whether or not a group of British Muslims were part of a plot to blow transatlantic airliners out of the sky.")

He asked why I was doubtful of the story. I told him some of the details I knew about 9/11 at that time – such as the destruction of WTC 7 and the general lack of any real evidence as a basis for the story. He asked me about details about myself. He asked "and your wife is a nurse, yes?" I confirmed that, asking him where he got this information "companies house" he said (I had a limited company at the time, through which I was doing Software Development work). I was puzzled by this as I don't think there was anything in my company records which documented my wife's profession. However, this proved that Gardham obviously had the facility to do research.

A day or two after this telephone call, an article was published in the Daily Telegraph with the title: "It's all a government plot, say internet 'truth activists'"[417]

When he published the article, he mentioned my Website, which I never even mentioned or discussed with him on the phone (I didn't even realise he knew it was my website, for example). He mentioned that my website "suggests men did not go to the moon". This statement is false. My website mentions the words of Neil Armstrong's 25th anniversary address at the Whitehouse (and includes a video clip of that address, so the evidence can be verified). He also lied when he reported that I had said "the London Tube bombers 'could have been going on a hiking trip in France'".

In other words, he wrote a hit piece and ignored the evidence I described to him personally - he didn't print Neil Armstrong's words either (which are also listed on a government website, linked on the same page of my website). This is the way the press work on issues of the greatest importance.

Below is the response I sent to Duncan Gardham, on the day the article was published.

From: Andrew Johnson < ad.johnson@ntlworld.com>

To: Duncan Gardham <Duncan .Gardham@telegraph.co.uk>

Date: 15 Aug 2006 - 8:44a.m.

Re:
http://www.telegraph.co.uk/news/main.jhtml?xml=/news/2006/08/15/nterror3 15.xml

Duncan,

Thanks for the article. I am glad you mentioned other people and the numbers of messages you received.

As regards what you wrote about me, it would've been fairer to include the words of Neil Armstrong from 1994 (not very long) and it would also have been fairer to include the words of Gordon Cooper, if you were determined to bring in such topics. You also omitted the "smoking gun" of WTC 7 that we did discuss.

I shall be advising my friends of these omissions, so that they know the balance of the article has been changed from what we discussed (i.e. we didn't discuss other items on my website, so I was not given the opportunity to highlight their importance and validity).

Thanks and regards

Andrew Johnson

Of course, there was no response from Mr Gardham and as with just about all mainstream "repeaters," he would never retract or correct what he said unless a court forced him to do so as punishment.

Jon Ronson - "A-Shilling for his Thoughts..."?

This UK journalist made several documentaries such as "The Crazy Rulers of the World[418]," about "conspiracy" topics. These programmes, in some places, have a sort of mocking tone, as I recall. Ronson has perhaps become most well-known for his (as far as I know) not-very authoritative book about the US Remote Viewing Program called "The Men Who Stare At Goats[419]." This was made into a film in 2009 (or maybe the book and the film were developed at the same time, I have not checked - and this is not important in relation to what is discussed below). In 1999, Ronson apparently managed to work his way into Bohemian Grove with Alex Jones - to film the "mock sacrifice to Moloch" ritual[420]. I suspect that Ronson is well-connected - and that the infiltration was not exactly "a surprise" to the elites in society who secretly frequent the Californian Campground.

My experience with Ronson was that he came onto our UK 911 forum in July 2006 and was insulted by many posters as a "Jewish shill" or something similar. (I have no idea, myself, if Ronson is Jewish - and his religious disposition, race and ethnicity are irrelevant to this section). However, I invited Ronson to discuss the 9/11 evidence, in the article he was preparing to write at that time.[421] My knowledge of what really happened on 9/11 started to change a few months after I made the post referenced above – as I became aware of Dr Judy Wood's research. (There are a massive number of trolls on the threads linked above – some of whom I met personally and took to be allies – but they turned out not to be). At first, I thought Ronson was genuinely interested in the truth, but like other journalists, this was not his real interest. He had his own agenda - to write a story - rather than discuss the truth.

On the forum thread, you can see Ronson agreed[422] that I was being "more reasonable" than other posters so I challenged him to discuss the actual evidence and he replied:

> *Andrew, I will contact you in the coming weeks. You are clearly among the sanest and easiest-to-talk-with people on this forum. I do find the rudeness and fundamentalism displayed by others on this forum to be terribly off-putting. You are doing your movement no service. And I mean that in the most constructive way possible.*

When I saw this post, I messaged him via his own website[423], giving him my contact details. He never replied. (In compiling this section, I notice that currently, Ronson's homepage, linked above, has a note at the bottom which reads "Site created and maintained for Jon Ronson by John Lundberg." This is noteworthy as Lundberg has been involved with the Circlemakers Group[424] - formerly known as "Team Satan" - who create Crop Formations by request.)

On 4 Nov 2006, almost 4 months after his "appearance" on the UK 911 forum, he published an article titled "We rationalists are the oppressed minority'" in the UK Guardian newspaper[425]. Feel free to read the whole article, but I will include a few brief quotes from it, to give you an idea of what he was doing.

> *"Ronson's strings are being pulled," somebody writes. "You can bet there is a Zionist agenda somewhere in what he does." Another poster adds that my Zionist overlords and I don't only control the media, we also control "the money supply" and "everything else as well". And it was us "Zionists" who orchestrated 9/11.*

> *I tell them to stop being anti-semitic….*

> *I stare out of the window a bit more. Then I have a very significant thought: "It is time for rational, sceptical people like me to get off the fence and make ourselves known. It is time for us to be publicly and assertively rational."…*

> *… Dawkins and I are the same. He's unshackled himself from any lily-livered residual respect for vicars. He doesn't buy the rose-tinted "country vicar*

coming round for tea" thing. He basically thinks vicars are no different to those 9/11 anti-semite lunatics. They're all part of the same problem.

The Guardian article mentioned precisely 0% of the evidence he was pointed at by some of the more identifiable forum members. Ronson did not contact me and, more importantly, did not mention a *single shred* of the 9/11 evidence. Instead, he made characterisations of a group of people and implicitly encouraged his readers to move to a position of "guilt by association," rather than giving them an opportunity to study the evidence. This is dishonest journalism at its worst. So perhaps the only truth in his article was that some of the accusations made against him were true. As far as I am aware, Ronson has never, to this day, written anything useful about what happened on 9/11. He's just one more reason that I no longer trust any mainstream media source.

Robert Fisk and "Society Matters"

At the time of writing this section, I have been a part time Associate Lecturer for the Open University (in IT subjects), since 2002 (see www.open.ac.uk, although it's unlikely you'll find me listed in the staff directory). No one in the University really knows about my research activities and website etc. However, back in August 2007, a short article I wrote about 911 was published in the Open University's Social Sciences (yearly) Faculty Magazine, thanks to the help of a contact. You can read it on page 5 of a PDF file on my website, [426]which is an archived version of the file that was available on the OU's own website until about 2017[427]. I also posted this article, entitled "9/11 and the War On Terror – Creating Official Reality"[428] on my own website.

Back in 2007, I was still talking about melting steel and "collapsing buildings" and in my article, I wrote:

Kerosene bums at about 820C under optimum conditions. The WTC towers collapsed in 8.1 and 10 seconds respectively – this is (essentially) at a rate of freefall i.e. they fell with no resistance – at all. For this to have happened, all 283 steel beams, which ran (in welded sections) from the top to the bottom of the building, would have to melt through or snap very suddenly. Unfortunately, for proponents of the official story, the melting point of steel is about 1480C so no kerosene or office-flotsam-and-jetsam based fire could have caused the steel to either melt or weaken to the point of collapse.

I concluded the article with the following remarks:

All readers are encouraged to check and study the information outlined here for themselves and draw their own conclusions. This may challenge many aspects of what you took to be true and it may make you ponder what former US Presidential Advisor, Karl Rove really meant when he said "We're an Empire now. We create our own reality."

My article of course mentions Dr Judy Wood and Dr Morgan Reynolds, thus:

The terms of reference for the production of the final NIST WTC report (NCSTAR 1) have now been the subject of a Legal Challenge by Professors Morgan Reynolds (Emeritus, Texas A & M University) and Professor of

Mechanical Engineering Judy Wood (formerly of Clemson University, South Carolina). Their challenge is made as a "Request for Correction" and they charge that, as it is framed, the NIST study of the WTC collapse will be fraudulent and deceptive.

(I was writing about these cases at the time - trying to draw serious attention to them, as I documented in "9/11 Finding the Truth.")

Curiously, a few days after Issue 10 of the OU's yearly Social Sciences Faculty Magazine was published, a well-known UK journalist named Robert Fisk[429] published an article in the UK's Independent Newspaper entitled "Even I question the 'truth' about 9/11."[430] In this article, Fisk reported that when he gives lectures, during the Q & A segments, "ravers" would often ask him why he doesn't tell the truth about 9/11 - that "the Bush administration blew up the WTC." Of course, there are several in-built assumptions and implicit problems here. For example, using the term "raver" implies that the person challenging Fisk to be more truthful is not an "average" person. (Fisk should simply have replaced this somewhat derogatory label with "some people" or "someone.") Also, he assumes that people who know the official narrative is untrue believe that the US government "blew up" the WTC with bombs - which is also not the case here.

Fisk, like myself, a graduate of Lancaster University, then goes on to note several "problems" with the official narrative of 9/11. He writes:

If it is true, for example, that kerosene burns at 820C under optimum conditions, how come the steel beams of the twin towers – whose melting point is supposed to be about 1,480C – would snap through at the same time? (They collapsed in 8.1 and 10 seconds.) What about the third tower – the so-called World Trade Centre Building 7 (or the Salmon Brothers Building) – which collapsed in 6.6 seconds in its own footprint at 5.20pm on 11 September

Fisk also wrote:

Two prominent American professors of mechanical engineering *– very definitely not in the "raver" bracket – are now legally challenging the terms of reference of this final report on the grounds that it could be "fraudulent or deceptive".*

Fisk concludes his article thus:

Let me repeat. I am not a conspiracy theorist. Spare me the ravers. Spare me the plots. But like everyone else, I would like to know the full story of 9/11, not least because it was the trigger for the whole lunatic, meretricious "war on terror" which has led us to disaster in Iraq and Afghanistan and in much of the Middle East. Bush's happily departed adviser Karl Rove once said that "we're an empire now – we create our own reality". True? At least tell us.

Now, if Robert Fisk was one of my OU students, it is quite likely that I would have warned about possible plagiarism and not referencing his sources properly. (He neither contacted me nor credited me in his article.) Much worse and much more significant, however, was that Fisk omitted certain facts - such as the names of Drs Wood and Reynolds. I don't think this was an accident. If one reads his Biography on Britannica.com, you will find the following information:

> *He was one of the few Western reporters to have interviewed al-Qaeda leader Osama bin Laden, a feat he accomplished three times during the 1990s.*

This means that he would have almost certainly had close links either with the Intelligence Services or military leaders in order to set up these meetings. Fisk, then, was either wittingly or unwittingly - willingly or unwillingly - part of the 9/11 cover up.

9/11 Conspiracy Road Trip – May 2011

This became yet another hit piece and psychological operation – for the viewing public as well as those who were directly involved in the "exercise".

I was contacted through my Website contact email form on 06 May 2011 thus[431]:

> *Dear Andrew,*
>
> *I came across your website whilst researching for a BBC project. I am developing a project for BBC Three, which is a one-hour documentary exploring the events of September 11th 2001, and we are looking for six enthusiastic young British people who are keen to go on a road trip to New York to explore some of the myths and conspiracy theories surrounding this tragic day. It would be great to speak to you if you think you can help - 0207 xxx xxxx*

I responded by telephoning the number given and I spoke to one of the producers for about 30 minutes. I explained to her, in some detail, about the evidence that I was aware of and, for example, Dr Judy Wood's 9/11 Court Case[121][Error! Bookmark not defined.]. I did this so that I could state that the producers *had* been told about the evidence. In common with most people from the BBC, she showed little or no interest and was keen only that I pass on her "fishing" message to other people. I also sent them a follow up email with relevant links and a quick summary of the evidence proving what happened to the WTC on 9/11[431][Error! Bookmark not defined.].

I kept my end of the bargain, as I sent their message to several people, but I was not so cavalier as to pass any of their names or contact details on to the documentary producer. I just passed on the contact details to the people I knew so that they could contact her if they wished.

The reason I did not pass on any contact details was because I no longer trust anyone connected with mainstream journalism. Even though 3 years had elapsed, nothing seemed to have changed since the correspondence I had with Conspiracy Files producer Mike Rudin in 2008 – who apparently also had no interest at all in evidence – he merely had an agenda to get an interview with Dr Judy Wood (he failed)… [432]

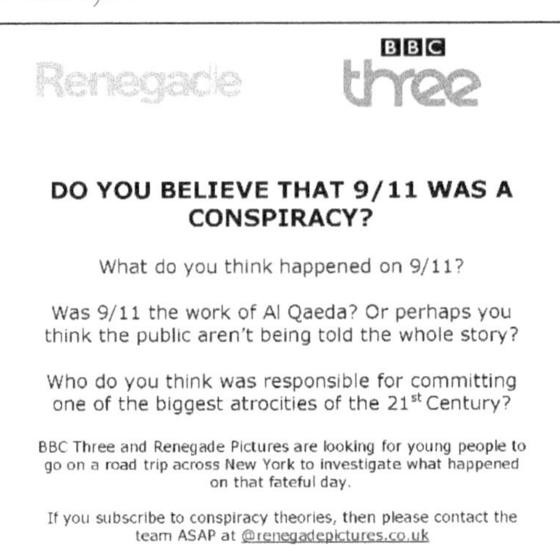

When the programme was broadcast, it was clear that it was another piece of propaganda – revealing none of the known truth. The request that was sent out (shown above) implied the programme was aimed at "younger adults." Can we deduce, then, that this programme was made specifically to influence some of the folks in that age group to disregard any questions of the official narrative that they may have.

After participating in the programme, a then popular speaker and activist Charlie Veitch seems to have made a peculiar "U-turn" with regard to ignoring 9/11 evidence.[433] I especially liked an analysis done by a Youtuber called CTAgenda[434], although he omitted the point that it is easy to show thermite had nothing to do with the destruction of the WTC. Charlie Veitch then declared that he had created the "truther" character to deceive people and his real name was Damien Rockefeller!

"…People Who Think… Let's Debate!"

On 3 April 2013, I was contacted about what seemed to be a similar proposed propaganda programme regarding the 7/7 bombings. It was again being produced by the inappropriately-named "Renegade" pictures. As you will see, my response to them was rather different this time.

Recipient: info@checktheevidence.com

Message text: Hi Andrew,

Im contacting you from a TV company called Renegade Pictures. I am working on a doc about people who think that the 7/7 bombings cannot be explained by the official report, which suggests that it was a terrorist attack committed in the name of Islam. We are currently in the process of casting for the prog, so are interested in looking for people who are between the ages of 18-35yrs who doubt the official account of events. Is there anyone who think might be keen to take part? Cheers

Here is the response I sent.

From: Andrew Johnson [mailto:ad.johnson@ntlworld.com]

Sent: 03 April 2012 18:52

*To: '***@renegadepictures.co.uk'*

Subject: RE: 7/7 Programme

Hi there,

I was contacted by your company last year re the 9/11 "road trip" film you made - and it is now clear what happened.

In your message you wrote:

> *We are currently in the process of casting for the prog, so are interested in looking for people who are between the ages of 18-35yrs who doubt the official account of events.*

Well, we have been in the process of pointing out that the government's (revised) narrative of the events of 7/7 cannot be true. This is the definitely the case (no "doubts" or "beliefs" are involved) - because the available evidence proves that the 4 alleged bombers cannot have committed the alleged crimes - someone else is responsible.

I would like to point you in the direction of John Anthony Hill's (JAH) film "7/7 Ripple Effect" which summarises the evidence which proves the official narrative of 7/7 is false.

http://video.google.com/videoplay?docid=87567952263359807776

You could also cover that JAH was detained without trial (accused of attempting to pervert the course of justice) for 140 days and finally brought to trial after that period had elapsed (and after the so-called 7/7 inquest had finished) and he was acquitted by a jury (they were shown the afore-mentioned film).

http://terroronthetube.co.uk/2011/05/12/muaddib-acquitted/

All the people I know are familiar with above story and, as far as I can tell, know that the BBC, news media and those production companies making films and documentaries NOT addressing this evidence are effectively (at best) then paid propaganda agents or (at worst) accomplices to a criminal cover up - being, as they are, complicit in attempts to pervert the course of justice.

History will record this - and the dishonesty of those unable to report on and investigate these matters appropriately and accurately when they "should know better". (A production brief given by a director or other person will not be seen as an valid excuse.)

History will also record others, like JAH, who have studied the details and the evidence and presented it fairly and accurately to those willing to listen:

http://www.richplanet.net/starship_main.php?ref=55&part=1

http://www.richplanet.net/starship_main.php?ref=56&part=1

I will be advising my contacts that a new BBC propaganda piece is in the works and they can then also "log" this as another attempt at smear, ridicule, distortion and so on in what is tantamount to fraud and conspiracy.

You, as a researcher, have a choice: continue to be paid money to help pervert the course of justice - or perform research openly and honestly and refuse to contribute to the project in any meaningful way. (All persons working on this programme have the same choice - perhaps once you have done the research, you can present this choice to them.)

I will be posting this on my website, deleting your name - so that you can privately make the choice above.

Regards

Andrew Johnson

This response came back:

*From: ***@renegadepictures.co.uk*

Sent: 04 April 2012 12:13

To: ad.johnson@ntlworld.com

Subject: RE: 7/7 Programme

Hi Andrew,

Thanks for your email. I fully appreciate your concerns, but wanted to let you know that we are not trying to make a one sided propaganda piece with this documentary. This is a programme which will allow five people the chance to tell the viewing public what they think really happened on 7/7. It is not a one sided programme, instead we wish to promote a genuine debate on the issue, which will enable five people who think the official account is false, to put forward their views, and present their case. It sounds like you know a lot on the topic, and it would be really helpful to talk to you about your views; materials that can help us in our research; and any points that you feel we should raise in the documentary,. If this is something you would be up for doing, you can reach me on ------.

Many Thanks,

I then responded again, trying to emphasise that debate was not necessary to establish what actually happened. That information and evidence was already available to anyone that wanted to study it.

From: Andrew Johnson [mailto:ad.johnson@ntlworld.com]

Sent: 04 April 2012 14:59

*To: ****@renegadepictures.co.uk*

Subject: RE: 7/7 Programme

Dear ----,

Thanks for your message and offering an opportunity to participate in a "debate". It's a bit like saying "should we debate whether 2+2 = 5". The government story of 7/7 is FALSE and the establishment has acted to PREVENT this being properly shown to the public. That is true. I don't want to discuss "a view" I want to discuss evidence - which won't be possible in a programme like that.

If your programme was to be called "7/7 - How the Government the UK Media lied and covered up crimes" and that title was going to be shown on air, then I MIGHT consider participating in some way. In any case, you won't retain editorial control yourself - and even if you did, a fair presentation of the evidence would either removed or compromised by including "experts" such as Chris French or Karen Douglas or someone else.

Other reasons for me not being interested in participating are:

1) Previous experience with your company, documented here:

http://www.checktheevidence.co.uk/cms/index.php?option=com_content&tas k=view&id=332&Itemid=60

2) Previous experience with the BBC - documented here:

http://www.checktheevidence.co.uk/cms/index.php?option=com_content&tas k=view&id=168&Itemid=60

3) Minor, but based on your criteria, I am too old (47 years old)

4) Reaction I've had to my posting (some from Facebook and some by e-mail) - see below.

So why would people react this way? All the information you need is "out there" - what I've given you is a starting point. Presumably, you get paid to do research - I do not (except for when I am researching into the nature of Student's health conditions for my student assessment work).

Regards

Andrew Johnson

When I posted this on my website and on facebook, the response I had from people was positive. One person said it well:

The fact that they ask for "people who think that 7/7 bombings cannot be explained by the official report" and not "people who have evidence about what actually happened on 7/7" tells you they are not interested in finding out the truth.

25. Video Fakery – Another Component of the "Second Tier" 9/11 Cover Up

In chapter 8, I mentioned Simon Shack's film "September Clues" and discussed my experience with Simon Shack (Hytten) himself and his statements about Dr Wood's research.

A friend and researcher, Mark Conlon, shared similar concerns about the motives and actions of Simon Shack and he began to question some of the content of "September Clues." This lead Mark into studying the "video fakery" aspect of the alleged plane crashes in a lot more detail. Since at least 2013, he has been collecting information and has posted a large selection of this in a number of articles on his blog http://mark-conlon.blogspot.com. I have edited and reposted a number of Mark's articles on my own website[435]. Below, I give a summary of some of these articles and what we think is going on.

Disinformation in Flight 175 Rare Video (Posted 11 September 2013)

This article analysed claims that the video shot by Michael Hezarkhani was fake. A shot from this video is shown below:

The video made by a poster called Markus Allen correctly states that the way the crash and explosion happens is impossible (if a normal plane was involved). However, the Markus Allen video claims that the Hezarkhani video must be fake, because the plane wing passes behind a certain building when it should not be able to do this, because it is claimed the building in question is behind WTC 2.

Mark Conlon carefully illustrates using maps and various photos where the buildings are in relation to the WTC and where they are in relation to where Michael Hezarkhani was standing when he shot the video.

Mark proves that Allen's claims are false – and it is easy to see this.

Flight 175 and The Truth about 'The Truth in 7 Minutes' in FIVE Minutes

Markus Allen had to admit that he made an error about the location of the buildings, but he then claimed that it was impossible to locate where Hezarkhani was when he recorded the video, hence, the video must be fake...

Mark Conlon, through careful research was able to locate with a high degree of certainty where Hezarkhani was located when he recorded the video.

Hence, Allen was again proven to be lying.

Markus Allen's Disappearing Buildings on 9/11

Here, Mark Conlon analyses a new claim from Markus Allen that the Hezarkhani video is fake because buildings are "missing." Again, Mark analyses the claim and shows that Markus Allen was simply using a cropped area from the Hezarkhani video – hence the buildings are missing because the video images have been cropped!

September Clues - Layers of Deception – Parts 1-3

Here, Mark Conlon carefully analyses several claims made by Simon Shack in the September Clues film to do with Layer Masking. He looks at the so-called "nose out" clip and shows that Simon Shack's explanation is not correct.

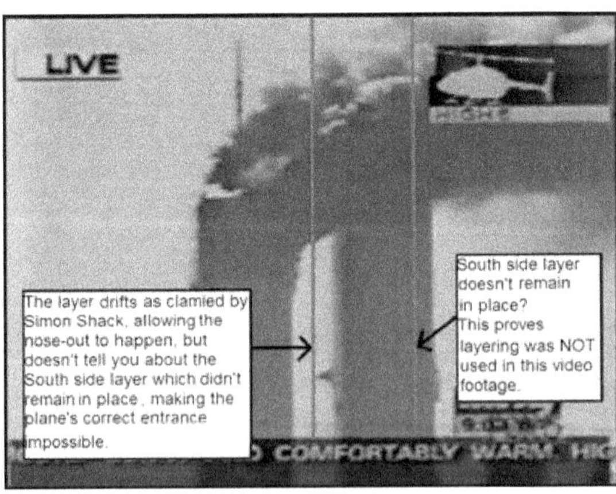

In part two, Mark studies further aspects of the "nose out" video and shows more errors in Shack's film.

In part three, Mark Conlon examines shack's claim that Pavel Hlava's video footage of Flight 175 impacting the South Tower is a re-edit of Michael Hezarkhani's video footage of the same event. Again, by analysing the shots in each carefully and looking at the maps of NYC, Mark shows this claim to be false.

Michael Hezarkhani's video camera was zoomed-in to capture the plane in his video footage. See the comparison of Michael Hezarkhani's zoomed-out video sequence which shows a different foreground location compared to Pavel Hlava's video below which is already zoomed-out when capturing the plane in his video

Pavel Hlava zoomed-out when capturing the plane. Different foreground location

9/11 "No-Planes" Perception Management Past & Present

In this article, Mark examines how various stories have appeared both in the mainstream and "alternative." All of these articles promote false information about the nature of the 9/11 plane crashes. They all seem designed to mislead people about what actually happened and also present them with a false choice of "real hijacked planes" crashing or "video fakery/CGI planes" being used to create a deception. As we can see above, there have been a repeated attempts to try to prove that the Michael Hezarkhani video is fake – perhaps because it is this video which most clearly shows the "anomalous physics of the crash – so declaring in to be CGI solves a problem for the perpetrators.

In summary, Mark Conlon and I agree that there has been a deliberate attempt to promote the 9/11 video fakery position in order to obscure or cover up the knowledge of the use of some type of image projection technology, which was used to create a very powerful illusion of plane crashes. The image projection conclusion is the only one which can explain the fact that some witnesses did not see or hear any planes at the WTC site (in circumstances when they should), whilst others did see and hear planes. (I discussed the witness accounts of planes at the WTC in the article "Going in Search of Planes in NYC" in *9/11 Finding the Truth*.)

Part 3

Other aspects of Deception.

Conclusions.

26. 9/11 and Global Warming Consensus

Since 9/11, in true Hegelian style, the promotion of the fake war on terror has allowed politicians to pass various laws and make wars. The UK has had

- Regulation of Investigatory Powers Act (2000)
- Serious Organised Crime and Police Act (2005)
- Terrorism Act (2006)
- Counter-Terrorism and Security Act (2015)

There have been Wars/Occupation of Afghanistan, Iraq, Syria, Libya and elsewhere and in the USA, the Patriot Act and the NDAA - National Defence Authorization Act have come into force.

Successful passing of these laws has been made possible through the use of the global trauma based mind control – the events of 9/11 caused the trauma. Another form of trauma that has been induced in the general population is from the fear about alleged changes in the climate. Again, mass deception has been perpetrated.

I wanted to include further a brief discussion of the global warming/climate change scam. I have written extensively about 9/11 research [110]**Error! Bookmark not defined.**and have seen in that work how "establishing consensus" is one of the main goals that needs to be achieved to propagate propaganda and lies – to close down questioning.

In the "climate change" field, one example of "consensus propaganda" is the "Agenda 21" document – which introduces concepts of sustainability. This talks about "security" of communities etc. This has now been used as a concept in local propaganda and certain cities are now being dubbed "Strong Cities" and "Smart Cities", but it is completely undermined by a knowledge of what really happened on 9/11, 7/7 etc i.e. how can a city be safe if some group has the ability to turn buildings to dust and direct weather systems towards a given city?

Funnily enough, Dr David Ray Griffin (discussed in chapter 12), is the author of several books sceptical of the official account of 9/11, has not been quite so sceptical about the "alleged CO_2 crisis". He is not a scientist – he is a theologian. Quoting from the "9/11 consensus" website[436] we find:

> *"David Griffin's 2015 book, "Unprecedented: Can Civilization Survive the CO2 Crisis?" was reviewed as "a great service to humanity," and was taken to the Paris climate summit in December by Panel co-founder, Elizabeth Woodworth, who has just made, with a professional film producer, a 2016 video entitled "A Climate Revolution For All. COP21: An Inside View." Griffin's book is featured for its section on mobilization.*

David Ray Griffin, as far as I am concerned, is part of the deception Grid.

COP21 – The Marriage of the "Terrorism" and Climate Change Scams

I also want to note the significance of the "Paris Climate Conference - COP21 – Conference of Parties" took place between 30 November 2015 and 12 December 2015. From their website[437] we read:

> *"The international political response to climate change began at the Rio Earth Summit in 1992, where the 'Rio Convention' included the adoption of the UN Framework on Climate Change (UNFCCC). This convention set out a framework for action aimed at stabilising atmospheric concentrations of greenhouse gases (GHGs) to avoid "dangerous anthropogenic interference with the climate system… The UNFCCC which entered into force on 21 March 1994, now has a near-universal membership of 195 parties."*

Just before the conference 13/14 Nov 2015 saw the alleged bombings and the deaths of over 100 people[438]. Paris then went into "Lockdown". However, terrorist incident drills were going on at the same time as the events happened[439] - just like they were on 7th of July 2005[440] – the date of the alleged bombings in London.

I suggest that, to notch up the "fear and trauma programming," and reduce any effects that scepticism might be having on the progress of the global governance and control agenda, what we experienced was the "interlocking" of 2 global psychological operations – in a major world capital. This was then blasted 24/7 across the world's media… to sear away any dissent and reinforce the previous decades-long programming. I have written more about this in my book "Climate Change and Global Warming: Exposed".

27. Uncritical Thinking – DEW and 2017 California Wildfires

29 Oct 2017

In October 2017, a number of serious and extensive wildfires broke out in areas of Northern California[441], such as Santa Rosa. (Around the same time, there were similar outbreaks of wildfires in Portugal[442] and Spain[443].) Very soon after the initial events, a number of YouTube videos appeared which claimed to show strange anomalies in relation to the fires – for example "toasted cars" and completely burned out houses with seemingly undamaged trees very close by. In more than one video[444], the appearance of these things was linked to the use of Directed Energy Weapons (DEW) – and parallels were drawn with some of the anomalies found in the evidence relating to the events of 9/11, as documented in Dr Judy Wood's comprehensive book *Where Did the Towers Go?* A clip from one of Dr Wood's presentations relating to the "toasted car" phenomenon was included in at least one video.

Both myself and Dr Judy Wood had people writing to us to point out these apparently strange anomalies – and others. A number of people wrote to me via Facebook.

Seeing as we were getting asked about it, Dr Wood and I decided to record an informal discussion (note: it wasn't an interview)[445]. I knew that what Dr Wood and I said in this discussion would not be popular, so I deliberately disabled comments on the video. (And such was the desire for people to express their "shock and dismay," they placed comments on other videos of mine – and even someone else's!)

The essential main points of our discussion were as follows. Most or all of the people posting YouTube videos and commenting

- were not specialists in investigating fires.
- had not visited California to study the site and gather evidence
- had not spent enough time collecting and considering the evidence carefully

Additionally:

- The effects that were claimed to be the result of DEW in some or all parts of some videos were clearly not the same as the effects seen at the WTC and were the result of ordinary (not "weird") fires.
- Trees that are still growing do not burn as readily as dry wood and the wood that houses are made of.

At one point in our discussion, I *speculated* that, for example, some type of weather modification or control could have been used to increase the damage caused by the fires and neither of us ruled out the use of "foul play" in the events. Indeed, some people have pointed out that many houses that were destroyed were in areas that were earmarked for "rezoning" under local Agenda 21-type plans.[446] (Though this has also come up before, in 2015, for example.)

[447]One thing I did find out is that at least one article about the 2017 California fires[448] (see the small thumbnail, which appeared larger on facebook shares) actually used an image from 2015[449].

In the discussion with Dr Wood, I stated had not investigated the events in enough depth to state whether there was "foul play". We stated with confidence that a number of the conclusions made in the videos were incorrect – and obviously so (listen to our discussion for examples). Apparently, this was not good enough for some people and so they wanted to send me/us accusatory messages (fair enough… it goes with the territory). I have included a few of these messages below – because some of them strike me as being rather peculiar. Also of note is that convicted felon[74]**Error! Bookmark not defined.** Jeremy Rys[450] has posted a new video to attack Dr Wood's character and research[451] and imply that we agreed with what is said in some of the "DEW Caused California Fires" type videos.

Thankfully, some people were still open to understanding how they could quite easily be manipulated into jumping to conclusions too quickly (see bottom of this article).

Again, the need for careful investigation – *before* jumping to conclusions is as strong as ever. Even if/when people write to me and express their frustration and call me names, I won't be jumping up and down and shouting "It's DEW again! It's DEW again!" If anyone wants to develop a comprehensive website about the California fires and do a forensic study, then put some of that into, say, a relevant court case[121]**Error! Bookmark not defined.**, then if it is relevant, in some way, to the research posted on this website, I will post a link to it or do an article about it!

For now, I will state that unless I make an agreement with someone, for a particular and sensible reason to investigate a given event, I am not obliged to investigate or comment on anything. I think the same can be said for Dr Judy Wood, but I don't speak *for* her – only *to* her.

As a final thought here, if people really want freedom, they have to respect the right for people to act freely. If they want freedom of speech, they have to be prepared to be on the receiving end of free speech.

Correspondence Re California Fires – 21st Oct 2017

XXX: She knows it wasn't DEWs? But she believes the media that the winds were 60mph! She hasn't investigated it beyond watching MSM and yt videos and she's automatically denying it's DEWs. IDK.

She knows DEWs and if she says it wasn't DEWs we have to believe her because she's the expert, but I doubt she even looked into the fires. She made up her mind before even looking into it. She seriously does NOT want anyone raining on her DEW parade.

ADJ: Indeed - but how many wildfires have you investigated and have you visited the site, collected all relevant data and published it?

Here's a good example -
https://www.facebook.com/permalink.php?story_fbid=10159743007055647&id=890945646

Tera Abraham shared a photo to your timeline.

[Note: the photo XXX refers to is from 2015[452]!]

https://www.facebook.com/photo.php?fbid=10208734661038559&set=p.10208734661038559&type=3

 I listened to your informal interview with Dr Judy Wood posted Oct 17/17. And I heard Dr Judy Wood say that we need to have more discernment. I agree, but I also think that when people ask the expert to comment re: the Cali fires an effort needs to be made to look at the evidence the public are questioning. What was the purpose of Where Did the Towers' Go? if not to wake the public up to things we were told was normal. Not everyone can have the education and experience that Dr Wood has and it is because of her work is why we are questioning these images now.

Tera Abraham

XXX: Andrew, common. It doesn't take a rocket scientist to see that those houses were NOT burned by normal fire. We need Dr Wood to investigate it. She's refusing without even looking into it. You saw the photos.

ADJ: So, it's now down to you to marshal all the evidence and collate it into a court case... Are you up to the job? You just implied you have the relevant background or qualifications, so ... off you go...?

XXX: For some reason Dr Wood thinks this is going to make her look bad. Does she even realize how many people are looking at her for the first time because of this?

I'm saying even a 3 year old can tell the fires weren't normal.

ADJ: I am sure she realises that - anyway, I will leave you to it for now. Let me know when you've submitted your court case or compiled your website etc

XXX: Why is she refusing to even look into it? She's letting her ego get the best of her.

Thank You for your work. Goodbye.

22 OCTOBER 00:14

XXX: Can someone investigate if "smart meters" had anything to do with it? What kind of expert would that be?

Something set 6,000 structures on fire at the same time. Someone needs to dig into this because we know the government wont.

http://stopsmartmeters.org.uk/resources/what-are-smart-meters/

What are 'Smart' Meters? « Stop Smart Meters! (UK)

Around the world utility companies are replacing wired analogue electricity, gas and water meters with new generation 'Smart' Meters at a rapid rate. The programme is already well under way in countries including North America, Canada, Australia, New Zealand and some European countries. Despite what...

stopsmartmeters.org.uk

22 OCTOBER 09:11

ADJ: Yeah - a good reason for you to investigate and make a comprehensive website then.

22 OCTOBER 14:19

But I don't have a piece of paper saying I'm a government indoctrinated professional, so what good is my work?

ADJ: Maybe you should get one then…?

I don't have any advanced degrees, but I still made and maintain a website.

People seem to value it (else why do people like you write to me).

XXX: Because you're the priest that has a direct connection to god, and having her call us stupid because we don't know as much as she does, while refusing to look into it, is making me into an atheist. I'm just giving her one last shot through you. She needs to look into the fires. She's the professional that everyone is looking to when it comes to DEWs and she just poopoo'd us away.

ADJ: Ah OK - well, if that's how you look at it, it ain't going to help your investigations much. Your problem is Dr Wood's fault or my fault then... right right I see now…

XXX: I preached Dr Wood every day for years, but no more. The tact that we don't volunteer for what you want us to do ... hmmm

ADJ: Well, we have no control over what you say to others about us

XXX: It's not for me.

ADJ: And when did Dr Wood say XXX is stupid? Ask yourself "Why did I identify with that comment?"

When you interviewed her about the fires. She said everyone who said it was DEWs is stupid.

Stupid or brainwashed.

ADJ: Anyway, I will leave you to do whatever you want to do… if you want to tell people the truth about 9/11, that's fine, but if you don't like the author of the research anymore, that's fine too… your choice

XXX: Right. What about the fires? You know it was DEWs.

Not one bathtub, sink, toilet…

What about smart meters? Who's looking into that?

She worked hard to prove DEWs did 9/11 and after all the hell they put her through she doesn't want all that to be trashed by people using her name for everything they think are DEWs. I can see that, but she didn't even look into it. That pisses me off.

Nearly 6,000 structures disappeared on the same day. Someone that's not part of the government needs to look into this. Smart meters and DEWs could take out most of the population worldwide. I'm not asking this for me or my ego. I have no website or ulterior motive. I connect dots but I have no paper saying I'm a good dot connector. We need Dr Wood to verify what's going on, or at least LOOK into it before trashing all our work.

FB Message – Sat 28ᵗʰ Oct

YYY: I will be doing a piece on this Andrew https://www.youtube.com/watch?v=5DOJtITaJ-c . Others are already in outrage over this. I wanted to give you a chance to respond before I publish my piece. My first and most obvious question is What on Earth could have possibly swayed you and Dr Judy Wood to create this painfully obvious hit piece?

ADJ: Hello there… I think the video is self-explanatory. Have you been to California to investigate the fires? Did you make a note of the time in the video where I mentioned that "foul play" could possibly be involved? You stated it was a "hit piece". Can you state clearly who it was a hit piece against? (Names of people or groups would be good to mention!) Best Wishes with your work!

YYY: Andrew you and Dr Judy Wood used the same tactics against InTruthByGrace and aplanetruth.info as those used by Alex Jones and Dr Steven Jones used to attempt to make Dr Judy Wood look like a raving lunatic. I followed all of her work and much of yours. I KNOW you two are lying. I am disappointed by this Andrew. I had a lot of respect for you as a journalist. A last thought. The two of you absolutely destroyed all your credibility when you made that video/podcast. I certainly hope it was worth whatever you two received.

ADJ: You didn't name any real people and didn't answer my questions. Hence, your comments are irrelevant. I don't class myself as a journalist either. I am a researcher and a writer - I don't regularly post stories about current affairs. I hope your comments mean you won't message me again and that some day you will be honest with yourself about what you know and what you speculate about.

Email received via Website:

It was submitted by addressnotgiven@checktheevidence.co.uk at 17:32:05 27-Oct-2017

Recipient: info@checktheevidence.com

Message text: Judy Wood, you Zionist pig shill. You should be ashamed of yourself! Rot in hell.

Char count: 1919

Further Facebook Comment Making <u>Good</u> Observations about the Fires

Has anyone heard of the Santa Anna Winds? I live here in northern California and we get them this time of year. We had a horrible fire in Oakland in the early 90s because of them. Look at those photos. Wind is directed energy but not a directed energy WEAPON. You tube is full of fear mongers doing MSM's job for them and they don't even realize it. Its very sad. Kudos Andrew and Rich Hall. (Y)

Like · Reply · 1 · 28 Oct 2017

One of the fires (The Cherokee Fire) came to within 3 miles of my home. The night before we had wind gusts up to 80mph. Power lines in the trees started many little fires that blended together in what became The Cherokee Fire. High winds just like in Santa Rosa, Petaluma, Napa and the Clear lake area sent these fires out of control. Wind and dryness from summer and steep terrain tend to do that with fires around here this time of year. We actually had a mild summer as far as fires go until these fires We had the wettest winter recorded in California's history. The level of ignorance and the increasing number of ignorant clowns with you tube channels is staggering. These people are much more stupid than they think I think they are. At this rate in the next 5 years the level of stupidity will become biblical.

Like · Reply · 1 · 28 Oct 2017 at 19:57

28. 9/11 – Another Dimension?

The WTC Site in 2017

I visited the site in August 2017 and noticed the following signs:

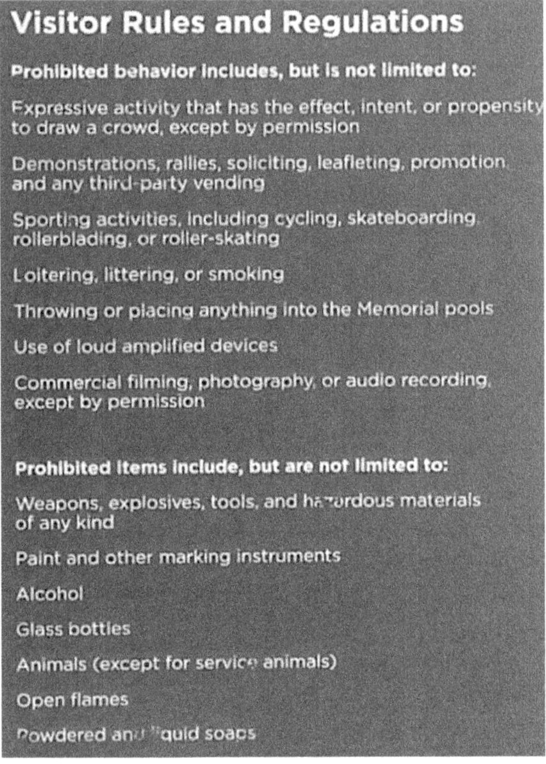

The museum subjects visitors to an "airport style" security check (as do the boats to the Statue of Liberty). The museum is expensive to enter and, of course, just re-asserts the official false narrative.

Some have commented that the WTC site now seems to contain something like "two black holes" which drain water into "an abyss."

Photo by Andrew Johnson

I think that the flowing water also has an additional purpose – to dampen down any residual energy from the ongoing reactions which started when the towers were destroyed.

Another observation is regarding the destruction of the Alfred P Murrah building in 1995. It also may have involved some type of energy weapon. The damage it experienced was quite similar to that experienced by WTC 6.

One picture of the inside of WTC6 and the other is the Murrah Building in OKC. Can you tell which is which? (Hint: one of them has a whcatchex at the bottom.)

Also of note were cars near the OKC building[453]:

Also of note is the state of the OKC site in 2017:

Alfred P Murrah Building – Memorial – Another Water Feature.

Numerology and Symbolism

For many years, people who have studied events like the JFK assassination and the murder of Princess Diana have discussed more esoteric considerations – such as the numbers associated with the events. Rik Clay, now deceased, presented some very compelling information about such things[454]. Rik Clay observed[455]:

- The World Trade Centre stood like an '11' on the New York skyline

- $9 + 1 + 1 = 11$

- September 11th is the 254th day of the year. $2+5+4 = 11$

- September 11th was 111 days until the end of the year

- The 1st plane to hit the World Trade Centre was 'Flight 11'

- Alleged total number crew on Flight 11 was '11'

- New York is the 11th state of the US Constitution

- September 11th 2001 stands '11' years from 2012 (Note that in the Mayan calendar, it was said that there would be 20 years of 'no-time'. A period of unrest where the planet is making a transition from one age to another. 9/11 stood 9 years from the start of this 'no-time' and 11 years from the end.)

I might also add that the number of floors in each building was 110 – or 111 if you count the observation deck etc.

The year 2001 was the first year of the New Millennium (as there was no year zero). We can also note the name of the building that is just across the street from where the WTC complex stood – the Millennium Hotel. On the old website for the building, it states[456].

The hotel is a high-rise black glass building which pays homage to Arthur C. Clarke's vision of the Monolith in "2001: A Space Odyssey" - complete with canopy, flags and ornamental trees at the entrance.

The Millenium Hotel – 31 Aug 2017 - Photo by Elizabeth Johnson

Photo by Andrew Johnson

Returning to the JFK assassination, it took place on 22 Nov (11/22 or 22/11).

Mark Passio has also spoken extensively about Occult Rituals and practices and their apparent usage in events like 9/11[457]. Passio is one of a relatively small number of researchers who has mentioned the research of Dr Judy Wood[458] in his talks, although I don't think he has mentioned the Hutchison Effect and weather-related phenomena.

Predictive Programming?

Though it is easy to write this off as a coincidence, one of the other unsettling areas of study is how images of the WTC towers being attacked, damaged or destroyed were shown in quite a number of films, TV shows and other media years before the events took place. A page entitled "The Shocking Advance Hints Of The 9/11 Attacks" by Mike King[459] displays the following examples.

April, 1967 - Newsweek Magazine

(Just before construction on the towers began).

Front cover: David Rockefeller, who pushed for the towers to be built, wearing a watch with hands on the "9" and the "11"

Back cover: Cigarette ad depicts towers and speaks of "a fight worth fighting"

1979 - Album Cover: Supertramp - 'Breakfast in America'

View from airplane window depicts Towers exploding (orange juice) at breakfast time (attacks took place in the morning).

1987 - Movie: The Squeeze - starring Michael Keaton

1993 - Movie: Super Mario Brothers

1995 - Card Game: Illuminati Cards

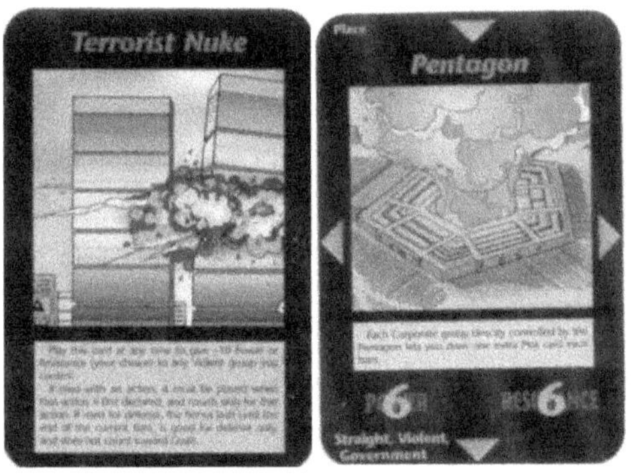

1997 - Donald Duck Comic Book

1998 - Movie: Armageddon - Starring Bruce Willis

March, 2001 - New York Magazine

Back to the Future – 1985 - 1989

Several observers have also pointed out a disturbing number of what seem to be thinly veiled references to 9/11 in all three "Back to the Future" films – the last of which was released 12 years before the events unfolded. Of particular interest is the analysis by Carl James[460] in his book *Science Fiction and the Hidden Global Agenda, Volume 2*[461]. He writes

Of all the films to contain symbolism and themes relating to 9/11, none have been scrutinized more closely than the "Back to the Future" trilogy – particularly part one of the film series. [Author's note: For the sake of avoiding repetition, I will refer to the "Back to the Future" films and trilogy as "BTTF" from this point on.] Numerous scenes and sections of dialogue appear to allude to the events of that day, often in combination with curious symbolism and on-screen appearances of the numbers nine and eleven. The key 9/11 allusions in part one of the film trilogy appear predominantly (but not exclusively) in several pivotal story sections. The first section takes place at the Twin Pines Mall in the early morning hours of October 26th 1985. The name of the Mall is analogous with the Twin Towers. When Marty McFly arrives at the Mall, the time on the Mall sign is 1:16 – an inverted 9/11. The sign carries the moniker "Twin Pines Mall" and two pine tree shapes. When the sign is inverted (as with the aforementioned time of 1:16) the tree "shapes" on the sign are loosely analogous with the iconic shapes that the WTC Twin Towers cast on the New York skyline

I should note that Marty comes directly to the Mall from his home on Lyon Estates, the entrance to which is flanked by twin concrete pillars of a sort. Marty arrives and becomes witness to a time travel experiment being carried out by his friend Doc Brown. Doc unveils his time machine – a modified DeLorean car – which emerges from the back of a van. The twin ramps which descend from the tailgate of the van are reminiscent of the WTC Twin Towers. The first thing the Doc does is to synchronize the experiment stopwatch with his control watch. The time on both of these watches is 1:19 (another quasi- inverted 9/11.) Marty and Doc Brown come under attack from Muslim terrorists – whose plutonium the Doc has stolen as part of his experiment. This inclusion of "Middle Eastern terrorists" is notable in the context of 9/11. However, remember that "terrorists" only equate to the "official" narrative / cover story of 9/11 - not to the evidence indicating a wholly different scenario on 9/11, such as the use of directed free energy technology at the WTC.

There is further analysis and information in Carl James' book. Other analyses of BTTF symbolism that have been done in various videos do not mention Dr Judy Wood's research.

Masonic Logos

Soon after I started to find out about the truth of 9/11 in 2004, I met a chap called Steve Collier. It was he that first alerted me to the use of masonic symbolism in logos and signs that are used by powerful organisations and companies. I later considered whether this symbolism was present in some of the "truth groups" that I had been writing about.

Architects and Engineers For 9/11 "Truth" Logo

Masonic Compass and Rulers

Masonic Lodge Banner, Alberta   Scholars for 9/11 Truth and Justice

An Attack on Human Consciousness

In several interviews, Dr Judy Wood has described that the events of 9/11 and their cover up were an attack on Human Consciousness[462]. I agree. These events were used to generate fear and ignorance – 9/11 was an implementation of global trauma-based mind control. You can read about smaller-scale trauma-based mind control in books by Neil Sanders[463], Walter Bowart[464] and others.

Some people have suggested that the events of 9/11 represent a "gateway" – through which our consciousness can pass and be transformed – so that we then learn the manipulation and control we have been subjected to in many ways.

Alchemy and Magic?

We have noted elsewhere that materials at the WTC during and after the destruction appear to have undergone some kind of transmutation. This is exactly what alchemists have talked about doing – turning lead into gold, and all that…

Are we now getting into an area which might even explain how the 9/11 perpetrators have been able to initiate and sustain a global cover up of the truth about 9/11 – and micro-manage this cover up? I'll leave the reader to think about that some more.

29. Conclusions

I have shown in this volume that even some of those who are supposed to be at the forefront of alternative research have refused to acknowledge or openly speak of the truth about 9/11. They have exhibited an unwillingness to learn from their mistakes. In some cases, this may just be down to their own personal issues. Beyond this, however, I have shown one or more examples of each of the following:

- Conferences being organised to promulgate 9/11 disinformation.

- Books being produced (which claim to tell the truth) and heavily promoted to deliver 9/11 disinformation.

- Efforts in the UK to promote 9/11 disinformation and cover up the truth.

- Research "going backwards" from promoting something closer to the truth to promoting 9/11 disinformation.

- Mainstream efforts in psychological operations to claim evidence is theory and belief is the only issue worth discussing.

These things have been done *within* the so-called "truth" movement. This should give you an idea, then, of the scale and effectiveness of the 9/11 cover up – which isn't going to end in the foreseeable future.

At this point, I would like to quote from John Lash's book "Not in His Image."[465] (p.210 - 211)

> *The Gnostic theory of error is one of the most sophisticated ideas ever conceived by the human mind in the mind's attempt to understand itself. It does not make Archons the source of human error, but indicates their intrapsychic influence as a key factor that causes error to run wild, extrapolating beyond the scale of correction. The Anthropos is a learning animal. To learn we must be free to err, to make mistakes, for in correcting our mistakes we advance the process of learning in a way unique to our species. We evolve precisely because of the extraordinary scope of error we have been allowed. We evolve not just by learning, as all sentient creatures do, but especially by learning from our mistakes. The exceptionally wide latitude for error typifies human singularity, the ennoia (intentionality) inherent to our species. But if we allow our mistakes to go undetected and uncorrected, we demonstrate the singularity of our species in a destructive way, a deviant way.*

I would suggest readers consider studying Lash's work (see www.metahistory.org) – which is about Gnosticism, primarily. It highlights the importance of *knowing* and once you *know* something, you no longer need to *believe.* Perhaps it is unsurprising, then, that John Lash is one of a small number of people who can correctly discuss Dr Judy Wood's research[466].

Guidelines for Researchers?

Considering, then, what can be learned from the research of Dr Judy Wood, it's vital for people to understand the connection between secret, weaponised "free" energy technology and the events of 9/11 - especially (but perhaps not exclusively) in the destruction of the WTC. This **knowledge** (not theory) can be used as a tool and "litmus test" of the openness and honesty of other researchers and, more often than not, will reveal if they (a) have another agenda or (b) are actually open to learning new things.

Due to the "problems" I have documented in this volume, related to accurate and appropriate referencing, reporting and characterisation of important research, I would like to see a voluntary "code of practice" for alternative knowledge researchers. Here's a draft. Is it unreasonable?

The researcher can declare these things:

- "I promise to do my best to speak and present the truth, the whole truth and nothing but the truth, so help me, Web."

- "If I find out that what I previously presented turns out to be incorrect or untrue, I will endeavour to post and point out corrections, when I become aware of them and, if applicable, apologise."

- "Where it relates to my own topic(s) of discussion or research, I agree to familiarise myself with the irrefutable evidence and state publicly that the Official Story of 9/11 cannot be true and, further, that the WTC was in fact, destroyed by an energy weapon of some kind."

- "If I haven't sufficiently studied the evidence regarding what happened to the WTC (or any similar issue), I will say, when asked, 'I don't know what happened.' "

- "I promise not to jump to conclusions too quickly - before gathering sufficient data and before completion of an appropriate amount of study."

- "I promise to separate speculation from "what I know that I know.""

We can simply, therefore, compare the actions and statements of, say, Steven Greer and Stephen Bassett to the statements and actions of Paul Hellyer and even Richard D Hall and Adam Dwyer. (i.e. make comparisons as to what these people have each done with the 9/11 evidence.)

Talk-show and Podcast Hosts and Disinformation

At the beginning of this book I asked a few rhetorical questions such as "does the truth matter?" Another question I often feel I have to pose is "Do you know the difference between theory, opinion and evidence?" I think that podcast and radio hosts should challenge guests when they are shown to be accidentally or deliberately lying. In the case of 9/11 it is, using evidence in this book and the WDTTG book easy to expose some lies and I recommend that this is done – unless people want the circulation of disinformation and lies to continue, unabated. For example, I essentially challenged Red Ice Radio and Henrik Palmgren and, latterly, regarding another issue, I have also challenged Veritas Show host Mel Fabregas to be honest about the evidence that is available[467] – evidence that proves a guest of theirs has lied about important topics.

Until these people take notice of these issues and this evidence, "disclosure" will not progress – indeed, in some cases, the process will continue to go into reverse and the internet will be used increasingly to get people to believe things (even ridiculous things) that are easily observably false/untrue.

Global Control Grid

As alluded to in chapter 28, 9/11 was part of an ongoing plan to keep the global populace in a state of fear and ignorance. Someone wants things on planet earth to operate a certain way. In the simple diagram below, I have sketched out a rough and incomplete representation of what might be called a "Perception Control Grid". I am not the first to do this and the diagram below is not even that comprehensive. I have included it merely to show a list of topics which "cross connect" and should be investigated by anyone who feels they have a need to learn as much as they can about the deception and lies which we have been victims of for centuries. I touched on this area in *9/11 Finding the Truth* – for example, in the chapter called "A World of Abundance or a World of Scarcity." The conclusions I came to then have not changed – they have only become "more-informed."

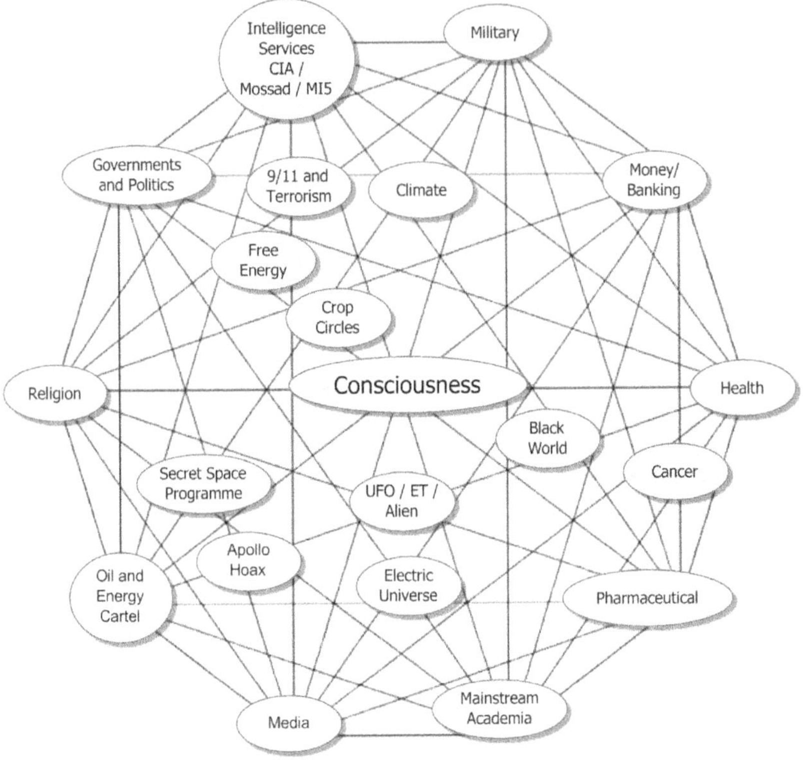

- Those people who are genuinely interested in knowing the truth are all-too-often perception-managed by researchers and other people who claim to be interested in knowing the truth, but are controlled or influenced by the "secret keepers" to keep important things covered up.

- Those who aren't actually co-opted or paid to do this are heavily influenced by those that are co-opted.

- Disingenuous speakers, presenters and researchers continue to promote speculative, false or incomplete information, thereby slowing down - or even reversing - any disclosure process (the "flat earth" Psychological operation has effectively destroyed and deleted knowledge in peoples' minds – by introducing doubt about what can be directly observed.)

- There are armies of "trolls" on the internet who, particularly in relation to the 9/11 evidence, will make so much "noise" that people cannot hear the truth and don't have time to "sort through" everything. They are STILL not able to talk about energy and 9/11 and weather control without omitting the details or getting them wrong or promoting false/wrong explanations.

If we are to ever live in a world where societies are run based on knowledge and truth then…

- Media organisations cannot be trusted to do any disclosure – indeed, they all need to be completely shut down and rebooted in some way, outside the control of the interests which currently control them.

- Secret Societies which are connected to globalist interests will have to become much more open and any advantages they hold in the power structure will have to disappear.

- The UN and similar organisations will need to be re-set and/or rebooted to operate on a completely different basis.

- The current basis on which all military organisations and those that concern themselves with secrecy or "national security" will have to be reset and re-booted and be transformed into something utterly different. They are all currently operating in a way not compatible with solving the world's biggest problems.

- Most or all religions will have to be revised and "reset" – because they currently operate on a partly or wholly false narrative – which has been set up to hide the underlying truths about who we are and where we came from.

- Military industrial contractors and organisations and others "in the know" will have to "fess up" not only about 9/11 but about the whole cover up of things like Human Abduction, Animal Abduction and Mutilations as well as all the tech they back-engineered and/or developed in secret.

Full disclosure about the events of 9/11 – how the WTC was destroyed and who did it will expose more about all the other secrets being kept and should help, ultimately, to free the human race from the physical, mental and spiritual abuse and even torture that it has been subjected to, by psychopaths and similar negative entities.

When the larger institutions and organisations start to truly operate on the principles they claim to hold dear – knowledge, integrity, honesty and truth, then perhaps the population in general will have a chance to operate on those same values.

In closing then, I would like to thank you for working your way through to the end, and for considering what I have presented to you. I hope it helps you to detect deception more easily and mitigate the effects it has on your thinking and the decisions you make.

30. References

In order to make access to links easier, I recommend you download an electronic version of this file and access the links therein, or find a copy of the links on http://www.checktheevidence.com/ .

---

[1] http://www.checktheevidence.co.uk/cms/index.php?option=com_content&task=view&id=314&Itemid=55

[2] http://www.drjudywood.com/

[3] http://www.wheredidthetowersgo.com/

[4] https://www.youtube.com/irrefutabletv

[5] http://www.debamboozled.com/

[6] http://tinyurl.com/911dvds

[7] https://www.youtube.com/user/PeteFD1986

[8] https://www.youtube.com/watch?v=U1Qt6a-vaNM

[9] http://www.countercurrents.org/larsen020711.htm

[10] https://www.paulcraigroberts.org/pages/about-paul-craig-roberts/

[11] http://www.vdare.com/articles/the-perfidy-of-government-evidence-v-denial

[12] http://www.intrepidreport.com/archives/author/eric-larsen

[13] https://www.youtube.com/watch?v=Xv8XB3qE8JM

[14] http://www.bibliotecapleyades.net/exopolitica/esp_exopolitics_ZZK.htm

[15] http://www.bibliotecapleyades.net/sociopolitica/dayafterroswell/dayafter.htm

[16] https://www.youtube.com/watch?v=25peG6F278A

[17] https://www.youtube.com/watch?v=vadSaWyiozg

[18] https://www.youtube.com/watch?v=1db-UqlBa8M

[19] http://www.paulhellyerweb.com/

[20] https://www.youtube.com/watch?v=coJdM9SU9Y8&feature=youtu.be&t=1h24m26s

[21] https://youtu.be/kip2w-DceV0?t=33s

[22] http://www.independent.co.uk/news/uk/politics/david-cameron-revives-moves-for-tough-action-against-nonviolent-extremists-10245592.html

[23] https://www.hopkinsmedicine.org/healthlibrary/conditions/mental_health_disorders/oppositional_defiant_disorder_90,P02573

[24] http://www.checktheevidence.co.uk/cms/index.php?option=com_content&task=view&id=226&Itemid=60

[25] https://www.youtube.com/watch?v=RV-clat5fZg

[26] http://www.travis-walton.com/

[27] http://www.starchildproject.com/starchild-skull-dna

[28] https://www.youtube.com/watch?v=cqsT5EoIk8U

[29] http://tpuc.org/forum/viewtopic.php?f=4&t=22984

[30] http://www.tpuc.org/forum/viewtopic.php?f=4&t=21827

[31] http://www.youtube.com/user/AlienScientist

[32] http://www.vortexnetworknews.com/Progressive_Tech_2011.html

[33] http://www.checktheevidence.co.uk/cms/index.php?option=com_content&task=view&id=238&Itemid=60

[34] https://www.youtube.com/watch?v=QAxTBQqhzfg&gl

[35] http://www.checktheevidence.co.uk/cms/index.php?option=com_content&task=view&id=328&Itemid=55

[36] http://www.youtube.com/user/WarCrime911

[37] http://www.youtube.com/watch?v=awy8cmcuBlk

[38] http://www.youtube.com/watch?v=nu68B7uzLUA

[39] http://www.drjudywood.com/articles/NIST/Qui_Tam_Wood.shtml

[40] http://www.youtube.com/watch?v=QAxTBQqhzfg

[41] http://drjudywood.com/articles/erin/

[42] http://www.checktheevidence.com/cms/index.php?option=com_content&task=view&id=337&Itemid=60

[43] http://www.disclosureproject.org/

[44] http://www.amazon.co.uk/Hunt-Zero-Point-Nick-Cook/dp/0099414988

[45] https://www.youtube.com/watch?v=6PIdgFnTbKw

[46] https://www.youtube.com/watch?v=YRkvCLMzdhE

[47] https://www.youtube.com/watch?v=Jy-3nSW9rbQ&list=PLmJCON6J2D5QSeFLU-7V5cQMFYEwix4Av

[48] http://www.bibliotecapleyades.net/ciencia/ciencia_extraterrestrialtech06.htm

[49] http://www.checktheevidence.com/pdf/The Case for AntiGravity-booklet.pdf

[50] https://www.youtube.com/watch?v=a9QrcV9-kA8

[51] http://www.youtube.com/user/efearfull

[52] https://www.wired.com/1998/03/antigravity/

[53] http://www.youtube.com/watch?v=AgyAFElQZcU

[54] http://www.americanantigravity.com/

[55] http://www.checktheevidence.com/audio/Eugene Podkletnov-July 27 2004 - - Tim Ventura - American Antigravity.mp3

[56] http://www.checktheevidence.com/audio/Eugen Podkletnov-Breakthrough-August 2nd, 2004 - Tim Ventura - American Antigravity.mp3

[57] http://www.americanantigravity.com/?s=podkletnov&x=0&y=0

[58] http://web.archive.org/web/20051003201453/http:/www.americanantigravity.com/index.shtml

[59] http://www.americanantigravity.com/audio/john-searl-on-the-searl-effect.html

[60] http://www.checktheevidence.co.uk/cms/index.php?option=com_content&task=view&id=286&Itemid=55

[61] http://www.americanantigravity.com/audio/john-hutchison-on-the-hutchison-effect.html

[62] https://www.facebook.com/Alienscientist/info

[63] http://www.nbcnews.com/id/33330516/ns/us_news-life/t/feared-lost-balloon-boy-found-home/

[64] https://www.youtube.com/watch?v=YcYGcBYzvWs

[65] http://edition.cnn.com/2010/CRIME/01/11/hccnc.balloon.boy/index.html?ircf=allsearch

[66] http://www.americanantigravity.com/link/alien-scientist

[67] http://www.r2controls.com/toc.htm

[68] http://www.invensys.com/en/AboutUs/

[69] https://www.youtube.com/watch?v=oTbSCUY1Z8o

70 http://www.alienscientist.com/forum/forum.php

71 http://www.theoutpostforum.com/tof/showthread.php?1495-Demise-of-alienscientist-forum

72 https://www.youtube.com/user/checktheevidence

73 http://www.checktheevidence.co.uk/cms/index.php?option=com_content&task=view&id=390&Itemid=62

74 https://web.archive.org/web/20140807121440/http:/patch.com/massachusetts/mansfield/police-log-road-rage-incident-involving-ax-reported-xfinity-center

75 https://www.facebook.com/jeremy.rys.1

76 http://www.drjudywood.com/pdf/080324_SAIC_AffdJW91_150.pdf

77 http://files.shareholder.com/downloads/SAIC/0x0x208149/64117BC7-5895-497E-A8EB-158A6E57012C/AR_2004.pdf

78 https://protected.networkshosting.com/depsor/DEPSpages/sponsors.html

79 https://digwithin.net/2014/06/04/andrews-and-saic/

80 http://aviationweek.com/awin/us-special-ops-command-psyops-related-contracts-go-saic-sycoleman-lincoln-group

81 http://tinyurl.com/somaero

82 http://web.archive.org/web/20080222044619/http:/www.aero2012.com:80/en/risk.mhtml

83 http://www.disclosureproject.org/docs/pdf/disclosure911.pdf

84 https://youtu.be/oHxGQjirV-c?t=3h45m32s

85 http://www.disclosureproject.org/transcripts/JeanNoelBassior-Nov2005.htm

86 http://www.bastison.net/RESSOURCES/Farce/57_Jones_Jesus.pdf

87 https://archive.org/stream/HiddenTruthForbiddenKnowledgeStevenM.Greer/Hidden Truth Forbidden Knowledge Steven M. Greer_djvu.txt

88 https://www.bibliotecapleyades.net/disclosure/briefing/disclosure13.htm

89 https://www.youtube.com/watch?v=NlWFnBGvMPo

90 http://exopolitics.blogs.com/files/steve.greer.dead.mans.trigger.pdf

91 http://911blogger.com/news/2007-09-17/2004-911-omission-hearings

92 http://www.911truth.org/article_for_printing.php?story=20110808073907849

93 http://www.drjudywood.com/articles/cc/Jenkinspanic.html

94 http://www.checktheevidence.co.uk/cms/index.php?option=com_content&task=view&id=28&Itemid=60

95 http://www.drjudywood.com/articles/cc/JJJ.html

96 http://www.checktheevidence.com/audio/911/Richard Gage Witchcraft Nuutjob - Ralph Winterrowd - 08 May 2011.mp3

97 http://www.youtube.com/watch?v=m-TZypcH9eg

98 http://www.drjudywood.com/articles/dirt/dirt4.html

99 https://www.amazon.com/New-Pearl-Harbor-Disturbing-Administration/dp/1566565529

100 http://www.cfr.org/about/membership/roster.html?letter=F

101 http://www.youtube.com/watch?v=-u7OhZIBd3A

102 http://www.checktheevidence.com/audio/911/SEJones/Paint on Thermate - 9-11 Debate-Air America - R Greene - S Jones 08 May 2008.mp3

103 http://www.youtube.com/watch?v=4Zp3wEm0R5k

104 http://www.checktheevidence.co.uk/cms/index.php?option=com_content&task=view&id=331&Itemid=60

105 http://www.drjudywood.com/articles/JJ/

106 http://www.drjudywood.com/articles/erin/

107 http://tinyurl.com/911qtam/

108 http://web.archive.org/web/20111219010736/http:/9-11cc.org:80/

109 http://web.archive.org/web/20111206181815/http:/9-11cc.org/index.php/about-us/contact-us/

110 http://tinyurl.com/911ftb

111 https://groups.yahoo.com/neo/groups/cognoscence/conversations/messages/2037

112 http://www.septclues.com/

113 http://www.garageband.com.sharedcopy.com/artist/f254dde97df981e52f5c6ca698cb83bc.html

114 http://www.youtube.com/watch?v=Mdkyk1up4ZA&t=1m43s

115 http://www.youtube.com/user/simonshack

116 http://acebaker.blogspot.com/2008/04/september-clues-9-blatant-disinfo.html

117 http://web.archive.org/web/20111209112437/http:/www.veteranstoday.com/2011/08/03/911-no-planes-v-planes-and-controlled-demolition/

118 http://www.septclues.com/SEPTEMBER CLUES COMPLETE 1.mp4

119 http://www.youtube.com/watch?v=5bNomV_8034

120 http://who.is/whois/septclues.com/

121 http://tinyurl.com/911qtam

122 http://www.checktheevidence.com/cms/index.php?option=com_content&task=view&id=349&Itemid=60

123 http://www.youtube.com/watch?v=zTy3anL7a3k&t=7m38s

124 http://www.youtube.com/watch?v=6aPvJSQtmoE

125 http://www.youtube.com/watch?v=edrTAh36Do8&t=0m55s

126 http://www.youtube.com/watch?v=6aPvJSQtmoE&t=6m47s

127 http://www.youtube.com/watch?v=6aPvJSQtmoE&t=6m57s

128 http://www.cluesforum.info/viewtopic.php?p=2353099

129 http://cluesforum.info/viewtopic.php?f=29&t=144&sid=c76925dcdbb3e2de39e1346899b0beb8&start=60

130 http://www.checktheevidence.com/Simon Hytten Skype Chat.pdf

131 http://www.checktheevidence.co.uk/cms/index.php?option=com_content&task=view&id=280&Itemid=60

132 http://www.checktheevidence.co.uk/cms/index.php?option=com_content&task=view&id=329&Itemid=60

133 http://www.richplanet.net/

134 http://www.richplanet.net/911.php

135 http://www.septclues.com/ANIMATED GIF FILES sept clues research/16SECONDS.gif

136 http://www.youtube.com/watch?v=RmSxi44b7Es

137 http://www.youtube.com/watch?v=5LvBEkmKVsE

138 http://cluesforum.info/viewtopic.php?p=2359186

139 http://www.septclues.com/SIMON SHACK PICS/

140 http://www.septclues.com/SIMON SHACK PICS/SeptCluesPARTYsept11_2011_F.JPG

141 http://www.cluesforum.info/viewtopic.php?f=17&t=807&p=2371650

142 http://projectavalon.net/forum4/showthread.php?42764-Nuked---New-free-e-book-on-9-11-by-Jeff-Prager-

143 http://www.veteranstoday.com/2012/03/21/intel-disclosure-march-21-2012/

144 http://www.checktheevidence.com/pdf/1 - 162 - 911 America Nuked.pdf

145 http://www.checktheevidence.com/pdf/163 - 247 - 911 America Nuked.pdf

146 http://www.checktheevidence.co.uk/cms/index.php?option=com_content&task=view&id=167&Itemid=60

147 http://www.checktheevidence.co.uk/cms/index.php?option=com_content&task=view&id=45&Itemid=60

148 http://www.spingola.com/April2012.html

149 http://www.checktheevidence.com/audio/911/2012-04-09 Dr Judy Wood - Andrew Johnson - Deanna Spingola - America Nuked Document etc.mp3

150 http://www.checktheevidence.com/Misc/P136America Nuked.jpg

151 http://www.drjudywood.com/articles/JJ/pics/Aluminum-Jellification1.jpg

152 http://www.drjudywood.com/articles/JJ/JJ4.html

153 http://www.drjudywood.com/articles/erin

154 http://www.checktheevidence.co.uk/cms/index.php?option=com_content&task=view&id=208&Itemid=60

155 http://www.checktheevidence.co.uk/cms/index.php?option=com_content&task=view&id=217&Itemid=60

156 http://nomoregames.net/2012/01/14/collapse-of-the-thermite-thesis/

157 http://en.wikipedia.org/wiki/Nuclear_fusion

158 http://www.facebook.com/pages/Muon-catalyzed-fusion/132880320080773

159 http://en.wikipedia.org/wiki/Muon-catalyzed_fusion

160 http://en.wikipedia.org/wiki/Steven_E._Jones

161 http://www.nucleardemolition.com/trouble.html

162 http://pages.csam.montclair.edu/~kowalski/cf/27conspiracy.html

163 http://wn.com/muon_catalyzed_fusion

164 http://www.scribd.com/doc/36911860/7/Generally-cold-locally-hot-fusion

165 http://www.infinite-energy.com/resources/keyexpdata.html

166 http://www.serendipity.li/wot/sft_wikipedia.htm

167 http://www.checktheevidence.com/audio/911/Prager Harris 1 031912 080000 c2.mp3

168 http://www.nytimes.com/2008/09/22/nyregion/22rocks.html

169 http://www.checktheevidence.co.uk/cms/index.php?option=com_content&task=view&id=288&Itemid=60

170 http://www.checktheevidence.co.uk/cms/index.php?option=com_content&task=view&id=290&Itemid=60

171 http://web.archive.org/web/20080313084235/http:/www.thepriceofliberty.org/07/03/05/ward.htm

172 http://www.checktheevidence.co.uk/cms/index.php?option=com_content&task=view&id=198&Itemid=60

173 http://www.bizjournals.com/phoenix/stories/1997/03/17/smallb3.html?page=all

174 http://www.checktheevidence.com/cms/index.php?option=com_content&task=view&id=347&Itemid=60

175 http://www.checktheevidence.co.uk/cms/index.php?option=com_content&task=category§ionid=6&id=20&Itemid=50

176 http://www.youtube.com/watch?v=wZYMCE3qbrE

177 http://publicdiplomacy.wikia.com/wiki/Smith_Mundt_Act

178 http://www.911vancouverhearings.com/?p=17

179 http://www.checktheevidence.com/911/judy-wood-clare-kuehn-vancouver-hearings-talk.pptx

180 http://www.checktheevidence.com/cms/index.php?option=com_content&task=view&id=352&Itemid=60

181 http://web.archive.org/web/20120805235417/http:/www.911vancouverhearings.com/?p=17

182 http://www.checktheevidence.co.uk/cms/index.php?option=com_content&task=view&id=278&Itemid=60

183 http://www.amazon.com/review/RC0R225GYLP3J/ref=cm_cr_rev_detmd_pl?ie=UTF8&asin=0615412564&cdForum=Fx192RWI9AF18BK&cdMsgID=MxSBTG0Y15KNLL&cdMsgNo=85&cdPage=9&cdSort=oldest&cdThread=Tx1Y9RDON1VV6ET&store=books

[184] http://wheredidthetowersgo.com/

[185] http://911scholars.ning.com/profiles/blog/show?id=3488444%3ABlogPost%3A4426&commentId=3488444%3AComment%3A4432

[186] http://www.youtube.com/watch?v=Kn3a--hf7_s

[187] https://www.youtube.com/watch?v=VK_z1K3x1WI

[188] http://911crashtest.org/

[189] http://www.checktheevidence.co.uk/cms/index.php?option=com_content&task=view&id=349&Itemid=60

[190] http://www.youtube.com/user/justin39641

[191] http://www.checktheevidence.com/911/911 Crash Test SteveDeAk - YT comments.htm

[192] http://www.youtube.com/all_comments?v=Kn3a--hf7_s&lc

[193] http://www.youtube.com/watch?v=gTAgKXwG1Dw

[194] http://www.youtube.com/watch?v=D9VvSBwVT_A&t=3m50s

[195] http://911crashtest.org/forumpress/

[196] http://911crashtest.org/faq/

[197] https://forum.davidicke.com/showpost.php?p=1061101394&postcount=1570

[198] https://www.youtube.com/watch?v=Nl8xTqTUGCY

[199] https://www.youtube.com/watch?v=CZ8uvQk1H9I

[200] http://www.checktheevidence.com/audio/911/DRG/DRG on Debris Filling Basements - Giani Hayes 24 Sep 2008.mp3

[201] http://www.checktheevidence.com/audio/911/DRG/DRG on Debris Pile - Giani Hayes 24 Sep 2008.mp3

[202] http://www.checktheevidence.com/audio/911/DRG/DRG on Erin and Scott Packs - Giani Hayes 24 Sep 2008.mp3

[203] https://www.amazon.co.uk/dp/B00SUIQDNC/

[204] http://drjudywood.com/articles/dirt/dirt4.html

[205] https://www.youtube.com/watch?v=m-TZypcH9eg

[206] https://www.youtube.com/watch?v=6m6ZVVlCK-0&feature=youtu.be&t=30m15s

[207] http://www.npl.washington.edu/AV/altvw36.html

[208] http://www.checktheevidence.com/cms/index.php?option=com_content&task=view&id=389&Itemid=60

[209] https://vimeo.com/57923364

[210] https://youtu.be/ufWggCESyDg?t=44m45s

[211] https://youtu.be/b5LW0vj2TV4?t=6m14s

[212] https://earthpulse.com/about-us/

[213] http://www.checktheevidence.com/audio/911/Nick Begich on Afghanistan - Coast to Coast - Dec 10 2006.mp3

[214] http://youtu.be/9FRrX6EWb0g?t=1h43m5s

[215] http://www.corbettreport.com/interview-539-mark-gaffney-on-black-9/11/

[216] http://www.corbettreport.com/episode-190-listener-feedback/

[217] http://www.checktheevidence.com/audio/911/Mark Gaffney Red Ice Radio - 911 Directed Energy Weapon 4 Oct 2012.mp3

[218] http://www.redicecreations.com/radio/2012/10/RIR-121004.php

[219] http://paulstott.typepad.com/911cultwatch/2011/09/conspiracy-theory-conference-25-september-conway-hall.html

220 https://youtu.be/1G__luSGw_A?t=1h16m21s

221 http://www.gnosticmedia.com/

222 http://www.gnosticmedia.com/dr-michael-labossiere-interview-logical-fallacies-the-critical-thinking-meme-part-1-062/

223 http://www.checktheevidence.com/articles/jan irvin-gnostic media correspondence.htm

224 http://jimmarrs.com/biography/

225 http://republicbroadcasting.org/?page_id=5

226 http://www.checktheevidence.com/audio/911/Jim Marrs on Thermite - Dave Hodges - The-Common-Sense - Caller Sheldon Day - 27 Dec 2009.mp3

227 https://www.newscientist.com/article/dn17288-crap-paper-accepted-by-journal/

228 https://www.youtube.com/watch?v=KWn6ZTiDe1w

229 https://books.google.co.uk/books?id=k4AMl1AGxjIC&printsec=frontcover&source=gbs_ge_summary_r&cad=0

230 https://www.prlog.org/10048184-scientists-see-wtc-hutchison-effect-parallel.html

231 http://www.paradigmresearchgroup.org/stephenbassett.html

232 https://youtu.be/MCSpgJNjop0?t=21m40s

233 https://www.youtube.com/channel/UCA9iiA4pxNRYxZDW_6oWbKw/videos

234 http://www.thehutchisoneffect.com/

235 http://www.johnbalexander.com/biography

236 http://www.checktheevidence.com/audio/911/Steve Bassett on 911 - UFO Truth Conf - 29 Apr 2017.mp3

237 http://www.redicecreations.com/radio/nonsubscriber.php

238 http://www.redicecreations.com/radio/2010/02feb/RIR-100202.html

239 http://www.arcconvention.org/ARCfeedback.html

240 http://www.amazon.co.uk/Dangerous-Man-Conversations-Free-Thinkers-Truth-Seekers/dp/1846943450

241 http://youtu.be/dhMPlJ9C__Q?t=19m22s

242 http://www.redicecreations.com/radio/2011/01/RIR-110118.html

243 http://www.redicecreations.com/radio/2011/09/RIR-110911.php

244 http://www.redicecreations.com/radio/2013/05/RIR-130528.php

245 http://www.checktheevidence.co.uk/cms/index.php?option=com_content&task=view&id=178&Itemid=60

246 https://www.youtube.com/watch?v=qedb0rctyis

247 http://youtu.be/M4XDN9sY3GI?t=47m15s

248 http://www.ae911truth.org/news/322-news-media-events-wrap-up-of-justice-in-focus-symposium-9-11-and-the-path-forward.html

249 http://www.redicecreations.com/radio/2013/04/RIR-130407.php

250 http://www.checktheevidence.com/audio/911/Kevin Barrett - Professional Interest in 9-11.mp3

251 http://nomoregames.net/2007/09/04/nice-guy-kevin-barrett-spins-911-planes-a-peer-review/

252 http://nomoregames.net/2012/02/29/barrett-versus-reynolds-on-bombs-did-not-unravel-the-towers/

253 http://www.redicecreations.com/radio/2013/01/RIR-130113.php

254 http://www.checktheevidence.com/audio/911/130528_RIR-130528-nielsharrit-hr2_ending3.mp3

255 http://911thermitefree.blogspot.co.uk/2009/10/thermite-free-rfc.html

256 http://www.guardian.co.uk/commentisfree/2007/feb/20/comment.september11

[257] http://www.guardian.co.uk/environment/georgemonbiot/2012/aug/29/day-world-went-mad

[258] https://youtu.be/GY-Nr9OGmzk

[259] http://www.checktheevidence.com/cms/index.php?option=com_content&task=view&id=376&Itemid=60

[260] http://www.checktheevidence.co.uk/cms/index.php?option=com_content&task=view&id=375&Itemid=60

[261] http://www.weourselves.org/xm169/092506.html

[262] http://www.youtube.com/watch?v=lPXcoqrCBvw

[263] http://www.thepowerhour.com/past_shows/schedule_03_22_2010.htm

[264] http://www.checktheevidence.com/audio/911/Dr Judy Wood - Andrew Johnson - WTC Destruction - Power Hour - 22 Mar 2010.mp3

[265] http://www.checktheevidence.com/audio/911/100323_Wood_Riley_t4a2c3.mp3

[266] http://911thermitefree.blogspot.com/

[267] http://www.checktheevidence.com/audio/911/Andrew Johnson - WTC Destruction - Power Hour - 31 Mar 2010 (2nd hour lost due to hosts phone failure).mp3

[268] http://www.drjudywood.com/media/100324_day1after.mp3

[269] http://www.drjudywood.com/media/100325_day2after.mp3

[270] http://www.checktheevidence.com/cms/index.php?option=com_content&task=view&id=380&Itemid=60

[271] http://www.checktheevidence.co.uk/cms/index.php?option=com_content&task=view&id=218&Itemid=55

[272] http://www.youtube.com/watch?v=6H3Bz7lseSI

[273] http://pesn.com/2010/11/09/9501722_Cold_Fusion_--_Answer_to_energy_problems/

[274] http://www.alienscientist.com/

[275] https://www.youtube.com/watch?v=dK8IHWJGaCc

[276] http://pesn.com/2012/11/20/9602226_Global_Breakthrough_Energy_Movement_Conference_2012_Exceeds_Expectations/

[277] http://www.checktheevidence.com/audio/911/SEJones/Steve Jones resume - on Alex Jones 7 Jun 2006.mp3

[278] http://newenergytimes.com/v2/sr/taubesfabrication/Krivit-Winocur-TritiumDiscovered.shtml

[279] http://pesn.com/2012/11/19/9602225_Steven_Jones_replica--Pons_and_Fleischmann_XS_Heat_not_from_fusion/

[280] http://newenergytimes.com/v2/sr/StevenEJones/JonesVote.shtml

[281] http://www.checktheevidence.com/audio/911/SEJones/01 Fleischmann - Dont call it fusion - the_people_speak_with_charles_giuliani_2013-06-25.mp3

[282] http://newenergytimes.com/v2/reports/LENR-FAQ.shtml

[283] http://news.newenergytimes.net/

[284] http://www.checktheevidence.com/audio/911/SEJones/02 SE Jones called it cold fusion - the_people_speak_with_charles_giuliani_2013.06.25.mp3

[285] http://www.checktheevidence.com/audio/911/SEJones/03 Pons and Fleischmann Visited Jones.mp3

[286] http://911blogger.com/news/2014-01-11/ae911truthorg-continues-grow-and-response-judy-wood

[287] http://www.checktheevidence.com/911/Thermite2.htm

[288] http://www.checktheevidence.com/audio/911/SEJones/S Jones Silvery Aluminium Molten All temps in daylight 07 Jun 2006 Alex Jones.mp3

[289] http://www.amazon.com/review/R1V39V3WU6J95D/ref=cm_cr_pr_perm?ie=UTF8&ASIN=0615412564&linkCode=&nodeID=&tag=

[290] http://rense.com/general39/coral.htm

291 http://www.checktheevidence.co.uk/cms/index.php?option=com_content&task=view&id=32&Itemid=53

292 http://pesn.com/2012/12/09/9602240_Ambulance-Survived_WTC1_911--Best-Evidence_Dustification_Free-Energy-Demo/

293 http://pesn.com/2013/09/11/9602370_Magnetometer-and-Hurricane-Correlations_with_9-11-2001/

294 http://www.checktheevidence.com/audio/911/SEJones/070131-Space Beams Joneses.mp3

295 http://www.checktheevidence.com/cms/index.php?option=com_content&task=view&id=382&Itemid=60

296 http://pesn.com/2013/08/13/9602355_Interview_with_Geoffrey-Miller_Energybat-Labs/

297 http://www.youtube.com/watch?v=TIwFhdqdMqo&t=2h11m40s

298 http://drjudywood.com/articles/DEW/StarWarsBeam7.html

299 http://www.checktheevidence.co.uk/cms/index.php?option=com_content&task=view&id=352&Itemid=60

300 http://www.heraldextra.com/news/local/crime-and-courts/fountain-green-man-sentenced-to-possible-life-in-prison-for/article_dc13e908-b078-58f7-b648-90df5e45d579.html

301 http://www.lulu.com/shop/andrew-johnson/9-11-finding-the-truth/paperback/product-16341476.html

302 http://www.checktheevidence.com/911/Caroline Louise - emails - 911 Scholars Group - Jan 2014.txt

303 http://www.checktheevidence.com/articles/Jones Grabbe Koonin Timeline2.htm

304 http://www.drjudywood.com/articles/JJ/JJ7.html

305 http://www.infinite-energy.com/iemagazine/issue35/ethics.html

306 http://willyloman.wordpress.com/2011/05/13/steven-jones-continues-to-demo-truth-movement/

307 http://www.checktheevidence.com/911/Caroline Louise - GooglePlus.pdf

308 https://www.youtube.com/watch?v=a0GBksJFmjI

309 http://www.infinite-energy.com/images/pdfs/Fleischmannobit.pdf

310 http://memoryholeblog.com/2013/07/16/stealth-terror-ii-hurricanes-911-and-geoengineering/

311 http://memoryholeblog.com/2013/12/17/sandy-hook-creating-reality/comment-page-2/

312 http://radiofetzer.blogspot.co.uk/2013/01/james-tracy.html

313 http://radiofetzer.blogspot.co.uk/2013/10/james-tracy.html

314 http://www.ae911truth.org/en/news-section/41-articles/851-want-to-hold-nist-accountable-become-a-member-for-just-250month.html

315 http://www.checktheevidence.co.uk/cms/index.php?option=com_content&task=view&id=259&Itemid=60

316 http://www.drjudywood.com/pdf/tritium_15002340.pdf

317 http://www.geoengineeringwatch.org/dane-wigington/

318 http://tinyurl.com/ccgwbook

319 http://www.checktheevidence.co.uk/cms/index.php?option=com_content&task=view&id=397&Itemid=60

320 http://www.checktheevidence.com/audio/911/2014-09-27-Wiggington Gage-clip.mp3

321 http://www.lulu.com/shop/michael-armenia/nanomanagement-the-disintegration-of-a-non-profit-corporation-sc/paperback/product-18804425.html

322 http://www.ae911truth.org/en/news-section/41-articles/854-ae911truth-to-present-wtc-evidence-in-17-stop-rethink911-canada-tour.html

323 http://globalskywatch.com/assets/mp3/gwradio/2014-09-27.mp3

324 http://www.bechtel.com/government-services.html

325 http://www.checktheevidence.com/audio/911/Dane Wigington on 911 - 02 Jun 2015.mp3

326 https://www.youtube.com/watch?v=Okk_1mJX6iE

327 http://www.amazon.co.uk/Methodical-Illusion-Rebekah-Roth-ebook/dp/B00PREI4Y8/ref=cm_rdp_product

328 http://www.amazon.co.uk/The-Shell-Game-Steve-Alten/dp/1599550946

329 https://www.youtube.com/watch?v=4Zp3wEm0R5k

330 https://www.youtube.com/watch?v=R5eyHCGv1CU

331 http://news.bbc.co.uk/1/hi/world/middle_east/1559151.stm

332 http://www.imdb.com/title/tt0831315/

333 https://www.youtube.com/watch?v=ijFAwzudIwI

334
http://www.amazon.com/review/R5SW3HVX4MQS0/ref=cm_cr_rev_detmd_pl?ie=UTF8&asin=0982757131&
cdForum=Fx32YQISVFM441H&cdMsgID=Mx2XF0G8MTBO0C9&cdMsgNo=35&cdPage=4&cdSort=oldest
&cdThread=Tx2SK97OFZMWDCJ&store=books

335 http://www.coasttocoastam.com/guest/roth-rebekah-/71823

336 https://www.youtube.com/watch?v=4VadAXNacNA

337 http://web.archive.org/web/20150512085122/http:/www.veritasradio.com:80/guests/2015/03mar/VS-
150326-rroth-p.php

338 https://www.facebook.com/groups/911TruthMovement/permalink/763459210428309/

339 http://www.bbc.co.uk/news/world-europe-32084956

340 https://www.youtube.com/watch?v=th4Jc92_FJE

341 http://www.checktheevidence.co.uk/cms/index.php?option=content&task=view&id

342 http://www.methodicalillusion.com/about-the-Author.html

343 http://www.methodicalillusion.com/Contact-Rebekah.html

344 https://wikispooks.com/wiki/File:Noevidence.pdf

345 https://www.youtube.com/watch?v=XGE2go6yhvA

346 http://kevbakershow.com/methodical-deception-roth/

347 https://youtu.be/HbIAZsfPUzI?t=7m6s

348 https://www.youtube.com/watch?v=993wlZ6XFSs

349 http://www.checktheevidence.com/audio/911/Rebekah Roth - Coast to Coast - 19 Mar 2015 - Tesla
Technology.mp3

350 https://www.youtube.com/watch?v=uQTO41K4E2s

351 https://www.naturalnews.com/052458_Rebekah_Roth_fake_identity_agent_provocateur.html

352 http://www.amazon.co.uk/review/R35RJTSD2X162E/ref=cm_cr_pr_perm?ie=UTF8&ASIN=B00PREI4Y8

353 http://noosphere.princeton.edu/911formal.html

354 https://www.youtube.com/watch?v=XCD7G9jPIWQ

355 https://www.podomatic.com/podcasts/alchemyradio/episodes/2013-09-17T05_24_32-07_00

356 https://www.youtube.com/watch?v=rj4DVMAp7_o&feature=youtu.be&t=1h13m00s

357 https://www.ukcolumn.org/oldforums/discussion/8978/neil-foster-dave-eden-community-press-group-
awake-radio-tv-live-pulse-news-june-30-2014?

358 http://www.richplanet.net/rp_genre.php?ref=231&part=1&gen=2

359 http://www.thecrowhouse.com/kcnokeefe.html

360 https://www.youtube.com/watch?v=_vQYjb-wVEk

361 https://www.youtube.com/watch?v=l23FWsCpp7U

362 https://www.youtube.com/watch?v=zeb6JNTfEWo

363 https://www.youtube.com/watch?v=VKdnJrN_dps

364 http://www.checktheevidence.com/audio/911/2013-11-04 time 21_44_22 Incoming Peer-to-Peer Call Ken O Keefe Excerpt.mp3

365 http://www.checktheevidence.com/pdf/Ken O Keefe Skype Chat Nov 2013.pdf

366 http://www.checktheevidence.co.uk/cms/index.php?option=content&task=view&id=46

367 https://www.youtube.com/watch?v=UYA2sVaNk-o&t=1h30m10s

368 http://www.bollyn.com/judy-woods-blatant-misrepresentation-of-9-11-facts/

369 https://www.facebook.com/marie.mcloughlin1962/posts/10153142794863595

370 http://www.checktheevidence.com/pdf/Ken O Keefe emails re 911 and Proposed Interview etc.pdf

371 http://www.checktheevidence.com/cms/index.php?option=com_content&task=view&id=208&Itemid=60

372 http://www.checktheevidence.com/cms/index.php?option=com_content&task=view&id=350&Itemid=60

373 http://petersantilli.com/

374 https://www.youtube.com/watch?v=gTlZDmwJ78g

375 https://www.scribd.com/document/121331717/You-Are-Under-A-Psy-Op-Gordon-Duff-Chief-Editor-For-VeteransToday-com

376 http://www.checktheevidence.com/audio/911/Pete Santilli - Episode-310-Jim Fetzer-911 Psyopping and Cover Up.mp3

377 http://thepetesantillishow.com/the-fbi-caught-red-handed-with-bogus-evidence-against-pete-santilli/

378 https://www.youtube.com/watch?v=MQNitCNycKQ

379 http://www.911forum.org.uk/

380 https://www.youtube.com/watch?v=xMncayPZqlE

381 http://www.911forum.org.uk/board/viewtopic.php?t=11268

382 http://www.911forum.org.uk/board/viewtopic.php?t=11609

383 http://web.archive.org/web/20070912004003/http:/shoutwire.com:80/

384 http://www.911forum.org.uk/board/viewtopic.php?p=137493

385 http://news.bbc.co.uk/1/hi/uk/691848.stm

386 https://cryptome.org/shayler-gaddafi.htm

387 http://news.bbc.co.uk/1/hi/uk/890450.stm

388 https://www.amazon.co.uk/Spies-Lies-Whistleblowers-Shayler-Affair/dp/185776952X

389 https://www.theguardian.com/world/2011/oct/23/gaddafi-last-words-begged-mercy

390 https://blackopinion.co.za/2016/05/09/real-reasons-killed-qaddafi/

391 https://www.theguardian.com/politics/2003/sep/06/september11.iraq

392 http://www.911forum.org.uk/board/viewtopic.php?p=75099&sid=c882d1c37b6837dcd726a5a01b944005

393 http://web.archive.org/web/20061104211712/http:/www.reopen911.org/compgraph.htm

394 http://www.checktheevidence.com/audio/911/BBC WM - William Rodriguez - Janice Long - 18 Feb 2007.mp3

395 http://www.checktheevidence.com/audio/911/WR Debunks Wood and Reynolds on Simon Mayo BBC 5 Live 23-Feb-2007.mp3

396 https://web.archive.org/web/20070621154622/http:/www.911researchers.com/node/555

397 https://www.youtube.com/watch?v=nguXc-NpyDI

398 http://911blogger.com/news/2006-12-08/david-shayler-sky-news

399 https://www.youtube.com/watch?v=IXQikj-C1tk

400 http://www.dailymail.co.uk/news/article-474737/David-Shaylers-partner-reveals-How-bullying-State-crushed-him.html

[401] http://www.dailymail.co.uk/news/article-1200089/Call-Delores-says-MI5-whistleblower-David-Shayler.html

[402] http://www.checktheevidence.com/cms/index.php?option=com_events&task=view_detail&agid=6&year=2009&month=12&day=12&Itemid=-1&catids=64

[403] http://www.911forum.org.uk/board/viewtopic.php?t=17612

[404] https://www.peacenews.info/node/3640/keith-mothersson-8-may-1948-ndash-3-july-2009

[405] http://www.opednews.com/articles/genera_keith_mo_080220_honouring_the_real_t.htm

[406] http://reinvestigate911.org/page/books.html

[407] http://www.checktheevidence.com/cms/index.php?option=com_content&task=view&id=358&Itemid=60

[408] http://www.reinvestigate911.org/content/court-victory-protestor

[409] http://news.bbc.co.uk/1/hi/programmes/conspiracy_files/7433017.stm

[410] http://www.youtube.com/watch?v=jeYPm8XzC3g

[411] http://killingauntiefilms.co.uk/

[412] http://www.checktheevidence.com/cms/index.php?option=com_content&task=view&id=373&Itemid=60

[413] http://www.dailymail.co.uk/news/article-2284337/TV-licence-evader-refused-pay-BBC-covered-facts-9-11.html

[414] http://www.richplanet.net/starship_main.php?ref=166&part=1

[415] http://www.checktheevidence.co.uk/cms/index.php?option=com_content&task=view&id=104&Itemid=60

[416] https://www.thetimes.co.uk/article/police-in-crisis-after-jury-rejects-pound10m-terror-case-fg60lbhxrm7

[417] http://www.telegraph.co.uk/news/1526379/Its-all-a-government-plot-say-internet-truth-activists.html

[418] https://www.imdb.com/title/tt0437000/

[419] https://www.amazon.co.uk/Men-Who-Stare-At-Goats/dp/0330375482

[420] https://news.avclub.com/read-this-jon-ronson-on-the-rise-of-conspiracy-theoris-1798249640

[421] http://www.911forum.org.uk/board/viewtopic.php?p=12402

[422] http://www.911forum.org.uk/board/viewtopic.php?p=12467

[423] http://jonronson.com/

[424] http://circlemakers.org/perpetrators.html

[425] https://www.theguardian.com/lifeandstyle/2006/nov/04/weekend.jonronson

[426] http://www.checktheevidence.com/pdf/SM 10 - 911 article.pdf

[427] http://www.open.ac.uk/socialsciences/main/__assets/kuzur9beeawzyzjo0v.pdf

[428] https://www.checktheevidence.com/wordpress/2007/07/31/9-11/

[429] https://www.britannica.com/biography/Robert-Fisk

[430] https://web.archive.org/web/20081224105622/http:/www.independent.co.uk/opinion/commentators/fisk/robert-fisk-even-i-question-the-truth-about-911-462904.html

[431] http://www.checktheevidence.co.uk/cms/index.php?option=com_content&task=view&id=332&Itemid=60

[432] http://www.checktheevidence.com/cms/index.php?Itemid=60&id=168&option=com_content&task=view

[433] http://www.atlanteanconspiracy.com/2011/07/charlie-veitch-and-shill-police.html

[434] http://www.youtube.com/watch?v=ogdi4m2Nywg

[435] http://www.checktheevidence.com/cms/index.php?searchword=conlon&option=com_search&Itemid=5

[436] http://www.consensus911.org/

[437] http://www.cop21paris.org/about/cop21

438 http://www.theguardian.com/world/live/2015/nov/13/shootings-reported-in-eastern-paris-live

439 https://www.youtube.com/watch?v=vKJWZaZL1ME

440 https://www.youtube.com/watch?v=JKvkhe3rqtc

441 https://www.nytimes.com/interactive/2017/10/10/us/california-fires-maps-photos.html

442 https://www.theguardian.com/world/2017/oct/19/portugal-interior-minister-resigns-wild-fires-dead

443 http://www.bbc.co.uk/news/world-europe-41634125

444 https://www.youtube.com/watch?v=Q2q7nN0JYWE

445 https://www.youtube.com/watch?=5DOJtITaJ-c

446 https://www.youtube.com/watch?v=pokPaIyuCGE

447 http://forum.prisonplanet.com/index.php?topic=285085.80

448 https://www.march-against-monsanto.com/why-did-cars-melt-while-trees-and-plastic-structures-remained-intact-during-california-fires/

449 http://www.gettyimages.co.uk/detail/news-photo/melted-metal-flows-from-a-burned-out-car-abandoned-on-a-news-photo/488103158

450 http://www.checktheevidence.com/cms/index.php?option=com_content&task=view&id=395&Itemid=53

451 https://www.youtube.com/watch?v=jU28kqkOzV0

452 https://www.f150forum.com/f118/melted-f150-copart-308862/

453 http://1.bp.blogspot.com/_zEi3fvPniFo/S7Scjk14OKI/AAAAAAAAFMQ/X1OZdu87Mpc/s1600/okc+bombing.jpg

454 https://www.youtube.com/watch?v=u83Y6op_1p8

455 http://www.whale.to/c/symbol11.html

456 https://web.archive.org/web/20080615015203/http:/www.hiltonfamilynewyork.com/millenium-hilton.php

457 https://www.youtube.com/watch?v=tXOJHZhoO68

458 https://www.youtube.com/watch?v=Qscqn-cVTRM

459 http://tomatobubble.com/id884.html

460 https://www.youtube.com/watch?v=oiB7xFPZAJs

461 http://www.lulu.com/shop/carl-james/science-fiction-and-the-hidden-global-agenda-2016-edition-volume-two/paperback/product-23209433.html

462 http://www.richplanet.net/rp_genre.php?ref=140

463 http://neilsandersmindcontrol.com/index.php/2014-01-02-21-10-30

464 https://www.amazon.com/Operation-Mind-Control-Walter-Bowart/dp/0440167558

465 https://www.amazon.co.uk/Not-His-Image-Gnostic-Ecology/dp/193149892X

466 http://www.checktheevidence.com/audio/911/John Lash and Dr Judy Wood - Thomas Malone 06 Sep 2011-1.mp3

467 http://www.checktheevidence.com/cms/index.php?option=com_content&task=view&id=454&Itemid=51